RAMPARTS

FORTIFICATION FROM THE RENAISSANCE TO WEST POINT

Marguerita Z. Herman

AVERY PUBLISHING GROUP INC.
Garden City Park, New York

Cover design by Rudy Shur and Janine Eisner-Wall
Cover art: Courtesy of the National Park Service; artist L. Kenneth Townsend
In-house editor: Linda Comac
Typesetting by Janine Eisner-Wall

Library of Congress Cataloging-in-Publication Data

Herman, Marguerita Z.
    Ramparts: Fortification from the renaissance to west point /
Marguerita Z. Herman
        p.   cm.
    Includes bibliographical references and index.
    ISBN 0-89529-511-3
        1. Fortification—United States—History. 2. Fortification-
-Europe—History. 3. Fortification—North America—History.
4. Fortification—New York (State)—West Point—History. 5. Attack
and defense (Military science)—History. I. Title
UG410.H47 1992
355.7'0973–dc20

Printed in Mexico

10 9 8 7 6 5 4 3 2 1

Contents

Foreword   vii
Preface   ix
Introduction   1

1 Fortification and the European Experience
Introduction   7
The Evolution of the Fortress From the Middle Ages
   to the Renaissance   9
The Transition Between the Renaissance and the
   Age of Vauban   22
The Basic Design of a Permanent Fortification   32

2 Vauban and the Golden Age of Fortification
Introduction   39
Vauban as a Defensive Engineer   41
Vauban and the Conduct of a Siege   45
Vauban's Contemporary Rival: Menno Von Coehorn   59
Vauban's Legacy and his Successors   61

3 Fortification in the New World
Introduction   79
Colonial Fortification in North America   82
The Transition Period of Fortification   89

4 Fortification and the American Experience
Introduction   115
The Development of the First System   117
The Corps of Engineers and West Point: The Formative Years,
   1794–1812   125
The Second System, 1802–1812   132
The Impact of the War of 1812   139

5 The Golden Age of Fortification in America

Introduction   147

The Role of the United States Military Academy in
    Theory and Practice   149

The Third System, 1815–1860   156

The Impact of the Civil War   162

6 Conclusion   169

Glossary   175

Bibliography   187

Index   195

To the many benefactors of the Friends of the West Point Library,
particularly the Trustees of the Cissy Patterson Trust whose generosity
caused this book to be created.

Foreword

In the nineteenth century, the United States Military Academy at West Point was the fountainhead for teaching American youth the art and science of building military fortresses, whose ramparts and ruins today dot the landscapes of America, Europe, and Asia. This ancient body of learning is now encapsulated in the fortifications collection of the Academy Library, more than 800 items that span the four centuries in which fortress building was raised to a sophisticated intellectual exercise while nearly ruining the economies of countless states.

When the Friends of the West Point Library undertook the publication of a book about the Library's extensive holdings on military fortifications, we soon discovered we had two invaluable assets. The Cissy Patterson Trust was to be more than generous in providing the financial support for research and publication. In addition, Marguerita Z. Herman became available to offer her wealth of knowledge in history as well as her ability to carry on research in a host of languages, and she became our author, adept at translating complex technical ideas into lucid prose.

Marguerita Herman begins her story in late medieval Europe when the advent of gunpowder caused Italian and French military architects to redesign fortresses so they would be less vulnerable, and conversely to refine the methods of siege warfare in order to conquer those fortresses. This new art spread throughout Europe and reached its zenith under the expertise of Maréchal Sebastien le Prestre de Vauban and King Louis XIV, who built some 300 forts on the frontiers of seventeenth-century France. The new knowledge further spread throughout Asia and the Americas, as the European powers built fortresses to secure their empires.

By the 1750s, nearly every European nation had its schools for training the builders of fortresses; military engineering with its allied studies in mathematics had become part of the education of French gentlemen of the military class, and was particularly important at the Ecole Polytechnique and the military school at Mézières. General George Washington had been forced to import European military engineers during the American Revolution, and urged the creating of an academy to train American engineers. In March 1802, President Thomas Jefferson signed a bill that brought such an academy into existence.

The War of 1812 only increased the public's perception of the need for seacoast fortifications, and a young officer named Sylvanus Thayer was dispatched to France to return with nearly a thousand volumes that would support the core of the Academy's curriculum. During Thayer's 15-year superintendency, West Point gained a reputation as the first engineering school in the United States, and in a few decades its graduates were using their training to construct seacoast fortifications, canals, harbors, railroads, and great public buildings throughout America.

By 1870, advances in military technology and engineering education had begun to spell an end to this unique 400-year sequence of fortress building in Western history. But, as the author points out, one cannot be a student of the politics, economics, education, and military affairs of those times unless one has a passing acquaintance with the issues of constructing and reducing fortifications that so dominated the minds of the leaders of that period.

We of the Friends of the West Point Library hope that this book will contribute to that understanding. The book is based on the holdings of the USMA Library's Special Collections devoted to fortifications and siege warfare, nearly 800 items that range from the library that Sylvanus Thayer brought from France in 1816 to gifts and recent purchases that have extended the collection back to the sixteenth century. In this book we have included representative illustrations from the USMA collection, with special emphasis on the color plates from John Charnock's *Military Architecture,* a gift from Major General George Smith Patton from his father's library. We have also included a selected bibliography of the most important holdings. A complete bibliography may be obtained from the USMA librarian upon request.

It is our hope that this book will further the use of this important collection, not only for scholarly research, but also for the pleasure that comes to all educated people who are conversant with the ideas of the past through the manuscripts, drawings, folios, and quartos that remain with us today.

Roger H. Nye
Colonel, USA (Ret.)
Chairman, Friends of the West Point Library

Preface

This volume had its origins in a project undertaken by the Friends of the West Point Library to produce a comprehensive catalogue of the U. S. Military Academy Library's holdings in military fortifications. However, it soon became obvious that a simple listing of the books on the subject of military fortifications, although ultimately useful, would fail to do justice to the extraordinary richness, depth, and historical significance of the Library's collection. West Point itself had played a unique role in gathering four centuries' worth of fortification literature from European sources. It had also shaped this material into an effective curriculum for the teaching of the art and science of fortification in America. To leave that story untold would have been a major disservice to the U. S. Military Academy's history and to the Library's collection. As a result, what began as a simple catalogue rapidly transformed itself into an essay, then into a longer piece profusely illustrated from the West Point collection, and finally into a full-fledged book. Every fortification text, manual, treatise, atlas, drawing, and manuscript referred to in this volume, ranging from the Renaissance to post-World War I, is available in the West Point collection.

Despite the availability of many works on military fortification, any novice who approaches the subject immediately encounters a major difficulty posed by the topic: a daunting accumulation of complex, technical vocabulary. Comprised primarily of a mixture of Italian, French, and English words, this nomenclature was developed over the centuries to explain the parts and theories of the art and science of fortification. In the same sense as the computer terminology of our day, this vocabulary has to be extracted, defined, and understood by an aspiring student of the subject. Indeed, I experienced a sense of some historical poignancy in realizing that I was tracing steps taken by so many others before me. It was quite appealing to contemplate the "homework sets" in the Library's collection, bequeathed by eighteenth- and nineteenth-century students and West Point cadets, because we all undertook to learn the process of fortification theory in precisely the same way: by analyzing a series of methodical questions beginning with the most basic question of all, "What is understood by fortification?" I hope that the addition of the illustrated glossary in this volume will aid the modern reader in pursuing the same path more efficiently.

In preparing this book, I have had the invaluable help and cooperation of many people. First and foremost, I must thank the Friends of the West Point Library for their encouragement and support. In particular, Colonel Roger H. Nye, the chairman of the Friends, has been unflagging in his guidance, support, and organization. I owe a special debt to the Military History, Manuscript, Rare Book, and Special Collections staff of the U.S. Military Academy Library: Alan Aimone, Marie Capps, Judith Sibley, Gladys Calvetti, Dawn Crumpler, and Pat Maher. Their extraordinary patience with my requests and ever-cheerful assistance over the months during which this project took shape are deeply appreciated. Colonel Paul F. Barber of the U. S. Military Academy's Department of Electrical Engineering and Computer Science generously donated his expertise in designing the graphics of the components and geometry of a military fortification, as well as the maps found in the illustrations. Finally, my thanks to Colonel Dean A. Herman, Jr. (Ret.), for his patience in proofreading, his technical knowledge, his computer expertise, and his willingness to eat cold meals.

Introduction

The history of the art and science of fortification aligns itself neatly into a period of roughly four centuries, from approximately 1490 to 1890. Very few periods of history demonstrate such clearly delineated parameters. Bounded on the one hand by the changes wrought when Europe entered the period of transition from medieval civilization to early modern times, fortification is flanked on the other by the technological advances of the twentieth century. The former represented the beginnings of fortification's golden age, the latter, its doom. During these 400 years, fortification achieved the stature of an art and science. Constantly responding to the changing events of the time, it acquired a large body of literature, a complex technical vocabulary, an international corps of theorists, and an active fraternity of engineers and military architects who vied for the chance to apply in practice the various theories and designs being advanced. In concrete terms, fortification's great achievement was the construction of many impressive fortresses in strategic locations all over the world. Both grandiose and modest, they flourished in Europe and the New World as integral elements of the foreign and domestic policies of their time. In theoretical terms, fortification's second lasting accomplishment was the legacy of historical works bequeathed to posterity. This literature included the detail necessary to guide a neophyte through the art and science of fortification. The fact that fortification may be considered irrelevant today does not negate the brilliance and effort that went into producing it.

Fortification's development into a mature discipline was rooted in a series of revolutionary events that profoundly altered European civilization in the fifteenth century. Between 1460 and 1560, Europe passed through a tumultuous period of change and discovery. It was a time when the combined impact of widely diverse discoveries, innovations, and rediscoveries propelled Europe out of medieval civilization, and began the transformation of its political, social, and economic systems into modern terms. Previously dependent upon the legacy and achievements of Greco-Roman and Eastern civilizations, Europe embarked upon the process by which it was to achieve and exert, along with political and economic leadership, the technical and scientific predominance of the world.

The changes experienced by Europeans from the mid-fifteenth century on were widespread, dramatic, and extraordinarily diverse. Some took time

Fortification, in the military art, is the art of fortifying a town, or other place; or of putting it in such a posture of defence, that every one of its parts defends, and is defended, by some other parts, by means of ramparts, parapets, ditches, and other outworks; to the end that a small number of men within may be able to defend themselves for a considerable time against the attacks of a numerous army without.

Captain George Smith, 1779

to make themselves felt, but others had an immediate impact. For example, between 1450 and 1500 the discovery and rapid spread of printing stimulated a growing demand for books and secular learning. In and of itself, this was revolutionary enough, but it also led to the emergence of new scientific theories that gradually altered medieval absolutes. Copernicus, for one, shook the cultural pillars of the age with his claim that the earth rotated on its axis and the planets orbited the sun. Indeed, because of the demand for the printing of original sources, much of ancient Greek science resurfaced. This secular science, free of church dogma and censorship, stimulated scholars and laymen to experiment in and study all sorts of scientific fields, including that of weaponry. One important development that arose from this heady atmosphere of scientific and technological experimentation was the appearance of new firearms between 1450 and 1525. Supported by metallurgical innovations, these weapons rapidly revolutionized European political structure and warfare, as well as fortification as it was then practiced. In fact, like so many other areas of European culture, fortification also found itself profoundly altered by the consequences of various discoveries and innovations. Primary among those that directly influenced the course of its development were the spread of books, which also fuelled interest in, and writing about, fortification theory and design; the appearance of the new firearms and artillery that radically altered previously held concepts of fortification; and the rise of the absolute monarchy and modern nation-state, whose wealth and power ultimately permitted both the building of huge, expensive fortresses, and the undertaking of massive sieges to capture them.

The development and spread of printing appeared, on the surface, to be the most unlikely to affect fortification during this period of change; yet, it was to be extremely significant. The invention of a mechanical process for duplicating texts was successfully completed by printers in Mainz in the 1450s, and was paralleled closely by the improved manufacture of paper. Printing spread quickly from Mainz to the rest of Europe—to Strasbourg in 1458, Cologne in 1465, Nuremberg in 1470, Italy in 1467, France and the Netherlands in 1470, and Spain and England in the years 1474–1476. The key factor in this expansion was the demand for books among merchants, artisans, lawyers, government functionaries, soldiers, and teachers—that is, among all those who made their living in the towns of Europe, and who needed some sort of education in order to conduct their affairs efficiently. A rise of secular literacy, fed by an insatiable demand by the bourgeoisie for self-improvement and education, nourished the demand for books. Works of all types, and on all sorts of subjects, in Latin or in the vernacular were printed. Encyclopedias, dictionaries, elementary texts, and manuals and treatises, many with splendid illustrations, represented just some of this output.

By the end of the 1490s, books on military fortifications were represented in all the categories just mentioned. Soldiers, engineers, military architects, and interested laymen all contributed to the growing literature on the subject, and printing presses all over Europe spread the topic to inquisitive readers. By the eighteenth century, it could be fairly said that no aristocrat or bourgeois gentleman could count himself educated if his library did not contain some sort of tome on the subject of fortification. This was also to be true for North Americans, as the bourgeois colonists followed the pattern of education set by Europe. This spread of books on the subject of military fortification was vital. It guaranteed an accelerated propagation of ideas on the subject almost as soon as someone formulated them. And conversely, the knowledge that there existed an audience of enthusiastic laymen with an interest in fortification theory stimulated individuals to publicize their concepts and designs for fortress building and siegecraft as extensively as possible. The revolution in printing and the growing availability of books meant that fortification had found its intellectual underpinnings, and was ready to progress to the true status of an art and science.

The changes in the technology of warfare in the 100 years between 1450 and 1550 also had a dramatic impact, particularly upon the design of fortresses and the theories of siegecraft. Gunpowder had been known in the West since about the middle of the thirteenth century, but the discovery that turned it from a novelty into a weapon was its use as a propellant. By the end of the fourteenth century, firearms were being manufactured all over Europe. Early guns were primitive, firing stone and lead balls, and weighing so much as to be virtually immobile. For example, at the siege of Constantinople in 1453, the Ottoman Turks had acquired German and Hungarian expertise to manufacture cannon. However, these guns required over 70 oxen each, and more than 1000 men, to move them before the Turks could manage to deploy them in batteries against the Byzantines. They included great bombards, 56 smaller cannon of various types, and 2 enormous guns that weighed over 800 pounds and fired stone balls of nearly 3 feet in diameter. So unwieldy and crude were these guns that it took seven weeks of sporadic, laborious firing to open enough breaches in the walls to render the Turks victorious.

The rapid development and spread of the new weapons were made possible by parallel improvements in metal production. Just as paper was vital for the spread of printing, so copper and iron were important for the spread of firearms. Early cannon consumed enormous amounts of metal. A gun, when combined with the metal used for its carriages, could easily weigh over 2 tons. In addition, by the end of the fifteenth century, iron had replaced stone for cannonballs. Taken together with the requirements of the other more traditional weapons—swords, lances, and armor—the demand for metal for military needs was extremely heavy. Fortunately, a series of technological advances combined to increase the production of European mines substantially. More efficient draining of mines, and the appearance of blast furnaces fanned by water-driven bellows—furnaces that could, for the first time, refine ore into an iron pure enough to be cast as skillfully as bronze—contributed to a huge increase in iron production between 1460 and 1530. Moreover, copper, an essential element in cannon manufacture until cast iron replaced it in the late sixteenth century, was also being mined more efficiently in Central Europe. The entire period was one of rapid innovation in the technology surrounding the use of artillery.

The reason for the acceleration in the technology of weaponry was simple. By the middle of the fifteenth century, the impact of even the first, rather crude artillery had been decisive against the stone castles and curtain walls of medieval towns. The French reconquest of Normandy from the English during the Hundred Years' War made use of artillery and siege warfare, and between 1449 and 1450, Charles VII of France actually conducted 60 successful, if rudimentary, siege operations. Although these sieges did not yet depict a streamlined process, they were a far cry from the old days of interminable sieges spent trying to pry rebellious vassals or enemies out of stone castles. One result of the dramatic proof of the mastery of cannon over medieval fortification was a rush by soldiers and engineers to meet the challenge with new designs for fortresses, and with new theories on how to capture them most efficiently. For the next two centuries, from Italy to the Netherlands, to France and England and beyond, those interested in the problem of military fortification labored enthusiastically and publicly, by means of Europe's printing presses, to redesign fortresses so as to restore the balance between the offense and the defense, tipped so precariously by the new artillery.

At the same time, while grappling with the implications of stationary artillery batteries—stationary because they were to remain limited in mobility and accuracy for some time—military tacticians also had to contend with the emergence of infantry equipped with portable firearms. During the fourteenth and fifteenth centuries, the mailed knight and cavalry of mounted and armored nobles had been gradually giving way to foot soldiers carrying pikes and firearms. The arquebus had become commonly used as early as the beginning of the fifteenth century, and in 1521 the Spaniards introduced the improved version that came to be called the musket. The pike and musket were designed to support one another militarily. The pike protected the arquebusier from cavalry during the dangerous moment immediately after he had fired his shot, while the musket cleared a path for the advancing pikemen. The first muskets were relatively crude. They consisted of an iron barrel sunk into a wooden butt, measured about 6 feet long, weighed 15 pounds, and fired lead bullets to a range of approximately 200 yards. For the new fortification theorists, as will be seen, the range and effectiveness of the musket had a direct bearing on the fortress designs they were advocating. The development of the bastion trace in Italy during the Renaissance directly reflected the importance of the new musketry and artillery as factors in fortification.

The historical movement of the period toward the dominant political form of the modern world—the sovereign territorial state—was also significant with respect to the development of the history of fortification. Although many factors played a part in the rise of the nation-state, the new weaponry and revolutionized warfare were among the most pivotal. In medieval times, private armies had been commonplace, and the landed gentry had enjoyed exercising both political and military power. However, the new weaponry signified an end to the military foundation of the independent power wielded by Europe's aristocracy. It was soon apparent that warfare in the age of gunpowder and artillery would require hundreds of cannon and thousands of well-equipped and well-trained infantrymen for a successful siege; and siege operations showed no signs of decreasing in magnitude in the following decades. Indeed, both defensive and offensive operations became enormously expensive, and were soon technically and financially beyond the means of any single feudal magnate. Eventually, only the rulers of important states of Europe had the means and resources needed to undertake this kind of warfare.

At the same time, the new weaponry benefited the ruler seeking to organize and dominate a large territory by providing him with the wherewithal for large-scale aggressions both at home and abroad. In effect, gunpowder technology royalized warfare by enabling the prince, by means of his greater wealth and power, to establish a monopoly on the use of organized force within his own territory. Feudal barons and lords could not compete with the prince in his acquisition of weapons and armies; with their military leverage severely limited, their political power diminished in turn. In the end, the appearance of the new artillery tipped the balance of power within each European state from the nobility in favor of the crown. In fact, the new technology hastened the decay of medieval chivalry and culture as a whole. The common foot soldiers with their pikes and muskets now fought more efficiently than armored knights, not by dint of glorious and individual feats of valor, but by collective discipline and tactics. The new amorality and impersonality of the state in war, coolly chronicled by Niccolò Machiavelli (1469–1527), began to supplant medieval concepts, which had valued the personal honor and valor of the knight above all.

The shift of power toward the absolute ruler and the nation-state had a powerful impact on fortification. Whereas most feudal lords had been generally able to afford the construction of a well-placed stone castle before the fifteenth century, 100 years later few could afford to build a large fortress, much less find the resources for a long-drawn-out siege of one. Europe's aristocracy continued to have an important military role. The nobility still served its kings by leading armies and theorizing about fortification and military tactics, but after the sixteenth century it could no longer exert independent power over men and arms. By the time these new elements had worked themselves into the fabric of European society, fortification had undergone a permanent change. A far cry from the stark and relatively simple castles of the Middle Ages, fortifications were, by the end of the seventeenth century, poised to enter their golden age. During that period, vast fortresses were built and subsidized by absolute monarchs; complex sieges were undertaken by national armies; and the entire enterprise was given a solid theoretical foundation by fortification specialists and a widespread audience of enthusiastic laymen.

Like most other elements of European civilization, fortification design was transferred in its totality to the New World. By the early eighteenth century, the bourgeois colonists of North America—at least those who could boast of a reasonable education—were as familiar with fortification literature as their European counterparts. In a practical sense, as will be seen, this knowledge played a significant role during the American Revolution and its aftermath. The difference between the European and American experiences lay in the smaller amount of expenditures the new American republic was willing and able to allocate to fortifications compared with the absolute monarchies of Europe. Fortresses were considered as vital in America as they had been in Europe, particularly since the new American government was both reluctant and unable to lavish great sums on standing armies or a far-flung navy. Seacoast fortifications, in most cases already established at strategic locations by the old colonial powers, appeared to be the most logical, prudent, and fiscally sound approach to the question of defense for the new nation. The issue in the early years of the republic was not whether to build fortifications, but *who* was to build them. The theories and designs for fortresses, buttressed by 200 years of European experience, had already been made available in America by various means. What was seen to be lacking immediately after the American Revolution was a method by which to develop a cadre of native-born engineers who could do in America what their counterparts had accomplished in Europe. It was in this area that certain far-sighted individuals and the U. S. Military Academy at West Point came to play a pivotal role.

The decades after the American Revolution up to the outbreak of the Civil War witnessed the development of a curriculum at West Point designed to institutionalize the teaching of fortification as an art and science. Fortuitous blunders and intelligent foresight played an equal role in this process, but ultimately, West Point graduates—some in the United States Corps of Engineers, others as civilian engineers—spread throughout the nation to build a series of fortifications that became the bulwark of American defense policy. A few graduates returned to the U. S. Military Academy to ponder and analyze fortification theory, and to devise the only national curriculum in the art and science of permanent military fortification. As a result, they directly influenced the style, size, and objectives of the forts that were built or redesigned all over America prior to the Civil War. Indeed, the history of the defense policy of the United States after the American Revolution and prior to the Civil War was that of fortification; and fortification constituted an integral part of the early training, curriculum, and history of West Point.

In the final analysis, however, the history of fortification is part of the history of military technology. The development of new weaponry stimulated the rise of modern fortification; exactly the same process toward the end of the nineteenth century brought about its demise. Four-hundred years had been a long and distinct period, one during which fortresses and siegecraft had flourished. It was to take less than four decades before modern science and technology were to render them strategically irrelevant, and to transform them into interesting but ineffectual museum pieces.

Fortification and the European Experience *1*

Introduction

In the twentieth century, technology has overtaken the art of military fortification. What was for many centuries an essential element of an educated man's body of knowledge has now become an obsolete, if interesting, subject of study for historians and military buffs. It was not always so. From time immemorial, military fortifications were built to perform the vital functions of protection, defense, and control. Fortresses enclosed towns and cities, housed garrisons, stored supplies and munitions, defended frontiers and strategic sites, and protected the populace. Whether the design involved the most simple enclosures of primitive times (earthworks, a perimeter of stakes planted in the ground, or rough stone walls), or the high castle walls of the Middle Ages, the strategy behind a fortification was always the same: to enable a small group of defenders to hold a place against the depredations of a larger force, ideally for an unlimited period of time. It is from this standpoint that the famous sieges of history—even those of remote antiquity such as Troy or Masada—have captured the imagination of each generation. The duel between the offense and the defense, between the besiegers and the besieged, is eternally gripping.

The history of military fortification presents another fascinating aspect as well: it is the only form of architecture that requires that its designer, while constructing a fortification, simultaneously take into account future attempts to destroy it. A military engineer did not have the luxury of straightforwardly building a fortress to achieve the strategic aims previously outlined, or of simply indulging in architectural aesthetics for the pleasure of it. He also had to consider at all stages of his work how best to counter enemy efforts to demolish each and every component of the fortress he was erecting. As a result, the art of military fortification represented above all a process of solving a problem: how to build a structure that would accomplish its strategic aims, and yet, through calculation and foresight, withstand not only the ravages of time and the natural elements, but also those ravages created by future attacks. No other form of architecture has labored under this dual burden; and, consequently, few other forms of architecture are as intrinsically fascinating.

Over the centuries, military fortification was also affected by another duality: the constant struggle between the offensive and defensive advances of technology. Every fortification was specifically designed to counter whatever level of weaponry existed to threaten it. This constant tension between the offensive and the defensive regulated the progress of fortification throughout history. Any step forward in the development of offensive technology—such as the appearance of the longbow, gunpowder and cast-iron shot, rifled ordnance, or the tank and the airplane of our day—tended to disrupt this balance and to provoke a frantic reaction. As one historian wrote, ". . . there are times when the offensive sweeps the defensive entirely aside, overwhelming it as a flood overwhelms all natural and artificial barriers in its path."[1] Those moments in history, when a change in the magnitude of the offense occurred so dramatically as to revolutionize warfare, are of immense interest to the historian for two reasons. First, the imbalance created at such times tended to rouse contemporaries to feverish activity to restore equilibrium (for, after all, their own lives might be at stake). Second, attempts to deal with the new offensive realities often spread into other fields, thereby enriching the culture of the time. Although primarily military, these efforts spilled over into related areas such as politics, technology, law, art and architecture, and even philosophy. The works of Niccolò Machiavelli (1469–1527) provide an excellent example. Disquieted initially by the dramatic impact of the new artillery in Italy during the Renaissance, Machiavelli expanded his military concern into a more general discussion of issues relating to politics, government, diplomacy, and warfare. His observations on a critical time continue to be of interest today.

Such a critical period in the history of permanent fortifications is that which extended roughly between the latter part of the fifteenth century and that of the nineteenth. The appearance in the 1490s of new, more powerful, and more mobile siege guns—which, with marginal improvements, lasted until the 1850s when the application of rifling to ordnance appeared—dramatically changed the art and science of permanent fortifications. This major breakthrough in technology necessitated a hurried reappraisal of the techniques used to attack fortifications and those used to defend them. For the first time in history, the concept of fortification was studied and analyzed by soldiers, engineers, and scholars with the intention of producing a set of theories and empirical proofs as to what sort of fortress might best withstand the new artillery. It was the beginning of an era during which the great military engineers of Europe transformed the art of fortification into a science, and ultimately turned its practice into a doctrine of elaborate rules and formalism. This explosion of ideas and activity in turn had a profound impact on the politics, the foreign policies, and even the urban development of sixteenth- and seventeenth-century Europe, as rulers were forced to ponder the lessons of the new technology and the new theories of fortification.

The Evolution of the Fortress from the Middle Ages to the Renaissance

The Impact of the New Artillery

The first radical change in the carefully crafted balance in warfare that had persisted throughout the Middle Ages occurred toward the end of the fifteenth century, when a series of technical improvements in the design and ordnance of cannon emerged in France and the Low Countries. Siege guns of about 8 feet in length, designed to fire an iron ball of between 25 to 50 pounds, were now capable of being hauled cross-country with a surprising ease. (See Figure 1.1.) Thanks to specially designed gun carriages, the new artillery could go wherever a heavy wagon and team of horses could pass. New techniques also provided a much more efficient transition from the travelling to the firing position. Equally as important as this improved mobility was the expansion of firepower achieved as various European foundries continued to experiment successfully.[2] These innovations gave a critical edge to those armies that first used them in the field.

In 1494, a French army invaded Italy to claim the throne of Naples for Charles VIII. The deadly efficiency of the army's offensive artillery stunned the Italian states as well as the rest of Europe. Francesco Guicciardini, the Florentine-born diplomat and historian of events in Renaissance Italy, wrote a concise, if disheartened, description of the impact of the French guns during this campaign:

When fortification was at this height, it stopped for many ages, 'till the use of gunpowder and guns was found out; and then the round and square towers, which were very good flanks against bows and arrows, became but indifferent ones against the violence of cannon.

Captain George Smith, 1779

Figure 1.1   Renaissance cannon (Dürer, 1527): these new siege guns of about 8 feet in length featured newly designed gun carriages that could be moved rapidly by horse and wagon, transforming sixteenth century warfare.

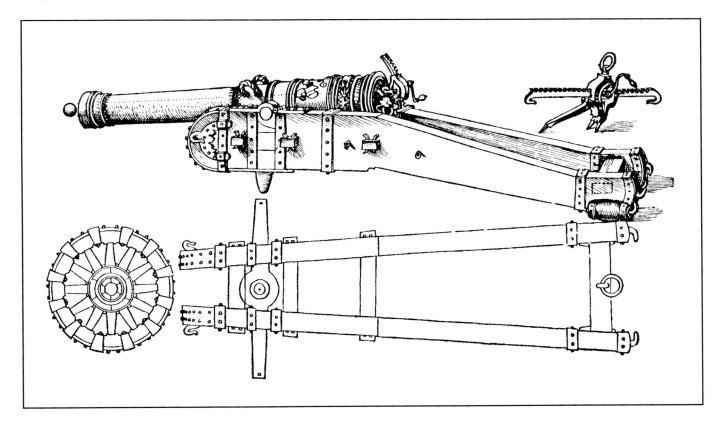

This new plague of artillery, developed many years before in Germany, had been brought to Italy for the first time by the Venetians during their war against the Genoese in the year 1380 . . . the biggest of these artillery pieces were called bombards, which were subsequently employed throughout Italy since this new invention could be adapted for attacking towns. Some of them were made of iron, some of bronze, but they were so big that large pieces could be dragged only very slowly and with the greatest difficulty. For the same reasons, it was difficult to plant them in position against cities; once placed, there was such an interval between one shot and another compared to later developments, that a great deal of time was consumed with very little reward. Consequently, the defenders of the place under attack had time to calmly make the necessary repairs and fortifications. . . . But the French developed many infantry pieces which were even more maneuverable, constructed only of bronze. These were called cannon and they used iron cannonballs instead of stone as before; and this new shot was incomparably larger and heavier than that which had been previously employed. Furthermore, they were hauled on carriages drawn not by oxen as was the custom in Italy, but by horses with such agility of manpower and tools assigned for this purpose that they almost always marched right along with the armies, and were led right up to the walls and set into position there with incredible speed; and so little time elapsed between one shot and another and the shots were so frequent and so violent was their battering that in a few hours they could accomplish what previously in Italy used to require many days. They used this diabolical rather than human weapon not only in besieging cities but also in the field, together with similar cannon and other smaller pieces, but all of them constructed and maneuvered, according to their size, with the same dexterity and speed.[3]

During this French campaign, the city-state of Florence and the Pope surrendered with only token resistance. Guicciardini unhappily recorded that the walls of one of the few fortresses that had resisted the French—namely, Monte San Giovanni on the border of the kingdom of Naples—were smashed to rubble after only eight hours of shelling. Monte San Giovanni was then brutally sacked, despite the fact that this same fortress had once withstood a siege of seven years.[4] It seemed that the balance between the defense and offense had indeed been fearfully altered to favor the latter. Wherever the new artillery appeared, existing fortifications struck observers as obsolescent. The other lesson taught by the French cannon was that the balance of power indubitably lay with those rulers who had the ability and the finances to integrate the new guns with the demands of their foreign policies. Unfortunately, the Italian city-states could not meet this condition, and subsequently became the prey of those powers that could.

Nevertheless, perhaps because Italy was the first area to receive its baptism by fire at the hands of the new weaponry, the initial efforts to resolve the imbalance between the offense and defense came from the ingenuity of Italian soldiers, engineers, scholars, artists, and architects. Actually, for some decades before they were confronted by the formidable French guns in 1494, various Italians interested in the art of fortification had been experimenting somewhat haphazardly with ways of making the old system better able to withstand gunfire. In fact, in the sixteenth century, the Italians became the acknowledged leaders and busiest exporters of all that was new and experimental in the art of permanent fortifications. The importance of this so-called Italian school lay in its achieving dominance not just by example, but also by being the first group to actually assemble the prevalent theories of fortification in books, treatises, and manuals, and to spread these works rapidly throughout Europe.[5]

Other factors equally encouraged the Italians to take the lead in experimenting with new theories in fortification. To begin with, politically, the Italian peninsula was divided into numerous independent and squabbling territories. This situation encouraged princes to build fortresses, first, to defend their frontiers, and, second, to make themselves secure from possible revolt by their own subjects. They were ready to pay handsomely for the design of a fortified place capable of achieving these ends.

In the second place, the Italian Renaissance was the cultural high point of the prestige and acceptability of the artist, as well as that of the architect and engineer. This meant that innovative concepts were given enthusiastic reception and rapid application by the popes and princes who commissioned such work. A look at the number of artists who tried their hand at fortification is both fascinating and revealing. For example, Michelangelo emphasized the artist's role in war, "especially in designing the form and proportions of a citadel and defensive work, and of bastions, ditches, mines, countermines, trenches, gun-ports, block-houses, etc."[6] Put in charge of the fortifications of Florence in 1529, he gallantly served as "governor of fortifications" during a siege that year.[7] Leonardo da Vinci inspected forts for Ludovico Sforza, the Duke of Milan, and for Cesare Borgia. And when Cosimo de' Medici wished to strengthen Florence's fortifications, he distributed the work among a number of artists, including Benvenuto Cellini.

Third, major civic building projects such as the Duomo in Milan or St. Peter's in Rome—projects that marked the Renaissance landscape—provided incomparable experience in the use of labor and materials on a vast scale, as well as a meeting ground where engineers and architects could exchange ideas about their designs. It is interesting that there was so little distinction between art and military engineering during these years. In fact, the mathematical training of artists was particularly suited to the development of a type of fortification based on geometrical principles. During the Renaissance, interest in scientific theory and mathematics was especially stimulated by the translation and dissemination in Italy of printed books of previously unknown Greek texts. After all, the Italian Renaissance preached the concepts of proportion, symmetry, and harmony—elements that neatly coincided with the need for precisely planned theories of angled fire and mathematically designed fortresses. At the moment that these elements combined with the practical experience of soldiers and military engineers, the new theory of bastioned fortifications began to take form.

The Development of the Bastion: From Medieval Castle to Mature Fortress

The process by which the siege gun modified the art of fortification as it was known during the Renaissance, and led to the development of the bastioned trace, was dramatic and fairly rapid. Until the arrival of gunpowder as a propellant in the fourteenth century, well-built castles were virtually impregnable. They contained a central **keep** (the innermost and strongest structure, or tower, of a medieval castle) to which defenders could retire for a last-ditch defense if the enemy penetrated the walls. This keep was surrounded by a deep ditch crossed at the main entrance by a removable drawbridge. Medieval castles often had more than one perimeter wall. Built tall and thin, these were called **curtain** walls, and were designed to be difficult to scale: the longer it took the enemy to climb, the greater the likelihood of picking him off before he reached the top. Medieval walls were also designed so that marksmen could walk freely upon them to shoot and ward off an attack. Since it was necessary to enable the defenders to fire from the wall, a raised platform, or **banquette**, upon which the soldiers might stand to shoot arrows and other missiles at the enemy, was built in the rear of the top of the outer face of the wall. To protect these soldiers as much as possible, a waist-high wall was built in front of them; but when the longbow was introduced, it was found necessary to provide slots—called **crenellations**—to nearly banquette level, through which the archers might shoot. Castle walls constructed with these crenellations were called **battlements**. To prevent attackers from working in comparative safety at the foot of the wall, the walls were sometimes **machicolated**—that is, the battlements and banquettes were projected forward into the face of the wall, and openings were made in the floor of these projecting galleries through which missiles, molten lead, oil, or other debris could be hurled from above onto the heads of the attackers. A direct assault against the walls was the usual technique for capturing medieval fortifications, and for many years, the castles survived with impunity the attacks of armored knights, bowmen, infantry, and catapults. (See Figure 1.2.).

Figure 1.2 Siege operations in the fourteenth century.

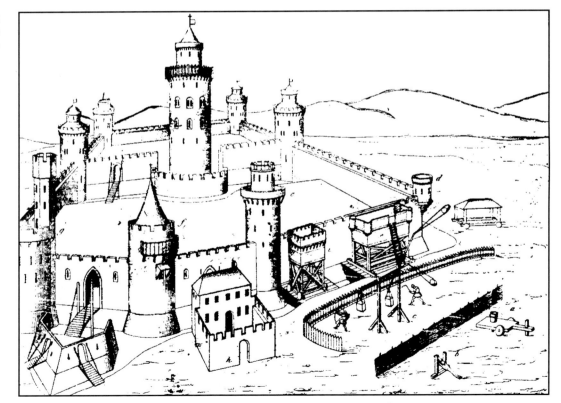

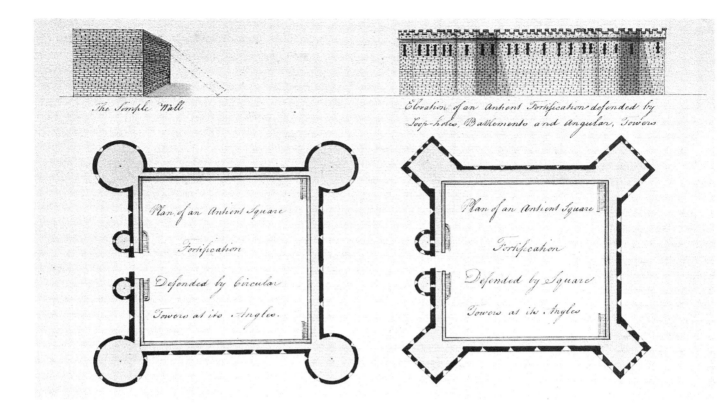

Another method of providing for defense close to the castle was the construction of circular or square loopholed towers at different junctures along the wall to overlook and guard the curtain wall between them. (See Figure 1.3.) These towers, built high in order to prevent scaling, were also intended as flanking positions to maintain fire against attackers. They allowed for effective firing upon any portion of the wall that might have temporarily fallen into the hands of an attacking force. The techniques of bombardment

Figure 1.3   Examples of castles with circular or square loopholed towers constructed at different junctures in order to provide defense for the curtain walls (Charnock).

during the Middle Ages were haphazard, crude, and mostly intended to harass the garrison. In this sense, early artillery did not really influence either the height or thickness of the walls. Those factors were determined purely by the desire to prevent their being scaled, by the needs of vertical defense, and by the need to provide some sort of effective fire by the garrison's muskets. Clearly, the advantage at this point in siege warfare, if the balance between the offense and defense is kept in mind, was generally with the defender. The capture of a strongly fortified town or fortress with a good garrison and ample supplies was a difficult task. (See Figure 1.4.) In a deliberate siege, the attackers first surrounded the town or castle with two lines of **fieldwork**—temporary entrenchments—to cut off all communication with the outside. The outer line, or **line of cir-**

Figure 1.4   Siege operations in the fifteenth century, illustrating the still haphazard techniques of bombardment of fortified places prior to the new artillery.

cumvallation, was designed to prevent a relieving force from surprising the besiegers' camp; the inner line, or **line of contravallation**, was intended to prevent a sortie from the castle or town from surprising these camps. (See Figure 1.5.) If the town were not well supplied with food, it might then be starved into submission. To shorten a siege, a breach in the wall might be attempted by undermining the wall, by battering it with rams, or by bombarding it with mortars and incendiary materials. Scaling the wall after first driving the defenders from it was difficult and bloody, and meant that even more labor, time, and men were squandered by the besiegers.

Once the power and efficiency of artillery increased because of improvements in the manufacture of powder and cannon and in the science of gunnery, change in the design of fortifications followed of necessity. The French siege gun could accurately bombard fortifications from a much longer range than was previously possible. Castle walls, looming high to prevent **escalade** (the scaling of fortified walls by means of ladders), were easy targets; and masonry walls simply shattered.

At the beginning of the fifteenth century, various tactics were adopted to protect castles from the relatively inaccurate bombardment of the early cannon, which hurled piles of stone and rubble. At first, because the new siege cannon functioned only semi-crudely, the fortification engineer sometimes attempted to make the walls stronger so that they might be able to

Figure 1.5 Attack of a place: the outer line, or line of circumvallation, was to prevent the surprise of the besiegers' camp by a relieving force; the inner line, or line of contravallation, prevented the surprise of these camps by a sortie from the castle, fort, or town.

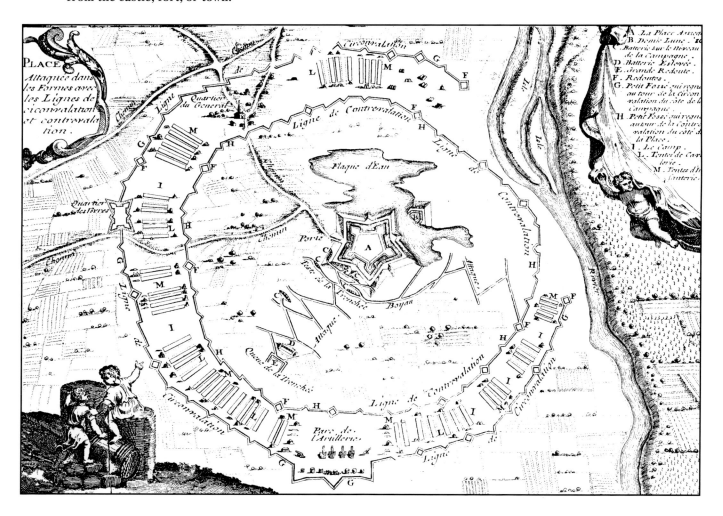

withstand the effect of cannon shot. The first attempt in this vein was simply to increase the thickness of the facing wall. However, it was soon apparent that this was too expensive a technique for the whole length of the wall, so it was done only at intervals in order to reduce the damage created by a breach. These reinforcing designs at the back of the wall were known as **counterforts.** In addition, several tiers of **relieving arches** were built into the rear of the wall and between the counterforts. Their object was to make it more difficult to cause breaches, and, if one were made, to greatly minimize the amount of earth that would tumble down. Too much wall rubble caused by a breach not only usually brought the rest of the wall down, but also created a makeshift hill of rubble that the attacking party could climb.

An important discovery occurred around 1500 when the Italians realized that loosely compacted dirt absorbed cannon shot and prevented massive devastation. An interesting new defensive tactic resulted: if the main walls were in danger of collapsing under assault, an emergency rampart of earth was thrown up inside the fortress, making a new obstacle that the besiegers would have to cross while under fire. At the same time, it occurred to engineers that if this great bank of earth were sloped forward and made high enough, a soldier could stand safely behind it to fire at the enemy. This was the origin of the **parapet**, and a **banquette**—a ledge—was immediately constructed at its base to enable the garrison to step up, fire over the parapet, and then retire safely to the lower ground behind it. The height of the parapet was further augmented by elevating it on another mound of earth—the **rampart**. The earth for both the parapet and rampart was derived from digging a deep ditch immediately in front of and parallel to the parapet.

In one sense, the parapet and the ditch represented the fortification engineer's reluctance to totally abandon the concept of a wall as an obstacle. Obviously, high walls visible to the enemy's fire were subject to destruction. But what if the wall could be hidden from the enemy? Thus, in a manner of speaking, the sloping outer face of the parapet and the ditch represented a negative or inverted wall. One wall of the ditch (the **scarp**) became the main obstacle; the other (the **counterscarp**) was constructed high enough to hide the scarp wall from sight and to protect it, to a great extent, from cannon fire. This fundamental idea, later embodied in more permanent forms, with masonry facings to the ditch (scarping or revetting), was a huge step in solving the problem of how to protect against gunfire. It so seriously reduced the effectiveness of vertical defense that machicolation rapidly became redundant. Thus, castle crenellations and machicolations were removed, not only because they were no longer needed, but also because they were too easily knocked off, with the debris falling and sometimes crushing the defenders behind the walls. Similarly, moats were widened so that falling masonry could no longer fill them and form bridges for the attackers. (See Figure 1.6.)

The older style of fortifications had, as mentioned, taken into account the need for providing flanking fire from the towers, and the initial reaction to the new artillery had been merely to modify castles sufficiently to allow more muskets and cannon to fire through the loopholes. The simple strategy of working to prevent a direct assault upon

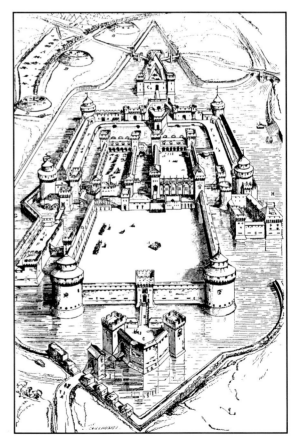

Figure 1.6 Bird's-eye view of the Castle of Milan (Viollet-le-Duc): an unusual example of old defenses mixed with the new, with its profusion of towers and ditches.

the walls remained unchanged for some time. Gradually, however, it was realized that artillery inside a fortress could also reach out in an active, offensive sense to destroy the enemy and his cannon. The theory was that if the volume of fire could be made sufficiently strong, a successful siege might be rendered impossible, since the defenders' superior firepower would destroy the besiegers' batteries as fast as they could set them up. Initially, then, an effort was made to mass as many cannon as close together as possible on the tops of the walls. To augment the volume of fire even more, relieving arches designed to strengthen the wall were used as emplacements for guns, and loopholes were added where necessary. This innovation was the origin of the first **casemate** batteries.

Although increased firepower was desirable, the old-style walls and towers made massing cannon on them a difficult tactic for several reasons. The width of the walls presented a problem in that they were only a foot or so wide in most places; the loopholes were too narrow to permit the efficient firing of the guns; and ventilation of the smoke produced was poor. To overcome these problems, a simple solution was proposed—the guns were placed on platforms on top of the towers. The moment this occurred, the concept of a bastion was almost complete: "It was not a gun tower, but a solid platform thrust forward to obtain as wide a field of fire as possible while retaining the tower's role of providing flank cover to the adjacent parts of a fortification. The tower was basically a defensive, the bastion [see Figure 1.7] an aggressive form."[8]

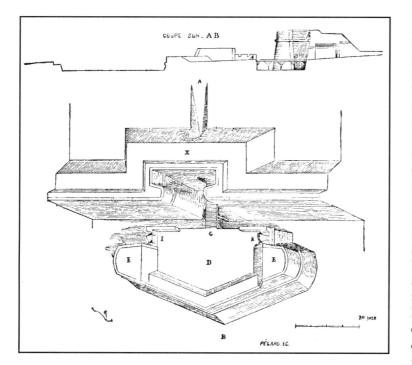

Figure 1.7 Bird's-eye view of a bastion.
AB. Line of the section
B. Parapet
C. Bridge
D. Solid earthworks
EE. Shoulders
IK. Flanking batteries
X. Ramparts behind the bastion
(Viollet-le-Duc)

To reduce the amount of surface and projections at risk to cannon fire, and to facilitate the necessary movement of guns from one area to another, walls and towers were lowered and were buttressed from behind with masses of dirt. Thus, among the first casualties of the new guns that fired iron cannon balls were the high curtain walls. Indeed, once the ability to defend vertically by dropping missiles from above was minimized, the question of how best to devise a sweeping flanking fire against assault became uppermost in the minds of the Italian engineers. The new profile of the towers—squat and thick—may have provided more space for cannon, but also correspondingly increased the amount of dead space, ground that could not be covered by flanking fire from some other part of the work. Because dead space could provide a staging area for escalade or the mining of the walls with gunpowder, it was imperative that the space be removed.

Eventually, the Italian engineers and military architects rejected outright the circular walls of medieval times, and opted instead for the angle **bastion**—a four-sided projecting structure that consisted of two sideways-facing **flanks** and two outward-facing **faces**, with the wall in between known as the **curtain**. It was determined that the meeting of the faces of the bastion in an **angular salient** effectively eliminated the area of dead ground that had existed in front of the tower, and opened clear fields of fire from the flanks of the adjacent bastions (see Figure 1.8). Thus, if the attackers' artillery attempted to breach the curtain, their guns would be exposed not only to fire coming directly from the curtain, but also to a brutal crossfire coming from the inner faces of the two adjacent bastions. The flanks of the bastions were the most critical elements of the **enceinte**—the main enclosure of a fortress—since they contained the cannon that **enfiladed** (swept with fire along the length of a wall, a line of troops, or a trench) the opposite faces of the bastion and crossfired on the ditches. This new design permitted a clear field of vision over every inch of wall, since the jutting sides of the bastions were themselves built along a line that was a continuation of the angle of vision available to the gun positions on the walls on either side of the tower. (See Figures 1.9 through 1.11.)

In the early 1500s, while trying to determine the most effective bastion design, the Italians initially drew all sorts of configurations. Some bastions were nearly round, with only a small projection. Some looked like the ace of spades. But, eventually, the angular salient came to dominate design as the most logical and popular shape. Like the bastion traces, the design of the flanks also evolved through many shapes. However, the key element that dominated flank design was the **line of defense**—the distance from the flank to the point of the opposite bastion, or, put another way, the line of fire from the re-entering angle of a bastion and a curtain to the salient angle of the next bastion. For the most effective flanking fire, most engineers felt that the line of defense should not exceed the range of musket fire, which was from 200 to 300 yards by the eighteenth century. A simple square with bastions was the first, most basic trace proposed by the military architects. However, the small flanks and sharp angles characteristic in the geometry of this design produced cramped interior spaces, limiting the number of troops and cannon that could be garrisoned there. On the other hand, if one tried to increase the size of the square bastioned trace, the permissible lines of defense (200 to 300 yards) were quickly exceeded. Thus, as a basic design, the square bastion trace was really only useful for citadels, detached forts, or small colonial forts in the wilderness.

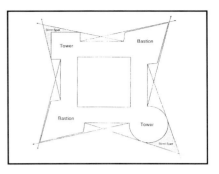

Figure 1.8   The meeting of the faces of the bastion in an angular salient eliminated the area of dead ground that had existed in front of the tower, and opened clear fields of fire from the flanks of adjacent bastions.

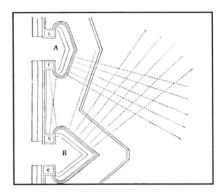

**Figure 1.9   Plans of bastions.
A. Obtuse angle
B. Acute angle
C. Casemated batteries
(Viollet-le-Duc)**

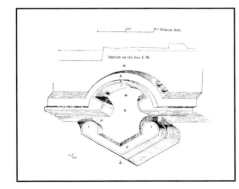

**Figure 1.10   Bastion isolated, with inner rampart.
A. Inner rampart B. Parapet
C. Escarpment D. Sloping surface
G. Lowest point H. Flanking battery
I. Masking shoulders K. Parapet
LM. Line of the section
(Viollet-le-Duc)**

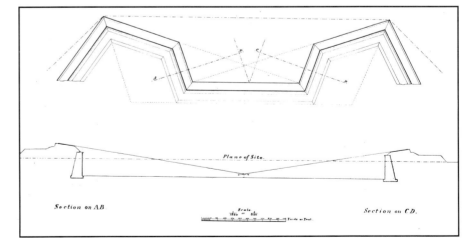

Figure 1.11   A sketch of a bastioned trace (Godson, Royal Military Academy, 1863).

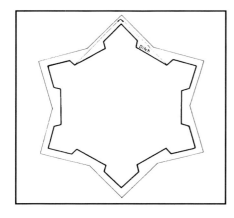

Figure 1.12   Bastioned fort.

Works traced on polygons offered more sides and were clearly easier to defend with men and materiel. To achieve even greater interior space within a polygonal fortification trace, the number of bastions was increased as was the length of the enclosing walls. (See Figure 1.12.) Thus, the number of sides on the exterior polygon was also increased, resulting in various bastioned enceintes ranging from pentagonal and hexagonal to even larger irregular polygons. When it was a question of enclosing a town, a large irregular polygon trace was obviously called for. Although most theories for tracing a bastioned fortress were based on tidy geometrical design, nature was often uncooperative. The proposed site for a bastioned fortress might include terrain with mountains, swamps, and rivers, often forcing basic readjustments in the original design. Thus, many fortifications were constructed from traces developed from irregular polygons in order to adapt to the conditions posed by the terrain. (See Figures 1.13 and 1.14.)

The first extensive and methodical application of the bastion design to the fortification of a town was the work of the Venetian architect Michele di Sanmicheli (1484–1559). In 1530, he consulted on the rebuilding of the fortifications in his home city, Verona, one of the key fortresses in Italy. In later years, he worked on the island of Crete to establish defenses against the Turkish threat, and eventually he strengthened various fortifications for the Republic of Venice, including the city itself.[9] At the same time, Francesco Paciotto da Urbino (1504–1576) was leading the way with bastion traces as he fortified the citadel of Turin. The official engineer for the Duke of Savoy, da Urbino was "the first engineer to make the curtains and bastions of reasonable size, and arrive at a rational allotment and distri-

Figure 1.13   Old and new fortification (De Fer, 1723).

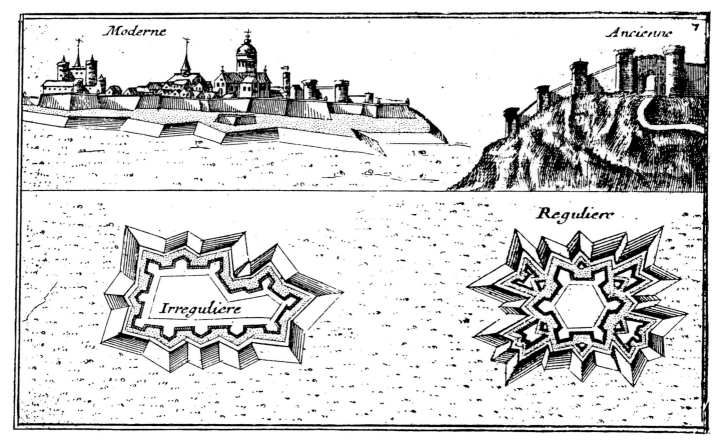

bution of the parts of a fortification."[10] He also helped fortify Antwerp for the Duke of Alva in 1568. (A revealing and piquant example of how far esteem for Italian expertise had spread in Europe was the 1585 appointment of Frederico Gianibelli of Mantua by Queen Elizabeth I to aid the burghers of Antwerp in *their* resistance to Alva's successor, the Duke of Parma.)

The New Italian School

By the end of the sixteenth century, all the experimentation of the previous years had shaped a coherent system of fortification, loosely called the new Italian school. Its practitioners were prominent architects, engineers, and a few soldiers, and included figures such as Pietro Cataneo, Niccolo Tartaglia, Girolamo Maggi, Fusto Castriotto, Francesco de' Marchi, and Pietro Sardi. In the course of their work (each published a book on the subject of fortification between 1546 and 1639), new elements were added to the bastion trace. **Outworks**, defenses located between the enceinte and the **glacis** (the cleared, long, sloping ground beyond the ditch), were developed. (See Figure 1.15.) A **ravelin**, a free-standing triangular outwork equidistant between the bastions, was situated almost as an island in the moat in front of the curtain. The ravelin was designed to protect the curtain as a whole, and to produce a crossfire over the ground in front of the neighboring bastions. If an attacker captured the ravelin, he would find himself isolated in the middle of the ditch, and would still have to attack one of the bastions in the face of vicious flanking fire.

The appearance of outworks represented a vital growth of the concept of a defense in depth. The objective was to prevent the enemy from reaching the curtain walls by establishing a series of outer defensive positions that augmented the firepower of the bastion artillery. In addition, an ingenious modification was proposed in 1556 by Tartaglia. Rather than the single line

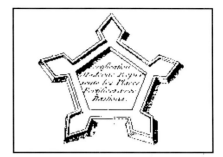

Figure 1.14 Types of fortifications (De Fer, 1723).

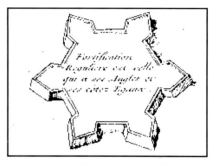

A modern fortification representing places fortified with bastions.

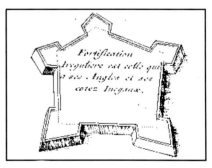

A regular fortification, one whose angles and sides are equal.

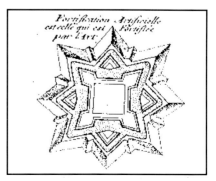

An irregular fortification, one whose angles and sides are unequal.

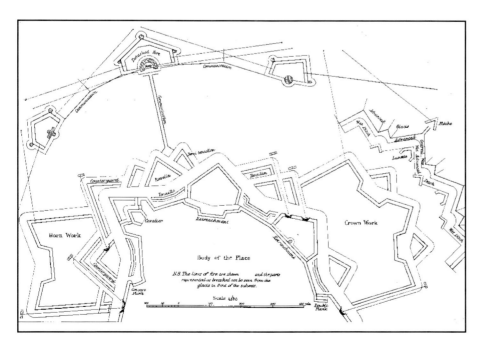

Figure 1.15 Depiction of some detached and advanced works and outworks.

An artificial fortification, one that is designed purely for art.

of defense of musketeers and cannon formed by the bastions and curtains, he suggested that some of the infantry be stationed in a walkway, **the via coperta or the covered way**, which was to be cut into the top of the outer rim of the ditch. In 1567, Pietro Cataneo, a Novarese engineer, added to the efficiency of this covered way by proposing the **re-entering place of arms**. This was a space left at the re-entrant angles of the zigzag pattern made by the **counter-scarp**—the slope or retaining wall on the outer side of the ditch—large enough for the assembly of troops and artillery needed to mount a sortie or ward off a besieger. As mentioned, the area in front of the ditch, known as the glacis, was heaped up into a bare slope of ground cleared of obstacles. The glacis acted as a massive parapet to the covered way, and helped to screen the masonry of the ravelins, bastions, and curtains from artillery fire. When considered as a unit, the main rampart, the ravelin, and the covered way made up a formidable defense in depth, delaying the movement of attackers toward the inner sections of the fortification.

With a defensive fortification structured in this manner, towns within the circuit of fortress walls were rebuilt or redesigned so that their streets radiated out from the town center to each bastion, and extended along the walls. In this way cannon and munitions could be moved with maximum efficiency from one

Figure 1.16   Design for pentagonal fort with ravelins (Francesco de' Marchi, c. 1545).

defensive point to another during periods of siege. The final shape of the new defensive structures resembled a star, and for this reason they were known as star forts.

One member of the Italian school deserves particular mention. Francesco de' Marchi (1506–?), an engineer from Bologna, served the de' Medicis in Florence, Pope Paul III, and, at various times, the Spanish monarchy in the Low Countries. In 1565, de' Marchi wrote his military treatise *Della Architettura Militare*, which was not published until 1599. In it, de' Marchi described as many as 161 systems of fortification, and discussed such practical topics as possible sites for fortresses under differing conditions of terrain; and, as was *de rigueur* during the Renaissance, he included the usual respectable references to Greek and Roman fortification. (See Figure 1.16.)

In addition to the traditional bastion motif, de' Marchi also proposed the idea of completely isolating the bastions from the enceinte so that they stood, like the ravelins, as detached works in the ditch, and served to slow an attack. He also made use of the refinement of an **orillon**, a sort of curved shoulder to the angle between the face and the flank of the bastion that gave the bastion its arrowhead shape. This innovation in design solved a significant problem that defenders faced during the early stages of bastion design: if the attacking forces reached the main wall, gunners on the bastions were forced to fire back on their own defenses in order to hit the enemy. Orillons permitted defenders to fire at the enemy along the wall instead of directly at their own defenses.

During the sixteenth century, the Italian engineer-cum-architect demonstrated a remarkable ease in shifting from one type of building design to another, whether a fortification or a city project. Although a distinct corps of engineers was not yet apparent, historians have identified a loose grouping of individuals based more on ties of blood and family.[11] Fortunately for the European landscape, the Renaissance engineer was not too concerned about national loyalties when it came to selling his skills, and happily exported his expertise wherever he was hired. When genuine Italians were not available, hosts of eager imitators copied their skills and ideas.

Italian ideas were not totally free from criticism, however. Detractors of the Italian techniques appeared in various places. In Germany, for example, the military architect Daniel Speckle (1546–1589) argued that the Germans were equally capable technicians and should not simply accept the Italian domination of the field of fortification without critical analysis. Speckle—one of the contributors to the fortifications of Ulm, Vienna, Prague, Hanau, and Strasbourg, to name a few—consistently argued against blindly accepting Italian theories. In 1587, he published *Architectura von Vestungen* (the frontispiece of which may be seen in Figure 1.17). The book began with an angry foreword about the lack of respect shown in Europe for any but Italian engineers. In this work, Speckle offered his new principles of fortifications, which he described as superior to the Italian. In fact, they differed very little from the Italian principles except in style.[12]

Figure 1.17   Daniel Speckle: Frontispiece of *Architectura Von Vestungen* (1587).

The Transition Between the Renaissance and the Age of Vauban

Unfortunately, it remained for a protracted and bloody European conflict, namely the 80-year war in the Netherlands (1566–1648) and the 1560–1660 upheavals in France, to provide a testing ground for the new theories of fortress defense and to standardize the new methods of siege warfare into almost the status of a science. Italian innovations in fortification design had been widely published and spread rapidly through Europe. Few of these designs, however, had undergone the practical, if brutal, experience of large-scale war. The period of religious, dynastic, and economic strife that began in 1560 and lasted for nearly a century, provided the opportunity for testing Italian fortification theory. The conflicts, especially in the Netherlands, were typified by cumbersome and slow campaigns aimed at seizing and holding large territories. As a result, the capture of towns and fortresses by means of sieges became paramount, as did the problems of adequately fortifying them against attack. The protracted warfare stimulated the beginnings of three particular styles of fortification—Dutch, German, and French. Each developed in response to the special circumstances created by the politics, military campaigns, and terrain of the nations involved, and helped produce a cadre of engineers and soldiers who synthesized and improved upon the existing approaches to fortification, and to siegecraft (as pictured in Figure 1.18).

The Dutch Style of Fortification

The Dutch efforts to throw off the yoke of Catholic Spain led to feverish fortification of their towns, while the Spanish attempted—often through trial and error—to refine the tactics of siege warfare in order to defeat the Dutch Protestant rebellion. During this conflict, the Spanish laid siege to many places, including Tournai in 1581, Oudenarde in 1582, Antwerp in 1584, and Ostend in 1601 (see Figure 1.19), and painfully became reacquainted with certain technical realities involved in attacking fortified places. Primarily, they were reminded of the importance of establishing lines of circumvallation and contravallation to prevent the relief of the place under siege, of the high cost of unprepared assaults launched directly upon the fortress, and of the absolute need for some form of cover, such as trenches, for the besieging troops.

The Dutch, in turn, attempted to refine their skills in both offense and defense and conducted many sieges of their own. For example, during a summer campaign in 1590 alone, the many towns besieged by the Dutch included Breda, Steenbergen, Oosterhout, and Westerloo. Between 1590 and 1600, the Dutch leader of the time, Maurice of Nassau, hastily tried to organize a new bureaucracy to supervise the progress of engineering works and fortifications. This new group of officials was directed by Simon Stevin, who had once been Maurice's tutor in mathematics and fortification—subjects by then considered an undisputed part of a gentleman's education. Now Stevin was appointed the quartermaster general of the army. To augment Dutch efforts against the Spanish, artillery was ordered from the

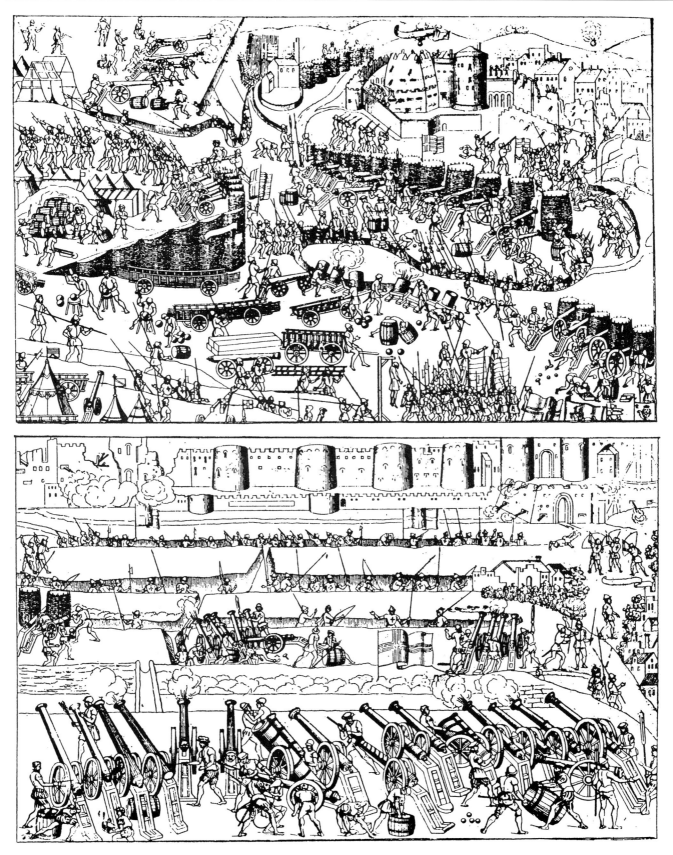

Figure 1.18   Two views of siege operations in the sixteenth century.

**Figure 1.19   A map depicting the
siege of Ostend, 1601.**

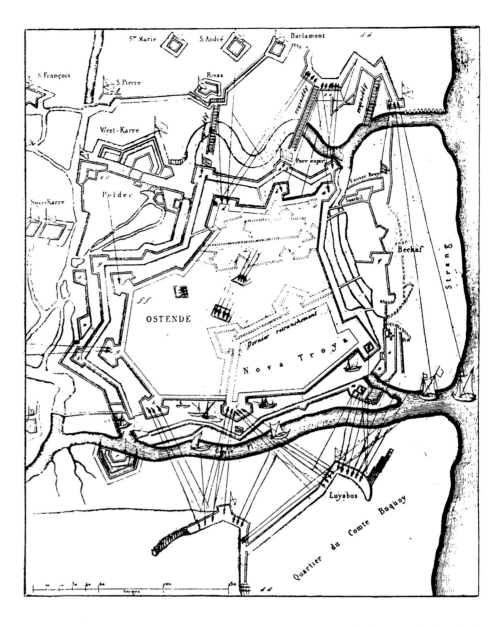

foundries in greater numbers, and towns were refortified or newly fortified
as their condition warranted.

However, the Netherlands' great and transitional contribution to fortification lay in the changes Dutch engineers brought to the Italian bastion
system. Dutch fortification evolved rapidly under the pressures of war and
featured two significant design innovations: an earthen rampart and a wet
ditch. These two concepts were logical in a countryside that was basically
flat and prone to flooding.

The most important defensive component of the fortification was the
thick, earthen rampart favored by Dutch engineers. To guard the rampart
against escalade, rows of horizontal, pointed timbers, known as **fraises** or
storm poles, were placed in front of it. Along the foot of the rampart ran
a low outer rampart, or **fausse-braye**, intended to give the defenders command of the ditch. A wet ditch, the prime innovation of passive defense of

the Dutch system, surrounded the entire enceinte. (See Figure 1.20.) The idea for the ditch, flooded by opening the dikes, derived from a tactic used in the sixteenth century by the Dutch rebels, known as the "sea beggars."

The more active aspects of the fortifi-cation's defenses were represented by the outworks—those defenses located between the enceinte and the glacis, or out-side the first enclo-sure. While the ravelin (essentially a detached triangular bastion) remained a close copy of the Italian model, the Dutch demon-strated an amazing ingenuity in their use of two other separate outworks. The first was the **demilune**, a

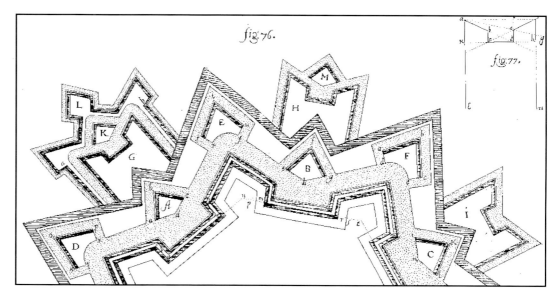

structure so similar to a ravelin that the terms often came to be used inter-changeably. The demilune was designed to be placed in front of the bastion to help cover the curtain walls, and was separated from the main body of the fortress by a ditch. The second, a sharply forward-projecting structure known as a **hornwork** (see Figure 1.21), was located beyond the main ditch to pro-

Figure 1.20   Dutch fortification (Freitag, 1631): Enceinte with fausse-braye, broad wet ditch, continuous outer enceinte, and elaborate detached works—ravelins (A, B, C), demilunes (D, E, F) and hornworks (G, H, I).

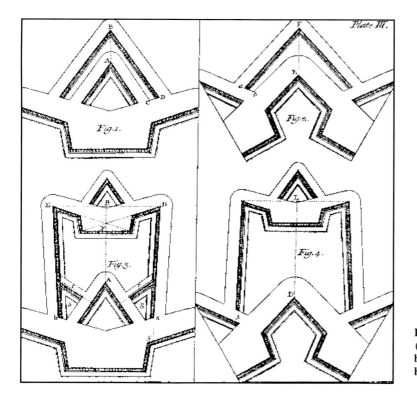

Figure 1.21   Hornworks and other outworks (Muller, 1746): Figures 1 and 2—ravelin and bastion with counterguards; Figures 3 and 4—hornworks.

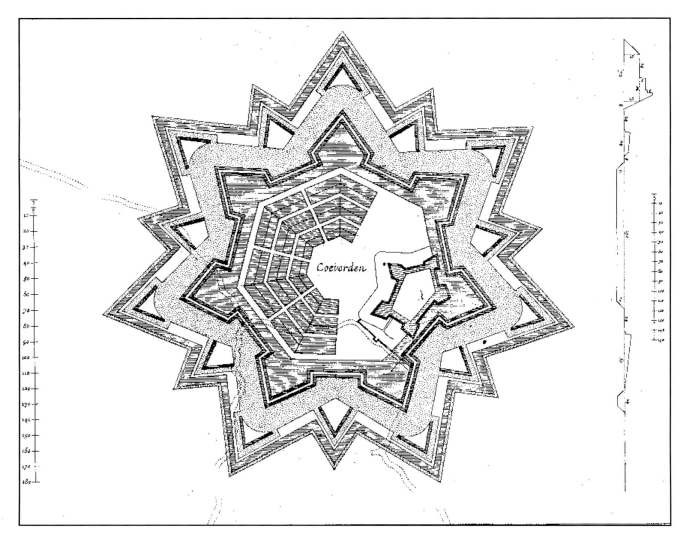

Figure 1.22 Coevorden as rebuilt by Maurice of Nassau (Dögen, 1647).

vide additional flanking fire. Basically, the hornwork design was simple. Its sides consisted of two parallel extensions, which connected at one end with two half-bastions, a curtain, and an outlying ravelin.

The fortress of Coevorden, refortified by Maurice of Nassau in 1605, best exemplified the Dutch style. Coevorden, pictured in Figure 1.22, consisted of seven bastions with salient angles so acute that the lines of defense—the theoretical line that traced the distance from the flank to the point of the opposite bastion—met the curtains virtually in the center. A thick faussebraye (the low, outer rampart) was bordered by a 180-foot-wide wet ditch, which was defended by a group of ravelins and demilunes, each preceded by its own 30-foot-wide ditch. These outworks were hidden from enemy view by a glacis. And, with an extraordinary attention to the concept of defense in depth, the Dutch had added beyond the main glacis another outer ditch full of water, and an outer glacis on the edge of the marshes.

This Dutch type of fortification had several distinct advantages over the basic Italian model. The wet ditches and earthen ramparts gave it substantial powers of passive resistance; the design's multiple systems and elaborate outworks created an interesting defense in depth; and finally, this style of fortification was relatively quick and cheap to build compared with the Italian plan. Because of these factors, the Dutch examples of fortification spread rapidly throughout Europe during this time, appearing in France and most particularly in Germany. However, several negative aspects inherent in the Dutch design prevented it from becoming the dominant system of fortification in the seventeenth century.

To begin with, as the war in the Netherlands dragged on, it often became apparent that small garrisons had difficulty defending such complicated outworks. If captured, those same outworks provided the besieger with a useful site to establish his own forces and to launch an attack. Moreover, while the wet ditches may have comprised a formidable barrier to the enemy, they simultaneously created an unintentional barrier to the supply and reinforcement of the covered way and the outworks by the garrison. The outworks could be reached only by means of rafts or over hastily rigged log bridges, which themselves ran the danger of being turned to good use by the enemy. Even a severely cold winter could be a threat to the Dutch design, for if the wet ditch froze, the storm poles and earthen rampart were no longer useful in hindering the enemy's attack. Eventually, too, the Dutch fortifications were discovered to be extremely prone to destruction by the ricochet artillery attack, which was developed in the seventeenth century. Ricochet bombardment forced the cannon shot to graze the top of fortress parapets and bounce along the length of the **terrepleins** (the wide upper part of a rampart), causing extensive damage to the fortress and its troops. The ricochet batteries turned out to be especially effective against the elongated sides of the hornworks and the faces of the sharply angled bastions, while batteries brought up to the counterscarp by attackers easily decimated the defenders who were still fighting in the low fausse-braye.

Ultimately, although the Dutch system was inexpensive and quick to build, it was apparent that such extensive use of the wet ditch was truly best suited to the Netherlands, where the water table was no more than 6 or 7 feet below the surface. Also, although the wooden palisades and earthen slopes of the Dutch system might initially have been inexpensive to construct compared to the "trace italienne," they had to be inspected and repaired constantly lest the fortification completely deteriorate. The Dutch system has consequently been described as merely an elaborate fieldwork, rather than a fortification built to endure.[13]

The German Style of Fortification

In Germany, during this time of transition from the Renaissance, greatest attention was focused on the bastion, with the general proportions given to it by Speckle, and on the Dutch fausse-braye. Unfortunately, there was no German engineer capable of uniting all the various designs floating around Europe into a coherent and workable system. Georg Rimpler (1634–1683), a German soldier-engineer who saw service in such disparate places as Sweden, Crete, France, and Vienna, left a number of writings on fortifications that most historians admit are a confused tangle of jargon, contradictions, and detail, without any plans that might help explain his designs. What came to be known as "the Rimpler trace" was actually the invention of later writers, such as Leonhard Cristoph Sturm (the frontspiece of Sturm's

Figure 1.23 Frontispiece, Leonhard Christoph Sturm, *Architectura Militaris*.

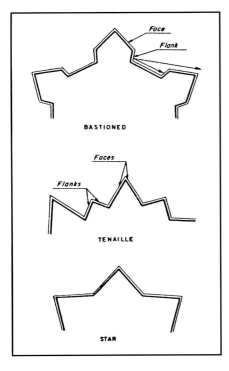

Figure 1.24 Types of traces.

Figure 1.25 Frontispiece, Matthias Dögen, *Architecura Militaris Moderna*.

Architectura Militaris may be seen in Figure 1.23) and L. A. Herlin, who purported to have understood and explained Rimpler's system in their own work.

Actually, until the late eighteenth century, when the theories of the Frenchman Montalembert made great inroads, the dominant trace in German design was the **tenaille** plan of fortification, which had originated in Italy. It was a simple trace, depicted in Figure 1.24, made up entirely of straight faces that were joined together as zigzags. The whole fortification took on the shape of a star, providing for excellent covering fire from the salients and the flanks. It was also a more economical way to enclose an area than any other shape except a circle. By the same token, however, its design, with those prolonged faces, made it exceedingly vulnerable to enfilading fire, which could make the long, unbroken ramparts untenable in a single day's bombardment.

During the seventeenth century, the Dutch fortification with its earthen enceintes made some inroads in Germany with the help of its foremost exponent in Brandenburg-Prussia, Matthias Dögen (c.1605–1672). Dögen, who wrote *Architectura Militaris Moderna* (see Figure 1.25) in 1647, learned the Dutch technique while serving in The Hague, and, beginning in 1658, used it to help refortify Berlin. However, during this period, Germany was greatly hampered by the fact that it remained a geographic expression, rather than a centralized nation such as France. Like Renaissance Italy, as long as Germany was composed of a myriad of squabbling states and bishoprics, fortifications on a massive, expensive, or even coherent scale were highly unlikely, as was the acquisition of any solid experience in the tactics and strategy of fortress warfare. In the seventeenth century, these advantages came to belong to France; under Louis XIV and his chief engineer, Vauban, France was to make the most of them.

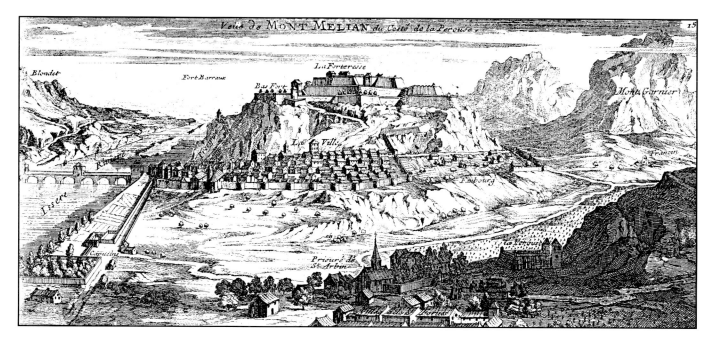

The French Style of Fortification

From 1560 to 1660, France was convulsed in the religious wars that pitted Catholics against Huguenots, and in the civil strife of the wars of the Fronde. During this time of turmoil, lessons about the strategy of warfare and fortifications were bitterly learned, and some of the groundwork that helped establish the absolute rule of Louis XIV was laid. Henri IV, one of the key figures of the time, was himself an acknowledged practitioner of fortress warfare.[14] He also had the good fortune to have in his service as chief engineer Maximilian de Béthune, Duke of Sully (1560–1641). Between 1596 and 1610, Henri IV and Sully—who simultaneously held the four offices of grand master of artillery, superintendent of finances, superintendent of building, and superintendent of fortifications—attempted to make progress in all four of these areas. They assembled a large force of infantry and attempted to regularize its training, and tried to better organize the methods of acquiring ordnance and stockpiling arsenals. Written instructions on theory and tactics were circulated among the engineers and gunners, and the artillery was given an official recognition of its new importance. These actions quickly bore fruit, and in 1600, to the surprise of Europe, a French army took the fortress of Montmélian in Savoy, pictured in Figure 1.26, by carving out battery sites on the steep mountain slopes. This event excited those engineers who had begun to understand the formidable possibilities inherent in the proper placement of artillery.

Sully and Henri also set up a bureaucracy to oversee fortifications in a systematic manner within France, especially on the frontiers. Revenues were raised and allotted to reinforce existing strongholds, while nearly 30 previously undefended towns—including Toulon, Grenoble, Boulogne, Calais, and Amiens—were converted into fortresses. Older fortresses, considered obsolete, were demolished.

Perhaps the most significant change that occurred during these years, despite the political upheavals, was the way the Italian School lost its pre-

Figure 1.26   Fortress of Montmélian (De Fer, 1690–95): taken by the French who astonished Europe by their placement of battery sites on the steep mountain slopes.

**Figure 1.27   Errard's fortification:
the lower bastions have his
characteristic right-angled
shoulders (Errard, 1594).**

eminence in France. It was gradually replaced by a home-grown constella-
tion of French engineers such as d'Espinai de Saint-Luc, who placed the
artillery in taking Amiens from the Spanish in 1597, and Claude de
Chastillon, who directed the sieges of Chartres (1591), Amiens (1597), and
Montmélian (1600). The most distinguished of this new generation of French
engineers was Jean Errard de Bar-le-Duc (1554–1610). Born in Lorraine,
he completed his education in Italy, studying the techniques and designs
then available. He was subsequently appointed by Henri IV to work on the
construction of fortresses in the northern and eastern sectors of France.
One of his fortifications is depicted in Figure 1.27. Errard's most notable
construction was the citadel of Amiens, which was begun in 1597 and finished by the time of his death in 1610. In 1614, in a compliment to Errard
and entirely in accordance with his principles, work began on the powerful citadel at Verdun. In 1594, upon royal command, Errard published *La
Fortification demonstrée et reduicte en art*, a work that was important in that it
was the first purely French book of any significance on fortification. In
Errard's opinion, engineers needed to have practical experience in both
defense and attack, and to have studied gunnery as a science. Nonetheless,
given his formative studies in Italy, it is not surprising that his designs were
basically a variation on the theme of the Italian styles. It is now apparent
that a glaring weakness of his design was his insistence on right angles at

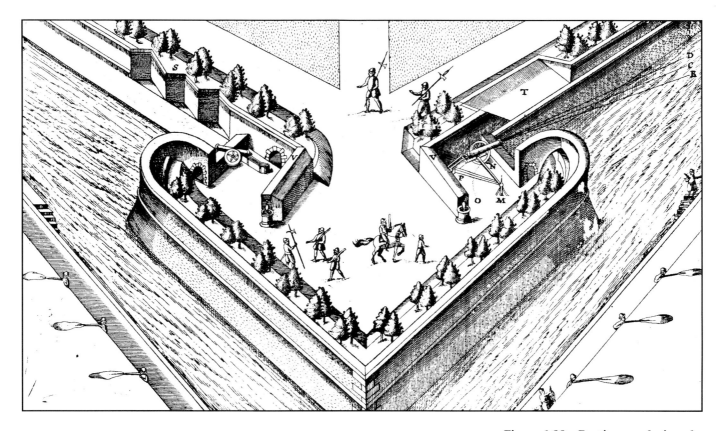

the shoulders of his bastions as shown in Figure 1.28. This produced a flank that met the curtain too acutely, resulting in poor covering fire for the face of the adjacent bastion. Also, Errard virtually ignored the value of outworks, despite the Dutch innovations in this area.

By 1653, Louis XIV, a 15-year-old, was on the throne of France, and the civil war was virtually over. No longer divided, France was able to gather her forces to make war on the Spanish and to regain the losses sustained in the Netherlands during the French civil and religious conflicts. Under the leadership of Maréchal de Turenne, the French handed Spain a series of defeats, the most noteworthy of which was at Dunkirk in 1658. At the same time, France also gained Oudenarde, Menin, and Ypres in the Netherlands. The Peace of the Pyrenées in 1659 ended a quarter-century of fighting between France and Spain, leaving France poised to expand her power and influence.

During this time, two Frenchmen in particular were well-known for contributing substantially to the theoretical literature on fortification. Blaise François, Comte de Pagan (1604–1665) was a veteran of the religious wars in the 1620s and had participated in many sieges. Although, as far as it is known, he never directed any important construction, he did succeed in changing the type of fortresses built by the French in the latter seventeenth century. Vauban's famous "first system" was in reality Pagan's style, executed with minor improvements and flexibly adapted to different terrain. Pagan's central ideas were presented in his treatise *Les Fortifications du comte de Pagan* (1645). All were founded on a single primary consideration: the increased effectiveness of firepower for both the offense and the defense. To Pagan, the bastions (Color Plate 1 on page 63) were the most important part of the

Figure 1.28   Bastions as designed by Errard: the right angles at the shoulders of his bastions produced a flank that met the curtain too acutely and resulted in poor covering fire for the faces of the adjacent bastion.

trace, and their position and shape were determined with the help of simple geometrical rules that he formulated. Pagan planned a new fortress by establishing the outer perimeter, measured from the outermost points of the bastions, before the inner perimeter of the rampart, reversing past procedures in which the inner perimeter was laid first.

The Chevalier de Ville (1596–1656) also wrote an influential text, *Fortifications* (1629), which went through many editions in comparison with Vauban's writings. (The book's frontispiece is pictured in Figure 1.29.) Vauban's works became known only gradually, through unauthorized printings of manuscripts circulated among a small group of engineers and officials. A seasoned old soldier like Pagan, de Ville differed from him in that he placed less emphasis on the importance of the bastion. De Ville laid out an enceinte in the Italian style with obtuse-angled bastions, and he encircled it with powerful outworks—both the ravelins of the Italians and the hornwork of the Dutch—that he believed were necessary for a protracted defense. He also argued that the design of the fortification should sensibly accommodate itself to the specific demands of the site.

Clearly, this period of transition between the Italian Renaissance and its development of bastion fortification, and the classic era of Vauban and Louis XIV, was a fertile, if confused, one with regard to the theories, strategy, and tactics of fortifications. The conflicts among the European states had given birth to assorted styles of fortification, and had provided those concepts with a baptism of fire. What remained to be accomplished was an organized re-ordering of all of these ideas and designs into a coherent system that would truly deserve the designation of not just the art, but also the *science* of fortification.

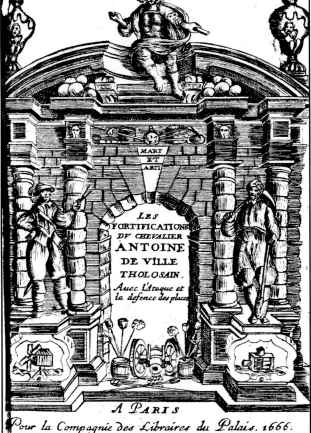

Figure 1.29 Frontispiece, Chevalier de Ville, *Fortifications*.

Modern fortification is the way of defence now used, turning the walls into ramparts, and square and round towers into bastions, defended by numerous outworks; all of which are made so solid, that they cannot be beat down, but by continual fire of several batteries of cannon . . . it is now almost a received opinion, that the art of fortification is at its height, and almost incapable of being carried to a much greater perfection.

Captain George Smith, 1779

The Basic Design of a Permanent Fortification

By the seventeenth century, most designs of a permanent fortification demonstrated essentially the same basic components. Certainly, the prolific fortification literature of the period featured all sorts of designs suggested by an amazing spectrum of theorists—ranging from soldiers and engineers to academics, and even to clergymen who were military buffs. However, what practical improvements or changes were made to fortification design were mostly variations on the common style that had gradually taken hold since the introduction of the new artillery. A large and permanent fortress, from inception to construction, had come to exhibit features that were universally accepted as basic principles by European engineers in the seventeenth century.

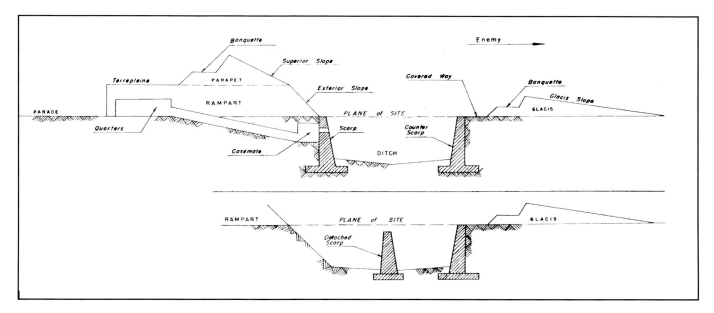

The first goal considered in the design of a fortress (see Figures 1.30 and 1.31), as has been discussed, was the establishment of maximum effective firepower. During the late seventeenth and early eighteenth centuries, all military engineers agreed with the basic premise that every sector of a fortress must be swept by converging fields of fire, from both cannon and firearms. But it was also expected that it would be possible to extend the firepower of cannon within the fortress to the outlying areas, and attempt to destroy the attackers at a distance from the fortress if possible—the concept of active defense. Acting upon these premises, fortification engineers were supposed to ensure that every position and outwork be carefully, even mathematically, designed to permit the most effective use of the defenders' weapons and the maximum degree of mutual support.

Second, the fortress had to demonstrate in its design the ability to protect its own garrison and the town within its walls. Compelled by these requirements, engineers had already abandoned the high walls of medieval

Figure 1.30   Profile of a fortification (Department of Art and Engineering, USMA, 1946).

Figure 1.31   A sketch of permanent profiles (Godson, Royal Military Academy, 1863).

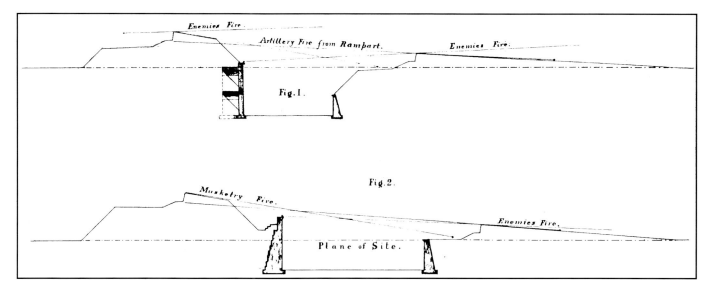

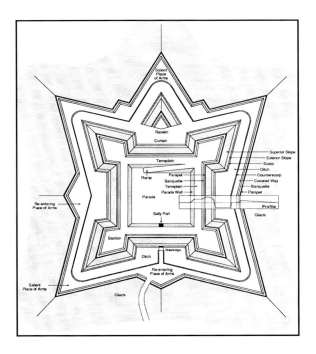

Figure 1.32 Elements of bastioned fortifications.

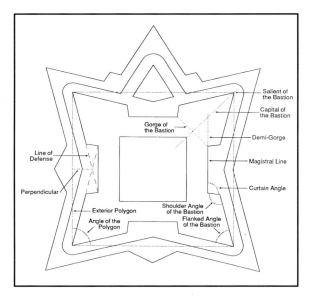

Figured 1.33 Geometry of bastioned fortifications.

castles for squat and tremendously thick bastions and curtain walls, constructed low to the ground in order to counteract the effects of enemy bombardment. Stone-reinforced positions of packed earth, along with deep ditches, had been added by engineers in order to reduce the damage done by artillery. And, as the cannon continued to be manufactured in greater numbers and become more powerful, defensive systems expanded into increasingly complex layers of outworks intended to force the enemy's batteries farther and farther away from the fortification itself. Thus, while the concept of effective firepower carried with it a component of active defense, the development of consecutive layers of outworks clearly revealed a growing understanding of the more passive defensive possibilities for the fortification. The design of a full-fledged seventeenth-century fortification combined elements of both active and passive defense, attempting to obstruct the enemy's approach by means of both firepower and physical obstacles. The object, of course, was to delay as long as possible the moment of hand-to-hand combat between the enemy and the garrison at a breach in the wall, so as to squander the enemy's resources, spare the garrison unnecessary bloodshed, and buy time in case a relieving army might arrive.

How were the general concepts of firepower, protection, and passive obstruction—recognized by engineers of the time as vital for fortress design—applied in practical terms? Let us start from the outermost perimeter and, keeping in mind what has been described so far, move inwards to the center of the fortification (see Figures 1.32 and 1.33).

The most distant part of the mature fortress was the glacis, an area of ground between 200 and 400 yards wide, designed to encircle completely a town or fortress. Sloping gently upwards toward the main defenses, the glacis was specifically cleared of all forms of cover in order to provide the garrison's sentries with a panoramic view of the area, and the guns with a clear field of fire. In some instances, especially with Dutch fortifications, the outer edge of the glacis was protected by a ditch, but many engineers disliked this design because of its tendency to interfere with sorties from the garrison. A ditch in the glacis carried with it a major disadvantage, for it could easily provide the enemy with a convenient, already dug cover for use as a place of arms. One of the few times the glacis was omitted was when the fortress was fortuitously situated on top of a hill or mountain, naturally providing a ready-made view for the garrison.

The first regular outwork of the fortification was the covered way, which merged with the inner edge of the ditch and continued all the way around the fortress on the outer side of the main ditch. The covered way consisted of a circular access road and a parapet built with a fire step, called the **banquette**, from which garrison troops could shoot at the attackers if they came within range. This parapet was constructed from a huge bank of earth, and buttressed by palisading. At various intervals, as the Italians had pioneered, places of arms were built into the glacis. These were large spaces constructed in the covered way, at the re-entrant or salient angles, where troops could be assembled for sorties or for the defense of the covered way.

Sloping down from the rear of the covered way was the counterscarp wall. Forming the outer face of the ditch, this steep bank was generally lined (**revetted**) with brick or stone. Galleries were sometimes cut into the face of the counterscarp. These galleries were firing positions intended to defend the bottom of the ditch and the foot of the facing scarp walls. The ditch itself represented the next consecutive defensive obstacle in fortress design. Although ditches varied in width and depth, in all cases the earth dug out of them was, in turn, used to construct positions beyond them. By the mid-seventeenth century, the most popular dimensions for a ditch were a width of 95 feet, and a depth of 18 to 20 feet below the ground level of the fortress interior.[15] Three types of ditches were common in fortification design. There was a dry ditch with a deep trench running down the center known as the **cuvette**. A narrow ditch sunk in the bottom of a dry ditch, the cuvette was intended to aid drainage, hamper enemy troops, and prevent mining attempts. In addition, there were two sorts of wet ditches—those filled with still water and those with moving water. Despite functioning as an obstacle to the enemy, each kind of ditch carried its own drawbacks. The ditches with still water posed hazards to health, and were disliked by engineers on exactly those grounds; while the ditches with running water, such as those at the great fortresses of Namur and Lille, were subject to erosion and flooding in bad weather. However, the wet ditch was commonly regarded as the best defensive obstacle, since, unlike the dry ditch, it was obviously difficult for the enemy to bridge easily under fire. It also became apparent to the defenders that the wet ditch could, to some extent, get in the way of effective sorties against the attackers. Bridges made from logs that were tied together (sometimes called sally bridges) were designed to counter this problem. Often, dry ditches also held a fausse-braye—a second low, outer earthen rampart running around the foot of the main rampart. But, despite the Dutch example, these were becoming passé by the 1700s.

The area surrounding the ditch contained the most important outworks of a fortress. Increasingly complex and elaborate, they all were intended to protect the various sections of the main position. The general objective of these designs was to force the enemy to start his operations farther and farther away from the main enceinte, thus sparing the interior from gunfire for as long as possible. Successive outworks also served to delay the progress of a siege by setting up a series of defensive works that had to be taken systematically before a real attack on the inner sectors could begin. The first outwork to be developed was, of course, the ravelin. Initially an enlargement of the covered way, it eventually became a separate detached work with a ditch, a scarp, and counterscarp walls of its own. When the ravelin formed part of the demilune but was separated from it by parts of the moat, it was often called a **redoubt**. Other outworks included demilunes and **tenailles**, long works parallel to the ramparts with ends canted out to protect the curtain. Because of the difficulties of providing a defense of the ditch solely from scarp or counterscarp galleries, a **caponnière** was designed. This was a low work built out into or across the ditch, entered by a tunnel from the main area of the fortress, and provided with loopholes for enfilading the ditch with musket or cannon fire. A final layer of outworks was represented by the immense addition of designs known as crownworks and hornworks, often constructed adjoining the glacis (as at the fortresses of Lille and Bouchain) to protect major entrances into the town or fortress.

Appearing inside the outworks was the scarp, or inner wall of the ditch. Generally faced with stone, the scarp wall, before long, also had galleries built in its rear. Loopholes for firing were then constructed through the scarp wall to help defend the ditch from assault parties. Scarp galleries had one great advantage—easy communication with the interior of the fort by means of tunnels through the rampart. On the other hand, both scarp and counterscarp galleries were exposed to breaching fire and to having their loopholes blocked by debris falling from above. Hence, the innovation of the caponnière. Often, too, a concealed walkway was designed behind the top of the scarp wall. Loopholes were then made in the upper scarp wall so that soldiers standing in the walkway could fire into the ditch or across the ditch into the covered way behind the glacis. This arrangement became known as a **semidetached scarp.**

Adjoining the scarp stood the main curtain wall, with its projecting bastions. Both the curtain and the bastions had been dropped lower to the ground by engineers to counter the effects of cannon fire, and they projected only about 12 to 15 feet over the edge of the glacis. When combined with the depth of the ditch, however, this height was enough to form a considerable obstacle for the enemy. The real advantage of the bastion design lay in its thickness, which measured as much as 66 feet at the base and tapered to some 30 feet at the level of the gun platform. Curtain walls were less massive, but still formidable, with an average thickness of 24 feet at the parapets. They were constructed of buttressed earth, and were usually provided with sloping outer faces to lessen the damage from bombardment.

Finally, in the center of the fortification stood the bastions themselves, projecting forward from the main trace to create the required configuration of flanking fire with the other guns positioned on their respective platforms. The two faces of the bastion, and the curtain wall between them, permitted fire to the front. The two flanks were intended to provide fire along the curtain and the face of the next bastion. For many years, the sharpness of the angle at the apex of the bastion, as well as the specific shape and length of the flanks, remained the subject of argument among rival schools of engineering. If the salient angles—the angles pointing out toward the field—were too sharp or too obtuse, they adversely affected the lines of fire and the length of the flanks. The fire from the flanks of the bastion was the most vital element of the defense of the ditch, and perhaps of the bastion system itself. In order for the volume of fire from the flanks to be powerful enough, the flanks had to be sufficiently long. However, lengthening the flanks too far tended to throw into disarray the proper relationship between the flanks and the faces of the next bastion, critically affecting the lines of fire. Thus, a good engineer constantly strove to ensure that all parts of the fortress were covered against fire, trying to keep in mind the line of defense at all times. In general, the line of defense was determined by calculating the musket range of the day from one flank of the bastions to another. Although the distance between the two bastions was theoretically not supposed to exceed the musket range of the time, this rule was not always adhered to. At the fortification at Maubeuge, for exam-

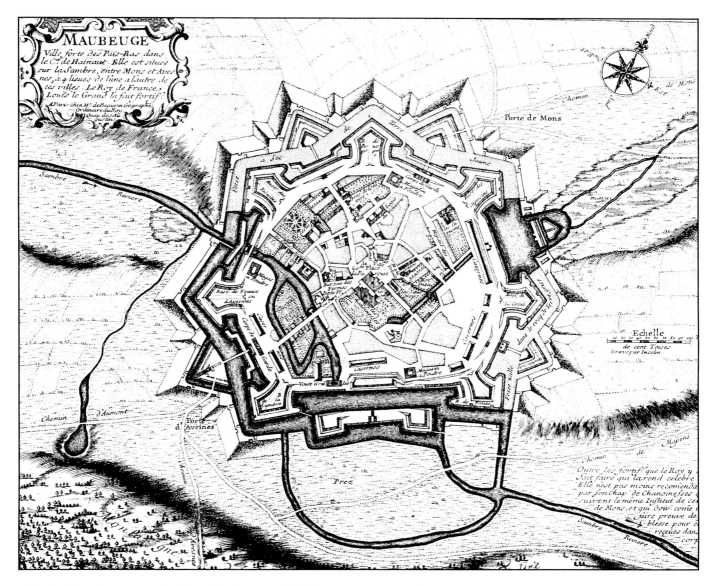

Figure 1.34   The fortified town of Maubeuge: note the tenailles designed to protect the exposed length of curtain walls. These were built when the bastion flanks were too far away from one another for effective fire.

ple, the bastions were designed to be over 600 feet apart; in such cases, tenailles were developed to provide cover for the dangerously exposed length of curtain wall. (See Figure 1.34.)

Situated within the bastions were the gun platforms, protected by a strong parapet. The parapet was furnished with a banquette (a fire step), and with sizeable gun embrasures for further firepower. As it became apparent that some sort of tower observation posts at the apex of the bastion or at intervals along the curtain wall were highly useful, **tours bastionées** appeared in the design plans. These towers, especially popular in France where they originated, were soon also used as additional places for batteries of guns. For better communication, a **chemin de ronde**—a sentry walkway—ran along the top of the rampart, while to the rear of the bastions ran an actual road. Provided with staircases up to the ramparts, or more simply with earthen slopes up to the gun platforms, this road was intended to allow the garrison to quickly and efficiently reinforce any threatened sector of the fortress.

Such, then, was the seventeenth century fortress—a vast, elaborate, and formidable stronghold whose very appearance represented a challenge to those who considered besieging it. Indeed, the history of fortification during its most mature period could best be characterized as a process of problem solving, in which engineers were constantly reacting to the changes in technology and warfare. As soon as a weakness in the fortress was noted, something new was added to correct it, only to in time develop its own flaws, which in turn had to be corrected if the fortress were to survive. As a result, by the middle of the seventeenth century, the complexity of fortifications had become enormous, and their very nomenclature was on the verge of becoming a science in itself. In fact, so complex was the field that the art of fortification risked becoming arcane. Fortunately, before this could happen, one individual—Vauban—succeeded in analyzing and communicating the theory of fortification and siegecraft with such clarity that he, in effect, prevented it from becoming the province of merely a few.

Notes

[1] Edward M. Earle, *Makers of Modern Strategy* (Princeton: Princeton University Press, 1943), p. x.

[2] Carlo M. Cipolla, *Guns, Sails and Empires: Technological Innovation and the Early Phases of European Expansion*, 1400–1700 (New York: Pantheon Books, 1965), pp. 1–73. The author provides an excellent and detailed account of the initial development of artillery in Europe during this period.

[3] Francesco Guicciardini, *The History of Italy*, trans. S. Alexander (New York: Macmillan Co., 1967), pp. 50–51.

[4] Guicciardini, *The History of Italy*, p. 72.

[5] John R. Hale, "The Development of the Bastion, 1440–1534," in *Europe in the Late Middle Ages* (London: Faber and Faber, 1965). This article offers a comprehensive look at the development of the Italian advances in bastion fortification.

[6] Hale, "The Development of the Bastion," p. 472.

[7] Guicciardini, *The History of Italy*, p. 418.

[8] Hale, "The Development of the Bastion," p. 475.

[9] Cristopher Duffy, *Siege Warfare: The Fortress in the Early Modern World* 1494–1660 (London: Routledge and Kegan Paul, 1979), p. 31.

[10] Duffy, *Siege Warfare*, a quotation from Gabrio Busca, p. 33.

[11] Duffy, *Siege Warfare*, pp. 38–39. The author provides detailed and comprehensive charts of these various "families" of Italian engineers.

[12] Duffy, *Siege Warfare*, p. 55.

[13] Duffy, *Siege Warfare*, p. 93.

[14] Duffy, *Siege Warfare*, p. 111. The author points out that Henri IV was closely associated with, if not the founder, of the explosive weapon known as the petard. It was actually a bronze bell packed with powder, attached to an iron beam with chains or ropes—all propped up against the wall or gate that was targeted to be blown up. A fuse strung back from the bell supposedly gave the petardiers enough time to scurry to a safe distance before the device went off, and propelled the beam through the target. That they often did not make it in time is evidenced by our use of the phrase "hoist with your own petard."

[15] Sebastien le Prestre de Vauban, *Traité de l'attaque et de la deffence des places*. MS copy, Executé par le Seigneur De Lussac, Ingénieur du Roy, undated, p.15.

Vauban and the Golden Age of Fortification | 2

Introduction

Indisputably, the great engineer of the golden age of fortifications was Sebastien le Prestre de Vauban (1633–1707), a man whose skill and fame became legendary in his own lifetime, and who wielded enormous influence during his life as well as after it. Vauban had the advantage of serving a king, Louis XIV, and his sympathetic *secrétaire de l'état de la guerre*, the Marquis de Louvois, at a time when France was ready to expand its frontiers and use its wars as instruments of state policy. The France of Louis XIV owed much of its ascendancy to the combination of an absolutist monarchical state that controlled a "de-feudalized" army, a fairly efficient bureaucracy, a comparatively wealthy agricultural economy, a busy commercial and capitalistic class, and a population of unprecedented size and efficiency. Vauban's career would advance inextricably entwined with France's increasing power in Europe.

Born to a relatively modest family of Burgundian gentry, Vauban first left his native province in 1651 when he volunteered to enter the regiment of the Prince de Condé, the rebel leader in the civil war of the time. Taken prisoner two years later, he was won over to the royalists by Cardinal Mazarin, and sent back to the wars to serve as an apprentice engineer under the Chevalier de Clerville, a highly competent military engineer. By the late 1660s, Vauban was by far the most famous soldier-engineer of his time, but he had to wait until 1678 before Louvois formally named him *commissaire général des fortifications*. Yet Vauban's power really derived from his integrity and authority, and from his professional relationship with both Louvois and Louis XIV. In 1688 he was promoted to lieutenant general, and in January 1703, toward the end of his life, he became a marshal of France. He died on March 30, 1707, having sustained 8 wounds in the service of France, directed some 48 sieges, and drawn up projects for about 160 fortresses.[1] Moreover, his abilities spanned an amazing spectrum of interests. Vauban wrote not just on military matters such as fortifications, weaponry, and the need for a trained corps of engineers, but also on issues dealing with government, social policies, and national economics.[2] His achievements represented an amazing contribution by any standard. Even the cynical Saint-Simon, whose biographies savaged so many prominent men of French public life in the eighteenth century, had kind words for Vauban: "For valour, bounty and probity, despite a rough and brutal exterior, he was by far the greatest man of his century in the art of fortifications and sieges, and also in the realm of handling men; whilst a further outstanding characteristic was his simplicity."[3]

Vauban's great contribution to the art and science of permanent fortification was his perfection and development of the ideas that had germinated in Europe in the decades before him. He himself freely acknowledged his debt to Pagan and the Italian engineers of the Renaissance. It was Vauban's successors, not Vauban, who insisted on breaking down his ideas into three "systems" of fortification, perhaps because elements from each were readily to be found in his work. (See Color Plates 2 through 4 on pages 63–64.) The first system comprised a basically simple series of defenses such as those already common in Europe—namely, polygon outlines with bastions, ditches, and outworks. The second system replaced the angle bastions with small tours bastionées, added a second ditch, and placed large bastions in detached positions before the rampart. The third modified the design of the tenailles, and added a hedge along the demilunes. Each demilune was further defended by a ravelin or redoubt built in the rear, thus presenting a ring of defensive works to the enemy. (See Figure 2.1.)

It must be stated, however, that Vauban himself would have scoffed at describing his ideas as a "system," for he always deplored a rigid approach. "The art of fortification," he wrote, "does not consist of rules and systems, but lies solely in good sense and in experience."[4] Fontenelle, who was his

Figure 2.1   Profile of Vauban's so-called "third system" of fortification (Muller, 1746).

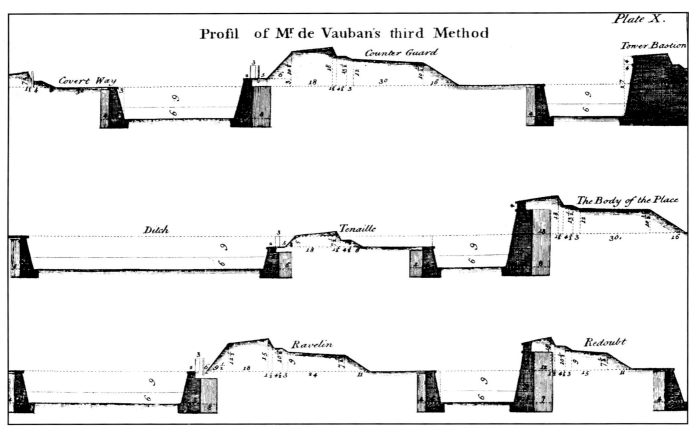

contemporary, commented: "He always said, and always demonstrated in practice that he had no particular system. Every various site provided him with a new idea, according to the differing circumstances of its size, its situation and its terrain."[5] The arbitrary ordering of his ideas after his death probably resulted from the confusion surrounding his written works. It is known that he wrote indefatigably about all sorts of subjects for the French government and for himself; yet he constantly denied the validity of many published works attributed to him that appeared during his lifetime, especially abroad—such as the work titled *La Manière de fortification de M. Vauban*, published in Amsterdam (1689) and in London (1691 and 1693).

Eventually, however, three works of which he was the author became public—namely *Traité de l'attaque des places* (1704), *Traité de la défense des places* (c.1706) and *Traité des mines* (1707). The first versions were probably written in the 1670s and were intended only for the eyes of the highest of the king's public servants. But in an age in which security was so lax that even Vauban was driven to complain, it was not long before more or less complete versions appeared in Paris and The Hague. In due course these ran into many editions in several languages, with many spurious additions to the text.[6] (See Figure 2.2.) The rapid spread of Vauban's work by the publishers of Europe, the clarity of his ideas, and the coherence of his presentation soon made him the most pre-eminent fortification theorist of his age. When this widespread admiration for his written works was added to his reputation for practical competence as a military engineer and fortress builder, Vauban's dominance as both a defensive and offensive engineer was assured.

Figure 2.2   Frontispiece, Vauban, *Traité de l'attaque et de la deffence des places (De Lussac).*

Vauban as a Defensive Engineer

Four broad principles or concepts formed the foundation of most of Vauban's work on defensive fortifications. The first was his primary tenet that any fortress design be adapted to the specific demands of the site, making the most of any natural advantages and adjusting to the negative ones. Vauban had little patience with those whose fortification designs were so perfectly symmetrical theoretically that they disregarded completely the practical demands of the terrain. In every case the problem of design was a simple one: to build and adapt a fortress with a bastioned trace to a terrain so that none of the basic principles of firepower were violated. During his career, he built an amazing variety of fortresses in every conceivable type of site. Some sat on mountains, such as Mont-Louis in the Pyrenées; some on rivers, such as Briançon on a rocky plateau above the Durance; and some were simply spectacularly unique, such as the Château-Queyras (1692), which perched on an isolated rock 4,000 feet above sea level. He renovated such coastal

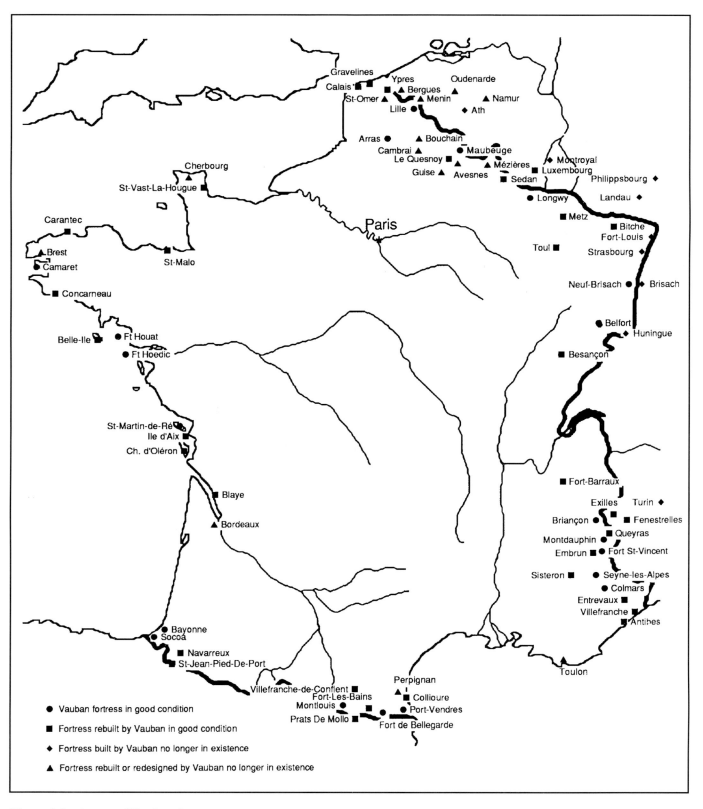

Figure 2.3   A map of Vauban fortresses.

fortresses as Dunkirk on the English Channel and Concarneau in Brittany (see Figure 2.3).

Indeed, the creation of coherent, defensible frontiers for France was one of Vauban's primary aims. Ideally, Vauban visualized France as enclosed in a simplified and rationally designed ring of fortresses, strong enough to resist any attack. He called this concept the **pré carré** (the square field), and over his 30 years of service, Vauban worked constantly to convince the king and his ministers to acquire—by means of wars or peace treaties—those places that could be fortified and simultaneously provide for France a frontier that, wherever possible, formed a straight line.[7] Toward this end, he established in the north a double line of powerful fortresses; in the east, Vauban built or refurbished another double row of fortresses designed to create a corridor between the contested lands of Luxembourg and Lorraine. On the line of the Rhine, critical fortresses such as Landau, Breisach, and Philipsbourg changed ownership continually, but Vauban built rearward supports at Belfort and Besançon, and strategically refortified Strasbourg. His one constant objective was to construct fortresses that would close the frontiers to hostile armies, and, conversely, provide French forces with an entry point into neighboring territories.

In every design, Vauban paid the greatest attention to a second principle: the ensuring of the maximum possible output of defensive firepower. He understood the engineer's prime directive that every approach to a fortress, and every sector of its defenses, should be covered by converging patterns of fire from the cannon and muskets. With this in mind, the design of his bastions in the so-called "first system" was essentially based on Pagan's model, with the bastions neither as obtuse as the Italian, nor as spiky and sharp as the Dutch. The flanks of his traces were usually straight, or sometimes retired and concave and supported by orillons. Where he thought they were necessary, hornworks and crownworks, evident in Figure 2.4, were used to strengthen the defense. Indeed, some

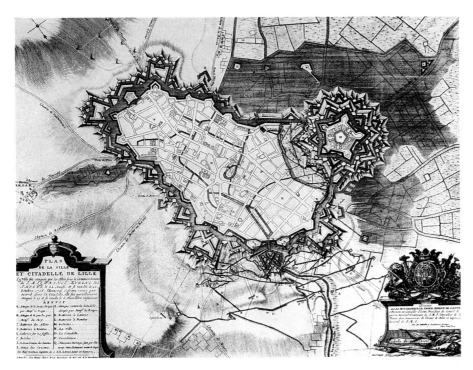

Figure 2.4   Lille: Vauban's "fille ainée" of fortresses. Note the profusion of outworks and crownworks.

of his great fortresses like Lille and Ypres so bristled with outworks that their appearance alone achieved a formidably threatening effect.

Third, Vauban advocated defense in depth in his "second system," designing successive layers of outworks and fortifications to push back the enemy batteries as far as possible from their main target, the bastion trace. The development of **tours bastionées**, seen in Color Plate 5 on page 65, was perhaps his most important original contribution in this area. These were strong towers, several stories high, enclosing gun platforms, and provided with flues to clear the powder smoke. Some historians have felt that with his conception of these towers, Vauban was able to achieve a synthesis between the fortifications of his time and those of the Middle Ages, even though his towers had a different function.[8] The point of their design was explained by Vauban:

> In essentials the bastion tower is a very strong retrenchment, which is capable of putting up a powerful resistance after the detached bastion in front has fallen. In an ordinary fortress, when the bastions are breached the whole enceinte is breached, and you cannot hold out unless you run the risk of seeing the garrison overwhelmed at the same time as the bastions.[9]

In other words, by concentrating the most powerful fortress artillery in the tower instead of in the bastion flanks, Vauban freed the bastion from its close link to the main wall and created a "detached bastion," also known as a **counterguard.** The point of this separation was, as Vauban had pointed out, to counter the most common siege scenario that had developed: it had soon become apparent that the curtain wall was inherently the most difficult target of attack. Assaults on it ran the certain risk of brutal crossfire from two bastions, and quickly ran up against the bristling complex of various outworks such as tenailles, ravelins, hornworks, crownworks, and demilunes (see Figure 2.5). As a result, the bastions themselves had become the preferred target. If a besieger breached the bastion rampart, he was in a position to threaten the

Figure 2.5 The city as fortified by Vauban (Department of Art and Engineering, USMA, 1946).

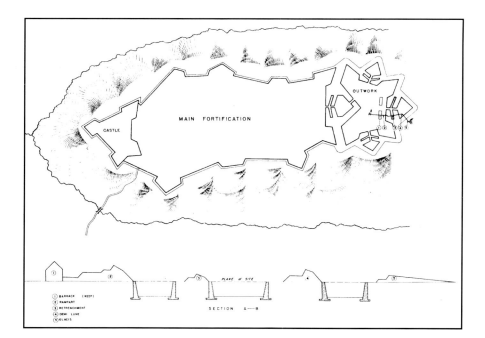

entire inner wall because the ramparts were contiguous to the curtain. Vauban's detaching of the bastion from the curtain wall by means of a narrow ditch enabled it to remain a firing platform for the fortress's muskets, but prevented the loss of the entire fortress if it were breached.

At Neuf-Brisach on the Rhine, the masterpiece of his later years, Vauban incorporated most of the elements identified with his name (see Color Plate 6 on page 65). Forest de Belidor, one of Vauban's successors, described its octagonal trace and recorded a detailed listing of all its measurements and features. Neuf-Brisach's internal diameter was 600 yards; each of the eight sides, bastions included, measured 360 yards, with the curtain walls stretching for 500 yards. The curtain walls were 10 feet 2 inches thick at the base, tapered to 5 feet at glacis level, and were sustained from within by 15-foot buttresses of stone and brick, around which were packed enormous quantities of earth to form a total thickness of 18 feet at the summit. At the angles stood the *tours bastionées*, with outer faces measuring 17 feet 5 inches, and with flanks 35 feet wide. The walls of the towers were 13 feet thick at the foot, tapering to 8 feet at the top. They were flat-roofed, were provided with a parapet, and stood two stories high. Beyond the main trace lay extensive outworks in successive series, making a defensive zone some 380 yards deep. To gain access to this fortress, the besiegers would have to cross over drawbridges and a hinged bridge worked by counterweights, and through petard-proof gates some 10 feet wide, 13 feet high, and 4 feet thick.[10]

Fourth, Vauban planned to permit the governors and garrisons to conduct a reasonably active defense by providing sally ports and bridges for sorties to hold up the progress of the besiegers. Despite the fact that his name became synonymous with a successful siege, Vauban firmly believed that it was the duty of the governor of a fortress to conduct as active a defense as possible, and that an engineer should design a fortress to provide as many advantages in this area as possible. And to these four principles, present in all his work, he added at times a fifth: he pointed out the usefulness of building large fortified encampments capable of holding a field army adjacent to fortresses, and experimented with the use of detached forts placed well beyond the regular defenses for even more support. This he did, for instance, at Toulon (1692), and he ascribed the loss of Namur to the Allies in 1695 to the failure to make the same provision there.

Vauban and the Conduct of a Siege

Vauban's work as a defensive engineer was obviously distinguished, but his contribution to the offensive tactics of siege warfare was even more so. As before, much of his work consisted of perfecting and regularizing the ideas of predecessors, but it seems certain that he was the originator of one important innovation, namely the parallel trench (see Figure 2.6 on page 46). The mechanics of siege warfare are nowhere better described than in Vauban's *Traité de l'attaque des places*. The whole process of besieging a fortress might be usefully summarized at this juncture with occasional reference to three colorful sieges of fortified towns of the period: that of Namur (May 26–July 1, 1692), with Vauban and the French besieging a force of 6,000 Dutch, Spanish, German, and English troops; Namur again (July 1–September 5,

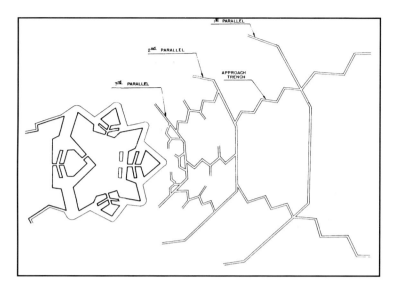

1st PARALLEL

2nd PARALLEL

APPROACH TRENCH

3rd PARALLEL

Figure 2.6   Diagram of a Vauban siege operation (Department of Art and Engineering, USMA, 1946).

1695), with William III and the Allies besieging the French; and finally, the siege of Lille (August 12–December 10, 1708), with Prince Eugene of Savoy, the Duke of Marlborough, and the Allies besieging the French. These particular sieges are of special interest because they exhibited almost all the classic stages as described by Vauban.

Every major siege of the seventeenth or eighteenth centuries commenced with daunting problems of logistics and intelligence. Massive organization was required to gather the necessary numbers of men, munitions, animals, provisions, and wagons needed for the coming campaign. As much intelligence as possible about the town and fortress to be attacked also had to be amassed, clearly a hard-to-conceal undertaking given the size of operations of the period. This usually meant that both sides had more than adequate warning of imminent siege. Vauban himself often deplored the lack of security involved in such projects:

> The foremost fault committed in siegecraft comes from insufficient attention to basic security and secrecy. For instance, when the King left for Dendermonde, although I was wounded at Douai and confined to my quarters, I knew two weeks in advance what was to be undertaken. It was so public that even the farmhands talked of it. Yet it is always of the greatest importance to keep one's intentions hidden, at least until the position is invested, for as soon as it is noised about the enemy is sure to be informed and to bend all his efforts to avoid it or at least to ameliorate the consequences.[11]

At the same time, however, Vauban himself often took advantage of poor security; he was known to reconnoiter a possible target personally, in order to pinpoint the weak sector of the fortification in advance—despite his own strictures that getting too close to the fortress was irresponsible, especially on the part of senior officers because it could lead to capture. As far as numbers were concerned, he felt that the besieging force needed to be at least ten times the estimated size of the garrison. In any case, the force should be no less than 20,000 strong if the lines of contravallation and circumvallation were planned. At a minimum, at least 15,000 peasantry and several thousand local wagons and horse teams were needed to commence operations.

Immediately after these already staggeringly large numbers of soldiers and materiel had been assembled, the question of how many siege guns were needed still remained to be solved. For example, to recapture Namur, the Dutch engineer Coehoorn was forced to amass at least 147 cannon and 60 mortars. Indeed, a minimum allowance of powder for a siege was estimated to be about 700,000 pounds.[12] All these cannon and powder supplies were then formed into huge, slow-moving siege trains that stayed in the rear, ready to be called up when needed. To gain a sense of the proportions involved in a major siege, consider the following preparations made for the allied siege of Lille: 80 siege guns drawn by 20 horses apiece, 20 mortars with 16 horses each, 3,000 four-horse wagons, and over 90,000 men.[13] The initial convoy, cumbersomely slow moving, snaked for almost 15 miles of road, and constantly required protection from possible French raiding parties. It comes as no surprise, then, that rulers were inordinately grateful to engineer-soldiers like Vauban who could successfully manage military undertakings of this magnitude.

Still, if the besiegers had to make elaborate preparations, so did the garrison commander. Although Vauban had stated that no fortress, however well defended, could hold out indefinitely, he still insisted that no fortress should have to surrender prematurely because of the irresponsible lack of preparedness of its governor. In *La Défense des places*, Vauban offered his detailed instruction on the duties of a garrison governor with respect to the laying in of supplies of food and gunpowder, the preparing of the physical defenses of his town and fortress against attack, and the bolstering of morale of his people before the siege should begin.[14] The burning question of the day, of course, was how long a reasonable governor and fortress should resist an attacking force before surrendering.

Lengths of sieges were erratic, being determined by many factors.[15] Besides the enemy's military and logistical resources and the condition of the fortress's defenses, defeatism and low morale among the townspeople and garrison sometimes led to early capitulation. For example, Louis XIV in 1691 at Mons successfully helped undermine morale by threatening to fine the fairly prosperous citizenry 100,000 crowns for each day of further resistance; the result was a surrender after only 26 days. Still, the duration of many sieges fell roughly into a period of between one and two months. This supported Vauban's rule that a defense of 48 days' duration was both respectable and likely. Ironically, however, so many fortresses surrendered after this period of time regardless of the state of their defenses that Louis XIV had to issue a threat in 1705 to all governors about beating a premature **chamade** (a drum beat indicating a desire to parley):

> Despite the satisfaction I have derived from the fine and vigorous defense of some of my fortresses besieged during this war, as well as those of my governors who have held their outworks for more than two months—which is more than the commanders of enemy fortresses have managed when besieged by my arms; nevertheless, as I consider that the main defenses of my towns can be held equally as long as the outworks. . . . I write you this letter to inform you that in the circumstances of your being besieged by the enemy, it is my intention that you should not surrender until there is a breach in the body of the enceinte, and until you have withstood at least one assault.[16]

Vauban's own timetable for the capture of a well-supplied and defended six-bastioned fortress (which he never meant to be taken entirely literally, since he fully appreciated the significance of unforeseen circumstances), is interesting in that it provides a step-by-step manual for commanders of the time:

> To invest a place, collect materials and build lines—9 days
> From the opening of the trenches to reaching the covered way—
>   9 days

The storm and capture of the covered way and its defenses—4 days

Descent into and crossing of the ditch of the demilune—3 days

Mining operations, siting of batteries, creation of a fair breach—
4 days

Capture and exploitation of the demilune and its defenses—
3 days

Crossing of the main ditch to two bastions—4 days

Mining operations and siting of guns on the covered way to
making a breach—4 days

The capture of the breach and its supporting positions—2 days

Surrender of the town after capitulation—2 days

Allowance for errors, damage caused by sorties, and a valorous
defense—4 days

Total: 48 days[17]

With the attacking army on its way to meeting its objective, the next step was to try to confuse the enemy with false reports regarding its real destination, or with feints toward a pretended objective—a difficult task given the size of the operations already under way. But once ready, the commander would begin the investment of the fortress, attempting to isolate it as completely as possible by cutting off roads and taking control of any high ground or waterways around it. This done, it was time to indulge in one of the specific rituals that had grown up around the conduct of sieges by the end of the seventeenth century, unless, of course, the siege was suddenly cut short by treachery with the opening of the gates, or by a sudden storming of the fortress. At this point, it was often the practice to beat a parley and invite the governor of the fortress to surrender immediately. Mild badinage was often exchanged during these conversations, since neither side took the other seriously at this early stage. In fact, even after the investment was complete, requests to evacuate noncombatants from the fortress were often honored, especially those with respect to women, whom Vauban nastily characterized as "always squalling and never good for anything." However, it must be added that while these events often showed this period at its most chivalrous and humane, if rather baroque, there were many sieges and campaigns that ended in brutal starvation and pillage of the garrison and the hapless civilians caught in the middle. Chivalrous behavior depended entirely upon the personality of the commander, or sometimes upon the force of public opinion of the day in Europe.

One of the reasons that the armies involved in sieges of this period appeared so incredibly numerous lay, in part, in the conventional wisdom of the time that the besieging forces should be divided in two lest there be an attempt at relief of the fortress from the outside. One force was to concentrate on the siege works, the other was to cover that operation. Thus, at Namur in 1692, the Duke of Luxembourg's army covered the siege organized by Louis XIV and Vauban; and in 1695, William III and Coehoorn supervised the trenches, while the Prince de Vaudément guarded the works. In 1708, Prince Eugene of Savoy undertook the siege of Lille with 50 battalions, while the Duke of Marlborough covered his efforts with 137 squadrons and 83 battalions.

The troops of the attackers were immediately put to work in various ways. While some were being kept busy making 6-foot **fascines** (bundles of branches), and 8-foot tall **gabions** (baskets of woven brushwood filled with earth) to be used in the trenches later (see Figure 2.7), others were constructing the traditional lines intended to isolate the fortress. The lines of contravallation—positions facing the fortification—were set up beyond cannon range. Usually consisting of a ditch and parapet, which were occasionally strengthened by redoubts, these lines, ideally, were intended to prevent the fortress from communicating with the outside. The line of circumvallation, facing outwards, was also completed to prevent the possibility of a field force's relieving the fortress. In the intervening area of ground, various components of the besiegers' forces, such as the headquarters, camps, siege trains, and magazines, would be situated. Whatever engineering was required by the surrounding terrain to link all sectors of the huge besieging force, such as temporary bridges over rivers or streams, was also being done. Vauban, as mentioned earlier, allowed nine days for the completion of this stage, but at Namur he amazingly took only three; in 1695, Coehoorn required ten days, and in 1708 at Lille, it was accomplished in seven days despite the added harassment of a French sortie.

In the meantime, other elements of the besieging forces were assigned specific tasks. The commander and the director of trenches were occupied

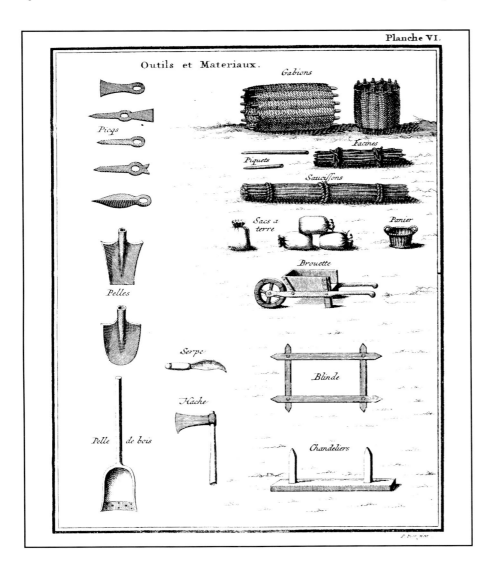

Figure 2.7 Vauban: tools and materials used during a siege.

with making a reconnaissance in order to decide which sector of the fortress was most vulnerable to attack, and with drawing up a detailed blueprint for each element of their forces once a plan was agreed upon. Elsewhere, the heavy gun batteries would have arrived, and would be at once mounted in place to begin firing upon the enemy soldiers to harass and make it difficult for them to man their outworks. Intended to destroy fortifications and enemy batteries, and to create breaches, siege guns were usually placed in five-, eight-, or ten-gun batteries. They featured either direct or ricochet fire. The latter, as mentioned, was Vauban's deadly innovation, which became widely adopted. It was not until the nineteenth century that the rather difficult art of ricochet firing, as illustrated in Color Plate 7 on page 66, became supplanted by the firing of shrapnel shells.

With the batteries in place, the next most important moment of a siege had arrived: the opening of the trenches. This was the beginning of the formal attack against the sector of the fortress that had been picked as the weakest point during the reconnaissance. Herein lay Vauban's major contribution to the art of siegecraft. Formerly, the attackers' approach to the fortification had been by means of trenches dug more or less directly foward, with an occasional zigzag to avoid enfilading fire. The usual result had been huge casualties when the fortress's guns opened up. Vauban's brilliant tactic of parallel

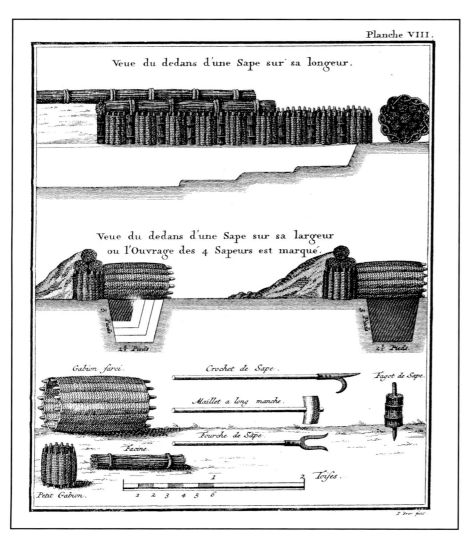

Figure 2.8   Vauban: the tools and techniques of constructing saps.

trenches provided for continuous movement toward the fortification walls, but also guaranteed cover for his men while doing so. Under the Vauban method, the attack was begun by the digging of a large trench *parallel* to the defenses at a distance of approximately 600 yards (maximum cannon range). The location for this first opening trench had been carefully marked, and the digging (see Figure 2.8) begun during the night to ensure secrecy and surprise, with the fond hope that daylight would not reveal any mistakes. (There is something piquant about the image of sappers [trench-makers] digging assiduously like moles during darkness only to discover at dawn, as happened upon occasion, that they had unfortunately dug in the wrong direction.) Two or three days would be spent forming a trench both wide and deep, with a fire step. Other workmen would be hastily digging a number of narrow approach trenches in a zigzag forward from the first parallel (see Figure 2.9) towards the fort. Opened cunningly in two or three places, these were intended to confuse the garrison as to which "attack" should be taken seriously. About 400 yards from the enemy defenses, the sappers and workmen would begin construction of the second parallel in the same fashion as the first. Meanwhile, the lines of the first parallel would by now be occupied by fresh troops, and be used as a supply point for tools, gabions, and other materiel.

The sappers were perhaps the unsung heroes of this first part of a formal siege. Volunteers, they were divided into four-man squads, each of which was made responsible for pushing forward one of the heads of the sap, seen in Color Plate 8 on page 66, or trench. The leading sapper covered himself and the rest of his squad by cautiously pushing forward a sap roller, or a wheeled timber screen. Then he took the basket called a gabion and carefully positioned it beside the screen. He then advanced the screen a little more and dug a trench 2 feet long and 18 inches wide and deep on the side away from the fortress, filling the gabion with the soil. He left a foot of space between the edge of his trench (see Color Plate 9 on page 67) and the gabion, and packed sandbags between it and the one before. After that he pushed the

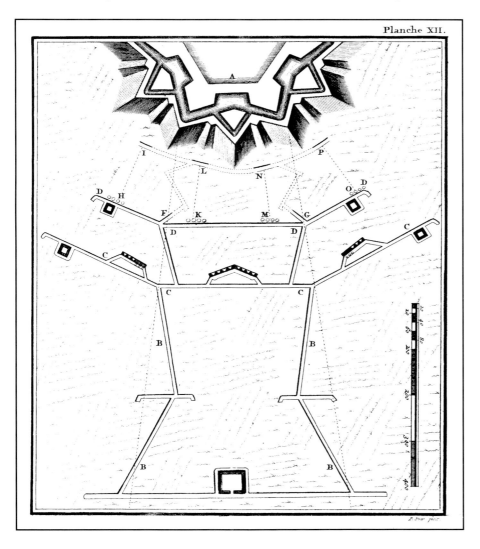

Planche XII.

Figure 2.9 Vauban: illustrates the placement of the parallel and forward attack approaches, with "places d'armes" for the troops.

screen forward and dealt with the next gabion, while the second sapper crowned the newly planted one with fascines, and widened and deepened the trench. This time, however, the excavated earth was thrown over the top to form a slope on the far side. The third and fourth sappers continued the process until the sap was 3 feet wide and deep, and the mass of gabions and fascines formed a rampart that could protect them against all musket balls and cannon shot. The same process continued until the third and final parallel, placed on the glacis itself, was reached (see Figure 2.10). This position had to be achieved with the most care shown thus far, because it was the most exposed to enemy fire. By this stage, however, it was expected that the siege batteries would have already successfully silenced a respectable number of the fortress guns. It is not surprising then, in view of the difficulties and dangers of their job, that the sappers had to be provided with bonuses for efficiency, and were cautioned by Vauban against drinking on the job to the detriment of their lives.

While the attackers were pressing their trenches forward, the governor

Figure 2.10   Vauban: illustrates the placement of the besiegers' batteries at the completion of the second parallel.

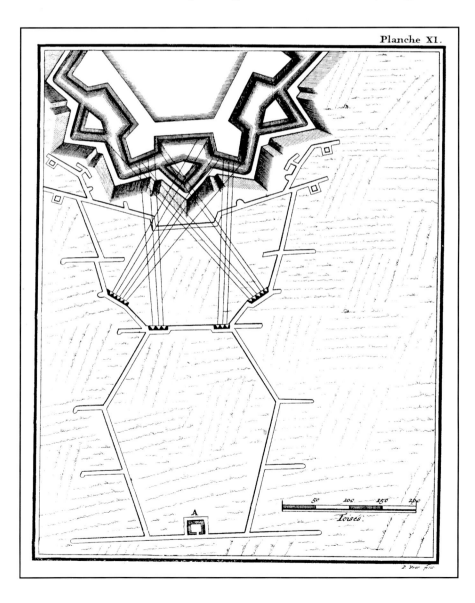

Planche XI.

of the besieged fortress, if at all a worthy opponent, was presumably busy arranging stealthy sorties by his troops to hamper the enemy's progress. The most desired objective was to damage the trench digging, and possibly lure the attackers close enough in retaliation to be swept by the fortress cannon. In addition, he could order smaller "internal" sorties, designed at various stages, to regain part of the covered way, reoccupy a breach, destroy enemy mine galleries, or prevent the besiegers' attempts to cross the ditch. These encounters usually occurred toward the end of a siege as desperate efforts by the garrison to stave off disaster for a little while longer.

If he wished to be even more active, the governor could order his troops to counterattack with several strategies of his own. For example, while the besieger's trenches moved closer over no-man's land, the garrison engineers and sappers could dig outwards from the covered way and attempt to force a trench across the exposed flanks of the enemy's parallel trenches, so as to rake the approaching forces with musket fire. This particular tactic on the part of the French gave the Allies a hard time at the siege of Namur in 1695. And finally, the defender could also use mines and countermines. If he were abandoning an outwork, the defender could rig mines to explode when the attackers arrived to take over the position. Otherwise, he could drive galleries under the glacis and place mines in chambers beneath the enemy, hoping to blow up something important, such as powder magazines or battery positions. Without question, this was dangerous and brutal work. At the same time, the defenders had to be alert for the sounds of the enemy's mine galleries, which were intended to help breach the fortification.

In the meantime, outside the microcosm of the fortress under siege, a friendly field army could well be in the process of launching various strategies to help the inhabitants of the fortress. These varied from a direct clash with the besiegers, to attempts at cutting off their supplies, to flooding the terrain where applicable (especially in the Netherlands), and even to the creation of a major diversion. The last maneuver generally involved a sudden attack on some other strategic enemy town or fortress in the hope that the besieging army would be withdrawn by the need to deal with the new threat. For example, the French attacked Brussels, capital of the Spanish Netherlands, in an unsuccessful attempt to disrupt the crucial siege of Namur in August 1695, and attempted the same tactic to disrupt the siege of Lille in 1708.

By this stage, the third parallel was expected to be nearly complete, and the saps to have reached far enough to begin threatening the integrity of the demilunes. At the same time, a group of mortar and **pierrier** (stone hurling) batteries, set up to the left and right of the main trenches, and the gun batteries mounted near the second parallel commenced firing in an effort to open breaches in the demilunes and in the curtain walls (see Color Plate 10 on page **67**). Vauban had argued that cannon set any further back in the first days of open trenches were largely a waste of time as the range was too distant. Indeed, the placing of batteries and the mechanics of gunnery was a skilled art that Vauban much appreciated. Besides requiring accurate placement to create a breach at the immediate objective, the other guns had to be firing simultaneously on all the nearby enemy positions in attempts to neutralize the defenders' crossfire.[18] Moreover, the object was to bombard the fortification's defenses, not to demolish the town, whose destruction would be a foolish luxury. Most governments of the time were fully aware that wholesale destruction of a fortified town was counterproductive, as it would effectively remove a possibly important bargaining pawn to be used in the eventual peace negotiations.

Thus, under heavy covering fire, the sappers and workmen continued to dig their way onto the glacis by creating a number of traverses (or sap heads). According to Vauban's blueprint, the time had arrived to try to take the covered way and counterscarp, either by an assault or by further digging (see Color Plates 11 and 12 on page 68). At the siege of Lille on September 7, 1708, when Eugene of Savoy attempted to storm the counterscarp with 15,000 men, he made only small gains for an appalling 3,000 casualties. The glacis was described the next day as being covered with bodies.[19] Still, Vauban was convinced that if the attack were properly prepared and correctly timed, the enemy should have already been forced to abandon that position. By this juncture, Vauban would have directed the sap heads to their final push of about 84 feet from the covered way; the trenches to the left and right would have been dug following the line of the fortress defenses (see Figure 2.11). Behind these positions, **cavaliers** were quickly erected—four-stepped entrenchments intended to sweep with firearms those enemy positions still defending the covered way and counterscarp. The object was to force the garrison troops to abandon this now exposed position. During their retreat, the defenders also commonly blew up their own mines as they went, a moment described by Vauban as the "signal that the enemy does retreat." Hearing this, the attackers would rush to take over the vacated positions, hurrying to make them secure against any last-gasp sorties from the garrison, and to find and defuse any remaining enemy mine galleries.

After the attackers secured the positions given up by the enemy, the big breaching guns would be moved up overnight, under cover of heavy fire, to what might be their final position on the edge of the counterscarp itself. Firing at pointblank range, day and night, against the angle of the demilune or bastion wall in front of them, these guns also covered the sappers who were methodically forcing a passage through the counterscarp down toward the ditch bottom of the demilune. If the ditch were a wet one, more time was expended in throwing huge quantities of fascines and other bridging materials into place to create bridges, or in constructing dams to stop the flow of water. Then, when ready, a storming party led by volunteers would assault the breach, and, in hand-to-hand combat, try to take possession of the positions on the demilune. The artillery fire would then be switched to the walls of the main bastion and beyond; that location would, in turn, be stormed and consolidated. This process would be repeated until the town, and even the citadel, if necessary, had

Figure 2.11 Views of bastions attacked (Viollet-le-Duc).
A. Bastions
B. Breaching Battery
C. Inner Rampart

been assaulted or had surrendered. The storming of the breaches represented the most costly part of a siege in terms of human carnage, and if attempted too prematurely could inflict huge casualties upon the attackers. For example, the Allied attack on the Terra Nova breach at Namur on August 30, 1695, cost over 2,000 casualties for small gains, and apparently appalled Vauban, who always preached the obligation of an officer to not, in his impatience to make the assault, needlessly waste the lives of his men. "Burn powder and spill less blood," was an oft-repeated dictum of his.[20] A vivid description of the carnage created at the siege at Badajoz in 1812, during which the British made 40 separate rushes against the breaches, depicted the effects of such storming parties in most cases:

> Hundreds of brave soldiers lay in piles upon each other, weltering in blood, and trodden down by their companions . . . the small groups of soldiers seeking shelter from the cartwheels, pieces of timber, fire-balls and other missiles hurled down upon them; the wounded crawling past the fire-balls, many of them scorched and perfectly black, and covered with mud, from having fallen into the cuvette [a trench cut into the floor of the ditch], where three hundred were suffocated or drowned; and all this time the French on top of the parapets, jeering and cracking their jokes, and deliberately picking off those whom they chose.[21]

Once the fortress had decided to surrender, the "rules of war" of the period went into effect, dictated by complex formalities that were generally accepted by all the combatants. It was widely held, for example, that a garrison that had held out for a minimum of 48 days had done its duty respectably and with honor, and was entitled to negotiate for the best possible terms of surrender if no relief help were in the offing. Similarly, once an obvious breach had been forced through the main defenses of a fortress and town, and once the besieger controlled the covered way and its area, a general storming was usually imminent. In this position, most governors considered themselves entitled to beat the chamade and seek a parley without losing face. Indeed, it was often common for the attacker to politely repeat invitations to the fortress to surrender during the various stages of the siege (see Figure 2.12 on pages 56 and 57), and the duration of the fighting sometimes depended purely upon the temperament of the governor. In any case, to continue the struggle past these points could be a dangerous gamble. By the commonly accepted rules of war, continuation meant that the siege commander was free to refuse to honor lenient surrender terms, and fully entitled to turn the town and its inhabitants over to pillage, rape, and destruction if he so chose. Most commanders preferred to avoid these situations for the mundane reasons previously mentioned, and those occasions when atrocities were allowed, such as Marlborough's devastation of Bavaria in July 1704, provoked such public outcry as to show that governments and societies of the time generally regarded such excesses as unjustifiable. Heroic last-ditch stands were not the fashion in the eighteenth century.

Once the offer to surrender had been accepted, negotiators designated by each side would meet to discuss the terms. Usually, the defenders presented a list of terms that the besieger would accept, reject, or change depending on his mood, the losses he had sustained, and how much he needed the town for future strategic considerations. If the victor were feeling magnan-

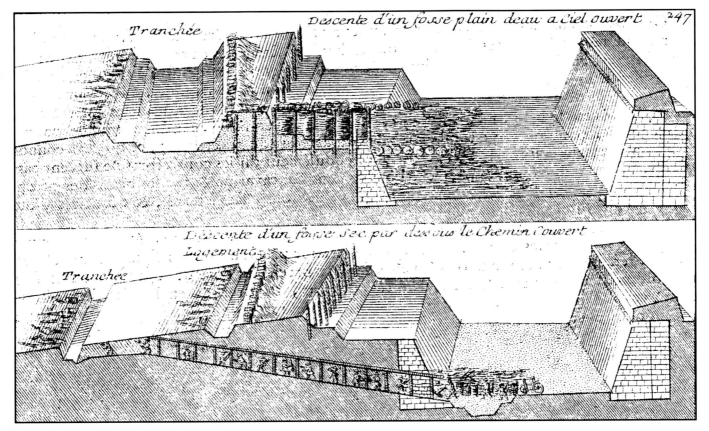

A. Descent and passage of the demilune ditch.

Figure 2.12   Views of a siege (Savin, 1735).

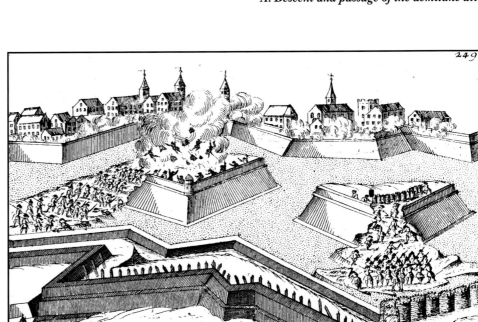

B. Assault and capture of the demilune.

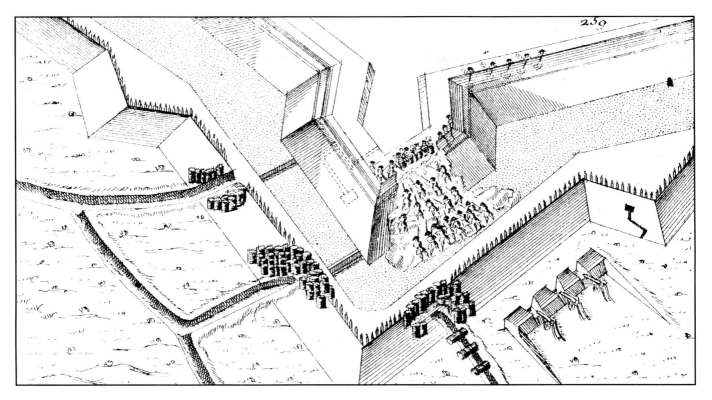

C. *Assault on the bastion and achievement of a breach.*

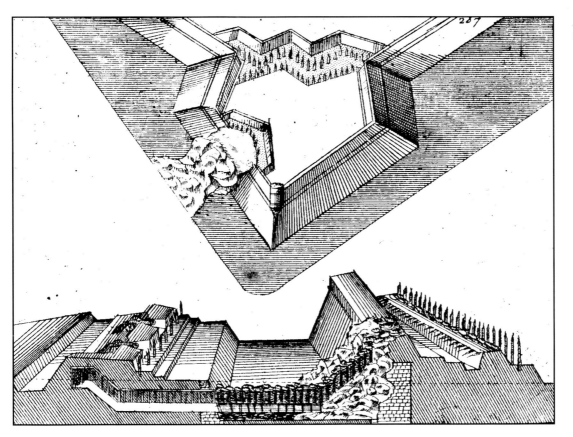

D. *Retrenchment in the bastion.*

imous, the garrison troops might be permitted to evacuate their positions with all the honors of war, marching out with drums beating, playing an enemy march (to show themselves as still able to pay their foe a compliment), with colors flying, and bayonets fixed. These customs were taken very seriously by contemporaries. For example, when the British refused to allow the Americans during the surrender of Charleston in May 1780 to play the drums or fly their colors, the Americans did not forget the insult. During the surrender at Yorktown, the British were required in retaliation to march out "with colors cased, the drums beating a British or German march."[22] Usually, the garrison troops would be escorted to a place agreed upon by both sides, after which they would be free to resume hostilities. Otherwise, the troops might be taken as prisoners of war, or disarmed and allowed to wander out, symbolically having had the waistbands of their breeches cut and their shoes removed.

Given the complexity of the siege warfare operations described here, it is not surprising that kings and commanders highly valued those engineers in chief who could manage to bring operations of such magnitude to successful conclusions. Louis XIV gave Vauban an outright gift of 40,000 crowns for capturing Namur in 1692. The "value" of Vauban's siege operations was, however, incalcuable in monetary terms. His innovation of parallel trenches became vital in several respects: they provided for the first time constant and efficient cover for the attackers at increments of 600, 400, and 200 yards from the ditch, thus helping to reduce casualties; and they enabled the mounting of several attacks (as the forward-going approach trenches were called) in order to confuse the defense as to where the point of greatest peril really lay. Vauban's larger lesson was that the fortress should be taken more by the shovel than by the sword, that patience was better than foolish impetuousness, especially when it came to the saving of lives, and that a commander should take as many days as needed to safeguard his troops. So efficient was his technique in view of what had gone before that the average time taken to finish a siege was reduced considerably in his day, and his "cautious" approach vindicated. Self-fulfilling prophecy also played its part. So famous was his reputation during his lifetime that a siege led by Vauban often induced a premature surrender on the part of a resigned and defeatist fortress.

It is probably fair to say that the enduring legacy and great service of Vauban was the systematic reordering of the various concepts and designs of fortification, and their application through practice until they almost achieved the status of a science. By the mid-eighteenth century, the imbalance between the offense and defense, created by the new artillery, had almost been redressed. No other age saw the erection of fortifications on such a vast and elaborate scale; and yet, ironically, the same period produced a lucid blueprint for how to destroy them. Much of the credit for this situation must go to Vauban. That is why he is such a towering figure in the history of fortification. Perhaps Vauban's historical impact can be best summed up in the characteristic that made him such a figure of integrity in his own lifetime: "Vauban survives as one of the most complete mortals whom history has to show. Hard-headed but warm-hearted, he was able to reconcile success in warfare and an inherently bloody trade, with the demands of common humanity."[23]

Vauban's Contemporary Rival: Menno Van Coehoorn

There were rivals to Vauban's pre-eminence in his own lifetime, of course. The most notable was Baron Menno van Coehoorn (1641–1704), also known as the "fighting engineer," who was very much a worthy descendant of the school of Dutch engineers that had flourished in the late 1500s in the days of Maurice of Nassau and William the Silent. Coehoorn was a veteran of numerous sieges and battles conducted between 1657 and 1688. His well-founded criticism to the Elector of Brandenburg of the way the siege of Bonn was conducted in 1688 made his name known, and in 1692 he was sent to improve the fortifications at Namur at the request of William III. His spirited defense of Namur in 1692, despite its unsuccessful conclusion, consolidated his reputation in Europe. Vauban himself, after the fall of Namur, sought to meet the wounded prisoner Coehoorn before his exchange was negotiated. Ironically, three years later their roles were reversed, and Coehoorn came to the aid of the floundering Allied siege of Namur on September 1, 1695. For this service he was appointed lieutenant-general and director-general of fortifications of the United Provinces. By this time a famous figure, he resisted Louis XIV's generous offers to enter the French service, and spent his time improving the Dutch frontier fortresses. When his royal patron, William III, died in 1702, Coehoorn's career also floundered without support until his own premature death in 1704. Vauban, of course, had the good fortune of serving a royal patron whose foreign policy required his services for almost five decades. Coehoorn, in contrast, had only seven years to accomplish what he could. Given their close historical proximity and their similar interest in the art and science of fortification, it is no wonder that the two men have been incessantly, and perhaps unfairly, compared.

In contrast to Vauban, Coehoorn's only publication was a small book, *Nieuwe Vestingbouw*, that appeared in 1685. The French translation was titled *Nouvelle fortification*, published in The Hague in 1706 and 1741; and the English version, translated by Thomas Savery, was *The New Method of Fortification translated from the Original Dutch of the late famous Engineer, Menno, Baron van Coehoorn*. Coehoorn's analysis of fortification generally advocated a close-range defense, with heavy and constant flanking fire, delivered from long, low-lying, concave, double-bastioned flanks, from loopholed redoubts in the re-entrant places of arms, and from earthen fausse-brayes. But, if necessary, his systems could sport elaborate outworks to expose the enemy everywhere to crossfire (see Figure 2.13). He also constructed huge wet ditches on the traditional Dutch model. Coehoorn remained faithful to these wet ditches, despite the difficulties involved in withdrawing over them if the defenders' position became untenable, and the difficulty in supplying the outworks beyond such a wide wet ditch.

When it came to actually fortifying on the ground, Coehoorn nonetheless ignored his own theories if the terrain did not permit their application. Elements of his traces with enormous ravelins and demilunes can be found in Nimjegen, Fort William at Namur, Coevorden, Groningen, and Mannheim. And at Bergen op Zoom, seen in Color Plate 13 on page 69, he completely accommodated his design to the demands of the site. The trace of the fortress looked like an hourglass laid on its side, with the eastern side featuring nine

Figure 2.13 Coehoorn's "first and second mehtods" of fortification as described by John Muller, 1746.

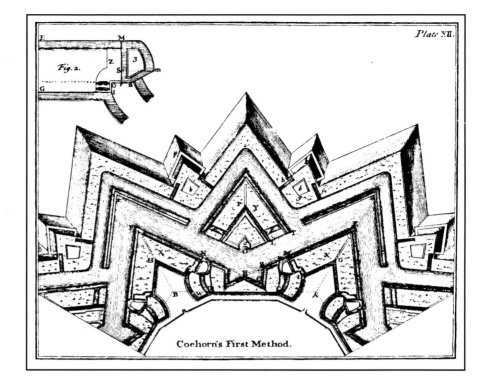

Coehorn's First Method.

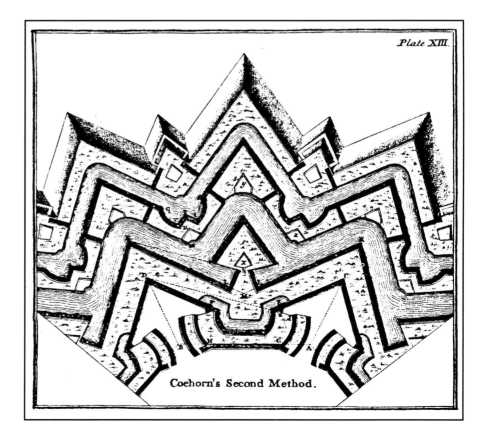

Coehorn's Second Method.

bastions, each with double concave flanks and small orillons. It also had a spacious covered way and casemated redoubts, evident in Color Plate 14 on page 69, that contributed to the huge amounts of firepower Coehoorn generally advocated.

In taking enemy fortresses, Coehoorn also deviated from Vauban's methods with a vengeance. Whereas Vauban was cautious and slow, advancing steadily after entrenching each foot of ground, Coehoorn liked to abridge a siege by employing overwhelming artillery fire, seconded by frequent and ferocious assaults in which casualties were usually heavy. Coehoorn preferred short cuts; stormings were performed at his request at both Namur (1695) and Liège (1702). At Namur, as mentioned before, over 2,000 casualties were incurred in two hours by this storming tactic, appalling and shocking Vauban who had methodically captured Namur three years earlier with only 300 casualties. Vauban consistently restrained his troops, allowing them to advance only under cover, and was able to show great concern for the welfare of his men without having to slacken the siege. Coehoorn, on the other hand, sent his troops across in the open to make assaults at a distance, and sacrificed everything in his eagerness to shorten the siege and frighten the defenders. And yet he often ended up not saving time, and certainly not men. It might be added in his defense, however, that the German troops Coehoorn often commanded were totally ignorant of fortress warfare, and not very capable of conducting a lengthy sap attack. As a result, he chose to use his best soldiers in mass assaults at the moment he judged that overwhelming Allied fire had breached the walls and shattered the morale of the defenders. More importantly, Coehoorn's tactic of *l'audace* required a brilliant commander to be successful; Vauban's merely required a competent one. Given the historical sparseness of true military greatness, it comes as no surprise that the latter dominated the siege warfare of the next century.

Vauban's Legacy and His Successors

Because of Vauban's inexhaustible energy and resources, and his amazing competence in varying conditions, his works soon gained an international reputation. Moreover, during his career he made every effort to train a corps of native engineers (280 of them by 1697) who rapidly disseminated his ideas across Europe and abroad.[24] His work ushered in the classic century of military engineering that lasted from the high point of Louis XIV's conquests in the 1680s and 1690s to the collapse of the old political, social, and military order after the outbreak of the French Revolution in 1789. During this period, French engineers enjoyed an undisputed authority in all areas of the art and science of fortification. Their prestige and influence sprang from the support of a centralized monarchy, from the continuity and direction that came from a large and well-organized engineer corps, and from the living tradition of Vauban, who seemed to have reduced siege warfare to an infallible routine. Vauban had been the first to insist that a special corps of engineers, not less than 200 strong, be established, and that it include trained officers. He also proposed that certain soldiers be enlisted from the ranks and trained specifically as sappers. His proposal, acknowledged some years after his death, provided the first step toward the establishment of the brilliant engineering service of France, the Ecole du Corps Royale du Génie, established in 1748 at Mézières by Louis XV. Rather than consider Vauban a prophet without honor in his own country, one might say that his ideas were ultimately overapplied by generation after generation, stifling new ideas and partially distorting his own. A *mythe Vauban* was created—one that regarded his work as infallible, and followed his designs almost obsequiously. "Vauban was God and Cormontaigne his prophet . . . and the School of Engineering at Mézières his scholasticism."[25] The reference is, of course, to the stringent and narrow adherence to Vauban's designs, teachings, and methods after his death.

Louis de Cormontaigne (1696–1752) was a working engineer who helped refortify Metz, among other places, and apparently dedicated his career in his considerable writings to delineating, preserving, and improving upon the methods of Vauban, whom he never met. His protégé was Charles-Réné de Fourcroy de Ramecourt (1715–1791) who, after much political maneuvering, was appointed in 1776 to a new office in the bureaucracy that, in effect, permitted him to function as the chief engineer of France. For the next 13 years, he zealously and totally dominated all aspects of engineering and fortification in France. Fourcroy turned to his early patron, Cormontaigne, and from the latter's works he extracted a so-called "authorized" version of what Vauban had proposed. Although adhering to the general proportions of Vauban's works, Fourcroy's design pushed the ravelins farther out, and replaced the *tour bastionée* with an elaborate retrenchment in the gorge (the space between the two curtain angles). In addition, the Fourcroy-Cormontaigne school argued for a reduction by at least a third of the artillery mounted inside the fortress to counter an attack. It was reasoned that an aggressive fortress defense was, by definition, a losing cause since the besieger could, in the end, always bring more guns to bear during a siege than could the defender.

Fourcroy and Cormontaigne also came up with what was a rather pointless scheme to analyze the cost of building fortifications. It was supposedly based upon Vauban's timetable for a siege, which Vauban had intended merely as a rough means to estimate the supplies and preparations a fortress should undertake. Maintaining that the theoretical duration of the defense in a siege should be 32 days, Fourcroy and his supporters then applied this analysis as the rule by which to measure the value of a fortification. Insisting that this was a truly scientific method, they divided the proposed building costs of a fortress (estimated in units of 100,000 francs) by the supposed 32 days of resistance to a siege.[26] This was nonsense, of course, and a far cry from Vauban's bedrock practicality. He would have been the first to point out that this theory relied upon entirely arbitrary and unknown factors, such as the actual cost of construction of any given fortification, and the unforeseeable elements that might affect the resistance of a fortress under siege.

As a result, the last years of the *ancien régime* before the outbreak of the French Revolution were ones of argument and dissension among the French engineers. They were grappling not only with the dictatorial control of the faculty at Mézières, which forbade any deviation from what were considered Vauban's theories, but also with the impact of continued minor innovations in the technology of certain fields. The changes they produced were often disruptive. For example, in the field of gunnery, Forest de Belidor

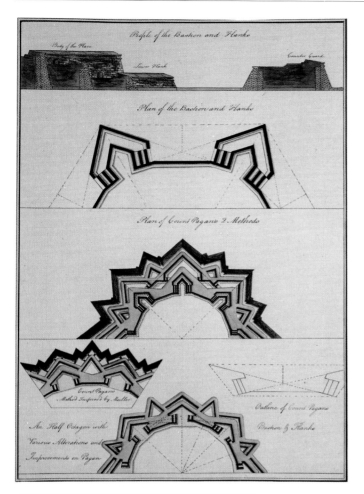

Color Plate 1   Bastion traces as designed by Pagan (Charnock).

Color Plate 2   Depiction of a trace fortified with a double ditch, covered way, and glacis "according to the first system of M. de Vauban" (Charnock).

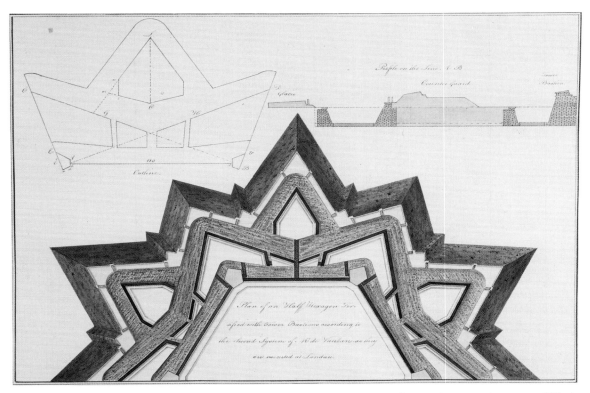

Color Plate 3 **Depiction of a trace fortified with tower bastions "according to the second system of M. de Vauban" (Charnock).**

Color Plate 4 **Depiction of a trace fortified with tower bastions "according to the third method of M. de Vauban" (Charnock).**

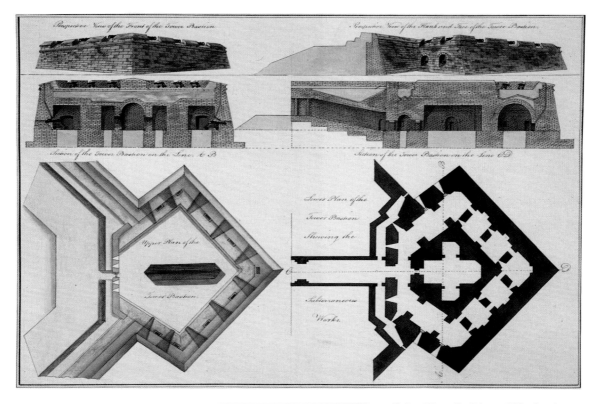

Color Plate 5   Plan of Vauban's "tour bastionée" (Charnock). Designed by Vauban to protect the ramparts and gun positions against attackers' fire from above (or even from flat country), these low, bastion-shaped towers with casemated artillery were set into the main walls of the fortress.

Color Plate 6   Depiction of plan of Vauban's "masterpiece of fortification," Neuf-Brisach (Charnock).

Color Plate 7 Profile and plan of a siege battery, and of the ricochet technique as established by Vauban (Charnock).

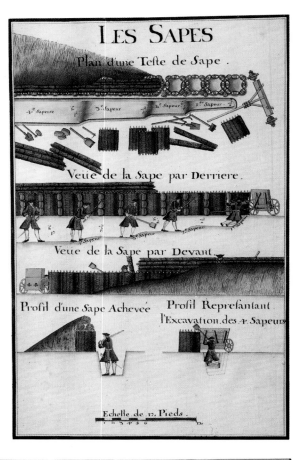

Color Plate 8 Vauban: views of sap from sides and rear.

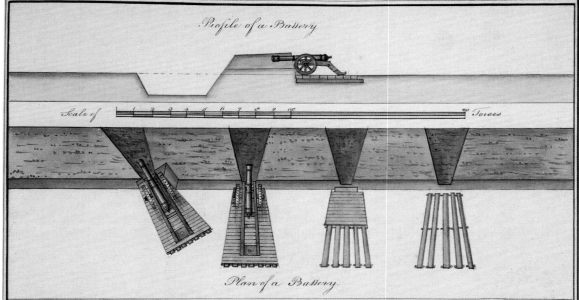

Color Plate 9   Various profiles of trenches and plans of batteries (Charnock).

Color Plate 10   View of a battery firing behind fascine construction (Charnock).

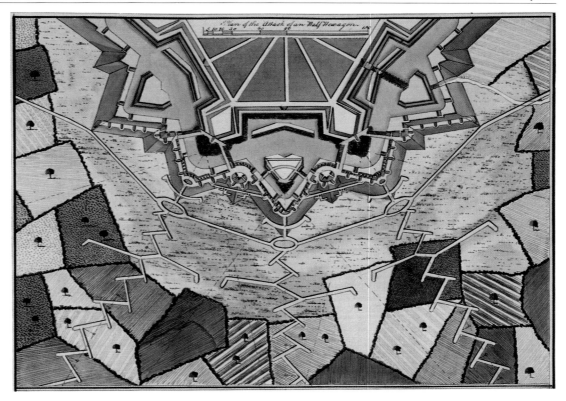

Color Plate 11   The last stages of the siege according to Vauban, illustrating the third parallel, crowning of the covered way, positions of breaching batteries, passages of the ditch, and lodgements on the breaches of the ravelin and bastion (Charnock).

Color Plate 12   Two depictions that show Vauban's methods of attacking the outworks of a fortification, and his placement of the elements of a siege (Charnock).

Color Plate 13   A fortification trace and the front of Bergen op Zoom, as designed by Coehoorn (Charnock).

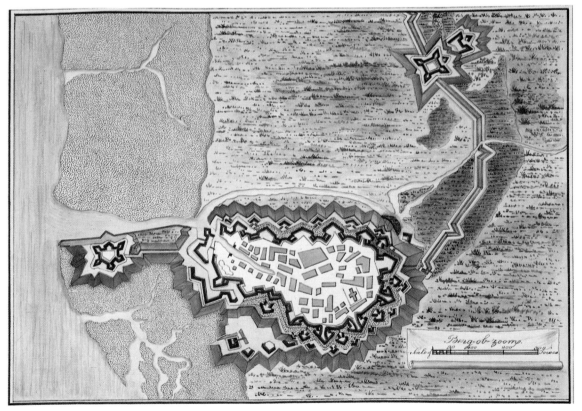

Color Plate 14   Bergen op Zoom (Charnock).

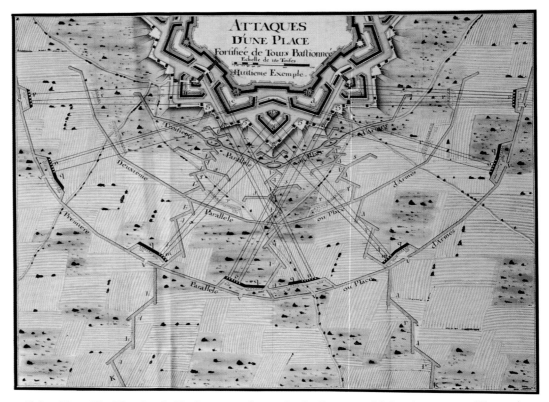

Color Plate 15   The classic Vauban: trench attack of a fortress with bastion towers, illustrating the zigzag approaches and three parallels.

Color Plate 16   Colorful depiction of an irregular fortification, illustrating several methods of approach, attack, and defense of the place (Charnock).

(1693–1761), who ultimately became inspector of artillery for the French monarch, published in 1731 *Le Bombardier français* in which he systematically laid out theories of gunnery as an empirically provable science. He criticized previous techniques of loading charges in cannon as wasteful and ineffective, much to the chagrin of the artillery corps, which was now being told that it had been doing things all wrong. Moreover, differing concepts of strategy—a few of which proposed by-passing fortresses completely—were also in the air. Some military men like the Marshal Maurice de Saxe (1696–1750), who conquered the Netherlands in the 1740s, felt that the fortification of towns was essentially a poor military tactic, and argued that it would be more effective to use the army to build entrenchments at vital strategic points in the open country.

Debates on the subjects of strategy and field tactics began to seem much more appealing than discussion of fortification, particularly since the fortress warfare that succeeded Vauban appeared to have been reduced to a dull and seemingly infallible routine, with the offense clearly superior to the defense. Vauban's legacy of success in siege warfare, and the efficiency with which French engineers spread it throughout the world, ironically brought with it a sense of contempt for the efficacy of artillery defense of a fortress among some of the French military establishment. It appeared that despite the many fortresses he designed and constructed to protect France from invading armies, Vauban was unable to cure the perceived defects of the bastion system during a siege. Had he not proven that a siege systematically undertaken upon the lines he advocated would inevitably take a fortress? Obviously, Vauban had not been able to add greatly to the endurance of a besieged fortification. In other words, he had done his work too well: his system of attack remained stronger than his system of defense. One soldier, bored with the dry fortification textbooks produced by such obviously unmilitary sources as the *abbés* Le Blond and Deidier, and convinced that Vauban's techniques had completely undermined fortress defense, wrote for many in the 1770s:

> At the present time nobody can doubt that the fate of fortresses depends entirely on the outcome of battles, that fortresses are just an auxiliary element, that the system of war has entirely changed, and that what matters in warfare is to have well-found, mobile and manoeuverable armies. From this it follows that artillery must participate in these fundamental changes, and that we must draw a distinction between fortress artillery and field artillery.[27]

In 1784, the young Lazare Carnot, a future minister of war who was at that time still a very junior engineer, argued while eulogizing Vauban in an essay, that fortresses were vital to the stability of France. The field tacticians and artillery officers who had become so contemptuous of siege warfare erupted in such a nasty squabble in print that the controversy finally had to be squelched by the then-minister of war.[28]

The Fortification Theories of Montalembert

Of all of Vauban's successors, one individual in particular deserves mention because his work directly affected the engineers and soldiers of Prussia in the eighteenth century, and eventually those of the fledgling American repub-

Figure 2.14   Frontispiece, Montalembert, *La Fortification perpendiculaire*.

lic. Marc-René, Marquis de Montalembert (1714–1800), essentially searched for some fresh means to restore the balance between the besieged and besieger, after Vauban's teachings had brought the art of attack to such apparent perfection and had caused the premature surrender of so many fortresses. He had taken part in a number of sieges during his 45 years of military and government service, and possessed a wide knowledge of European fortification acquired during his travels and postings abroad. During the 1770s, he began to write openly that while Vauban was indeed a great man, it was time to move on and improve upon his theories. After being studiously ignored by the official military establishment of his day, Montalembert lost patience, and in 1776 published the first polemical volume of *La Fortification perpendiculaire*, the frontispiece of which is seen in Figure 2.14. This undertaking eventually comprised 11 large volumes and 165 engravings, and used up most of his personal fortune.

The more innovative aspects of his theories were interesting and quite comprehensive. Aware of the arguments about the inability of fortresses to hold out after the development of the Vauban system of attack, Montalembert set himself the task of analyzing why that was so and what could be done about it. First, he isolated artillery as both the basic offensive and defensive component of fortification—the weapon that "takes fortresses" and, by the same token, the one that defends them. In his view, it was vital that the post-Vauban fortress regain superiority of fire. To accomplish this, he proposed setting up an immense number of guns in the fortress—between 300 and 400 of them—housed in casemates. These casemates were galleries with loopholes or embrasures for musketry or artillery, and were constructed to have overhead cover. In Montalembert's design, the guns were placed behind the scarp wall rather than left exposed on the open rampart as in a bastioned fortress. For coastal fortifications, he envisioned soaring lighthouse-type towers, depicted in Figure 2.15, and high

Figure 2.15   Montalembert's coastal towers, *La Fortification perpendiculaire*.

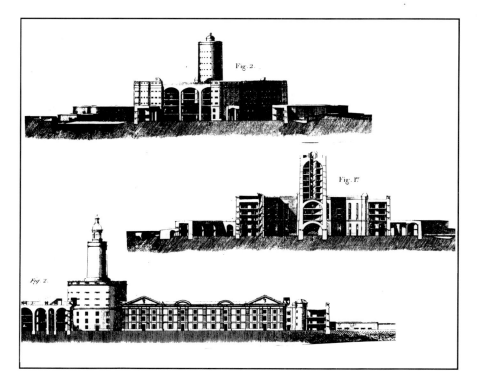

triangular forts with guns intended to deliver, over a short interval, massive fire against threatening ships.

Second, he proposed changing the indented, all-purpose front of a bastion trace to a long, straight curtain. It would be designed with two stories of artillery casemates to help provide the long-range defense required. To project at right angles from the center of the curtain, he designed a massive caponnière, seen in Figure 2.16, with 27 artillery casemates on each side arranged in 3 stories. The caponnière's sole purpose was to command the length of the ditch. Montalembert felt that the simple fronts of this **polygonal system** were more efficiently adapted to the ground than was the bastioned trace, which required in its essential design that every dimension and every angle be closely connected with the other in order to produce maximum firepower.

Third, impressed by the speed with which besiegers had been able to reach the glacis crest of a fortress despite all the outworks, and taken aback by the fall of some fortified towns after a simple bombardment because of damage supposedly preventable by the fortress, Montalembert also came up with the idea of some small, self-sustaining works beyond the outworks—namely, detached forts. These were meant to augment the depth of defense by permitting the occupation of outlying heights and by slowing down the enemy approach to the fortress proper. The detached works could be circular or three- or four-sided, as called for by the particular terrain. And once again, the simple, uncluttered polygonal trace was especially conducive to such small works. In these ways Montalembert tried to solve the problems he had identified in the fortresses of his time: the casemated curtain was designed to apply to long-range defense, the caponnière to short-range defense, and the detached fort to defense in depth.

Montalembert spent his later years, before and during the turbulent events of the French Revolution, immersed in fierce polemics trying to get his ideas accepted in France. When faced with criticism that the huge numbers of cannon his system called for would produce so much smoke inside the fortress as to make firing impossible, he arranged a successful test firing on the Ile

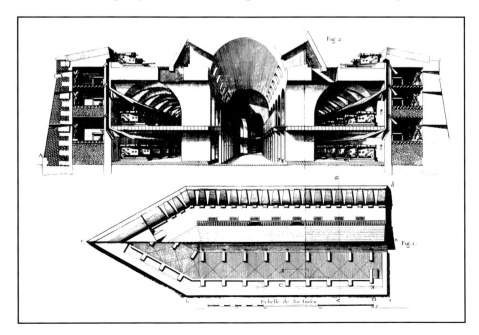

Figure 2.16   Montalembert's caponnière, *La Fortification perpendiculaire.*

d'Aix to prove his point. Despite this experiment, Fourcroy assembled his minions to criticize Montalembert's work by means of the usual tactic of invoking Vauban's legacy. The engineer Michaud d'Arçon published a tract belittling Montalembert's concept of heavy firepower as an interesting idea in theory, but too exorbitantly expensive in its use of gunpowder in reality. At one point, the young Lazare Carnot was caught in the crossfire of the squabble, partly because he was sympathetic to Montalembert's belief in the necessity of fortresses, and partly because he too resented the "oppressive regime" of the corps at Mézières. In the end, however, more pressing events overtook the course of this intellectual skirmishing when the French Revolution broke out, and the crusty old aristocrat was allowed to write in peace and obscurity until his death in 1800.

It may have been of some consolation to Montalembert that his ideas spread rapidly to Germany, where they were enthusiastically accepted by Frederick the Great, who instituted many of these ideas in the Silesian fortresses he had constructed. The Germans had no misapplied legacy of Vauban to live up to, and they were quick to adopt Montalembert's ideas. In 1788, a Prussian engineer translated Montalembert's work for instructional use in the officer corps, and at the same time casemates were tried successfully at various fortifications. During the nineteenth century, simplified forms of the polygonal system were built all over northern Europe and in the new American republic. (See Figure 2.17) And after the Napoleonic wars, the Prussians constructed detached forts in great numbers, 300 to 600 yards in front of the glacis as an outer line of defense. In this way, they not only compelled the attacker to begin hostilities farther away from the fortress and town, but also provided a protected area in front of the inner defensive line for the assembly of troops that would undertake a more active defense than had so far been possible. The area between the detached fort and the inner line was called an **entrenched camp**, a term thereafter applied to every fortified place with detached forts. In any case, the Germans straightforwardly acknowledged their debt to Montalembert, and registered their surprise at his lack of acceptance in his own country:

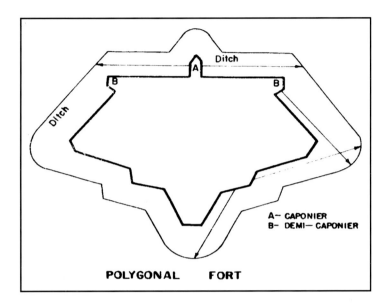

Figure 2.17   The polygonal system of fortification (Department of Art and Engineering, USMA, 1946).

> All foreign experts in military and engineering affairs hail Montalembert's work as the most intelligent and distinguished achievement in fortification over the last hundred years. Things are quite different in France. The French engineering corps is a very considerable organization which controls everything that has to do with the real and practical side of engineering in the kingdom. This corps was brought to its present high standing by a man who is justly famous [Vauban]. The prestige which was endowed on the corps by this great man had been maintained by mighty deeds in the attack and defense of fortresses . . . but it is extraordinary that such an important corps has failed to advance the state of its knowledge by so much as an inch. Its officers have not produced a single book on engineering, and its fortifications are still built according to the old forms and rules.[29]

This appraisal, made in 1800, was essentially correct. Michaud d'Arçon, although an aristocrat, had managed to win the confidence of the Jacobin government, and was thus able to continue the conservative control over engineering in France. His work *Considérations militaires et politiques sur les fortifications* continued to extol the Vauban trace as the ideal fortification—in the manner in which it had been reworked by Cormontaigne and Fourcroy. Indeed, as late as the reign of Louis-Philippe (1830–1848), a continuous line of traditional bastioned forts was still being constructed around the city of Paris.

The Fortification Theories of Lazare Carnot

Despite all the upheavals in France during the years of the French Revolution and those of the Napoleonic wars, the traditions of the engineering corps managed to survive the political changes. Perhaps the most significant reason for this survival lay in the fortuitous competence of the French engineers. It ensured their being in demand regardless of the regime in power. Lazare Carnot (1753–1823), for example, managed to serve in various capacities in such wildly different regimes as the French Republic, the Napoleonic Empire, and the Bourbon restoration. Trained as an engineer and holding the rank of captain when the French Revolution broke out, Carnot served first as a representative of the legislative assembly, and then in 1793 as a member of the notorious Committee of Public Safety. He himself was thus able to preserve a line of continuity between the military traditions of the *ancien régime* and of revolutionary France. Upon him fell the task of calling up and organizing the military resources of France at a time when that nation was endangered by the Allied threat on the Rhine and Dutch frontiers, by a Spanish invasion, by the British capture of Toulon, and by the insurrection in the Vendée. During this period, Carnot organized 14 armies, gave them leaders selected from all ranks (Vauban would have approved of this selection on merit), furnished the commanders with detailed instructions, and supervised campaigns and fortifications himself. Under Napoleon he became minister of war, and served until 1801 when his republicanism led him to oppose the newly announced Empire.

Still, in 1809 he published his work *Traité de la Défense des places fortes* in response to a request from Napoleon that he compile a special manual of instruction for the governors of fortresses. In this work, Carnot, who, it will be remembered, had earlier written an essay praising Vauban, maintained a link with that legacy by rejecting the widely held, post-Vauban assumption that surrender of fortresses was inevitable, and that the length of a siege could be more or less calculated in advance. Instead, he called for the defense of a fortress to the last extremity. Carnot realized that he had to respond to the debate that had been raging over the question of fortress defense. Like Montalembert, he attempted to re-examine the component parts of a fortification in order to adapt them to serve their purposes more efficiently, and he was clearly receptive to the idea of a stronger fortress defense in order to prevent surrender. He differed from Montalembert, however, in that he retained the conventional ground plan, while suggesting a more efficient use of artillery concentrated on the rampart. This he took apart, detaching the scarp wall from the rampart, and positioning the masonry revetment as a free-standing "Carnot wall" in the ditch. The main body of the rampart behind the wall was not lined with stone or masonry, but was left as a sloping wall of earth in order to achieve more defense in depth. In addition, Carnot called for frequent, aggressive, and systematic sorties from the fortress to demolish the besiegers' positions as quickly as they were established.

The importance of Carnot's theories and service lies in the fact that he, like Vauban and Montalembert, deeply believed in the efficacy of fortresses to provide various defensive functions for his nation. For a time it had appeared that the future of fortresses had very much been in question, especially after Napoleon Bonaparte came to power. It was likely that Carnot and others in the French military establishment could not help but perceive the impact of mobile and maneuverable field armies, raised by mass conscription, and turned into instruments of strategy by a brilliant general like Napoleon Bonaparte. During the Napoleonic wars, classic Vauban-style sieges certainly took place.[30] But as often as not, Napoleon's strategy was simply to by-pass fortresses and march his armies rapidly to battle on sites of his choice, settling the campaigns by victories in the field. After such victories, fortifications in the disputed territories tended to surrender. Too often during the Napoleonic campaigns, a fortification served only to slightly delay the attacking force, while a small portion of the field army was detached to observe or check its garrison.

Nonetheless, the continuity of the engineering corps with the traditions and legacy of the past survived intact the French Revolution and the Napoleonic upheavals. The faculty at Mézières and its proponents, individual engineers such as Montalembert, Carnot, and even Napoleon—their squabbling over tactics and fortress design aside—still found much to admire in the military achievements of the *ancien régime*. Despite the speed of Napoleon's campaigns and the sweep of his strategy, it was generally still believed that the fortresses that ringed France's frontiers continued to be vitally important, and that Vauban's defensive chain had been instrumental in saving France from conquest by the Allies during the darkest days of the Revolution when the nation had been encircled by her enemies.

Thus, the building of fortresses in Europe had managed to survive criticism and political upheavals, and had emerged in the nineteenth century as far from obsolete. Indeed, the traditions of fortification now found an entirely new area of expression in the New World to which they were initially exported, for colonial governments enthusiastically adopted the designs and techniques of their European models. Political upheavals in the New World in the eighteenth century also failed to derail the art and science of fortification that, as in Europe, had become an essential part of the culture and education of the time. It remained for the New World only to copy the professional engineering side of the European experience, and to borrow unabashedly from the knowledge and traditions that had been established.

Notes

[1.] Michel Parent and Jacques Verroust, *Vauban* (Paris: Editions Jacques Fréal, 1971), p. 315.

[2.] A comprehensive account of the widespread nature of Vauban's interests and writings is detailed throughout Parent and Verroust, *Vauban* .

[3.] Sir Reginald Blomfield, *Sebastien le Prestre de Vauban* (London: Methuen and Co. Ltd., 1938), p. 174.

[4.] Blomfield, *Vauban*, p. 60.

[5.] Blomfield, *Vauban*, pp. 163–164.

[6.] Spurious works claimed to be by Vauban were widespread. A 1799 purported edition of Vauban's *Attaque des places*, for example, contained a chapter on the attack of *tours bastionées* that, as the author and engineer Leblond pointed out in his own treatises, obviously contradicted Vauban's own rules for the placing of batteries.

[7.] Blomfield, *Vauban*, p. 74.

[8.] Parent and Verroust, *Vauban*, p. 99.

[9.] Christopher Duffy, *The Fortress in the Age of Vauban and Frederick the Great 1660–1789: Siege Warfare, Volume II* (London: Routledge and Kegan Paul, 1985), p. 83.

[10.] Forest de Belidor, *La Science des ingénieurs dans la conduite des travaux de fortification* (Paris: Jombert, 1729), pp. 50–55.

[11.] Sebastien le Prestre de Vauban, *A Manual of Siegecraft and Fortification,* trans. G. R. Rothrock, (Ann Arbor: The University of Michigan Press, 1968), p. 161.

[12.] Christopher Duffy, *Fire and Stone, The Science of Fortress Warfare 1660–1860* (Newton Abbot: David and Charles, 1975), p. 91.

[13.] David Chandler, *The Art of Warfare in the Age of Marlborough* (New York: Hippocrene Books, 1976), p. 243.

[14.] Sebastien le Prestre de Vauban, *Traité de la défense des places* (Paris: Anselin, 1829), pp. 51–54.

[15.] Chandler, *The Art of Warfare*, p. 245. The author provides examples of some of the longest sieges—Milazzo in 1718–1719, during which the Austrians held out for 219 days; the siege of Prague, during which the French resisted for 152 days—and of the shortest, such as the 6-day siege of Huy in 1705.

[16.] M. Augoyat, *Aperçu historique sur les fortifications, les ingénieurs et le Corps du Génie de France*, 2nd ed. (Paris: Cd. Tanera, 1860–64), Vol. I, p. 290. See also Lazare Carnot, *A Treatise on the Defence of Fortified Places*, trans. from the French by Lt.-Col. Baron de Montalembert (London: T. Egerton, 1814), pp. 5–6. Louis XIV's letter was translated into a law on July 26, 1792, which read, "Every commandant of a fortified place, who surrenders to the enemy, previous to there being a practicable and accessible breach in the body of the place, and before his having sustained, at least one assault, (supposing an interior intrenchment behind the breach), shall be punished with death, unless he shall have been in want of ammunition and provisions." p. 8.

[17.] Maurice T. Sautai, *L'Oeuvre de Vauban à Lille* (Paris: Librairie R. Chapelot et Cie., 1911), p.146. This list is included with others, all intended to guide governors of fortresses about the provisions they needed to make when threatened with a siege.

[18.] Vauban, *Mémoire pour servir d'instruction dans la conduite des sièges et dans la défense des places* (Leyden, 1740), p. 119. The methods of placing cannon and mortar for the most effective fire and the minimum of destruction is described in detail.

[19.] Duffy, *Fire and Stone*, p. 131.

[20.] Blomfield, *Vauban*, p. 134.

[21.] Duffy, *Fire and Stone*, p.149.

[22.] John W. Wright, "Sieges and Customs of War at the Opening of the Eighteenth Century," *American Historical Review*, Vol. XXXIX (July 1934), p. 643. Lieutenant-Colonel John Laurens, appointed by Washington as one of the commissioners to draw up the capitulation at Yorktown, had been at Charleston in May 1780 when Benjamin Lincoln's army was forced to surrender to the British under Sir Henry Clinton. When the British protested the harshness of the terms at Yorktown, Laurens replied, no doubt with some relish, that they were in retaliation for the insult at Charleston.

[23.] Duffy, *The Fortress in the Age of Vauban*, p. 97.

[24.] Chandler, *The Art of Warfare*, p. 278. Peter the Great, for example, hired one of Vauban's pupils to design the fortress of St. Peter and Paul to protect his new capital of St. Petersburg; and another engineer who learned his trade in France in 1700, the future Field Marshal Münnich, served a long line of Russian rulers.

[25.] Parent and Verroust, *Vauban*, p. 104.

[26] George S. Clarke, *Fortification*, (London: Murray, 1890), pp. 7–8.

[27] Duffy, *The Fortress in the Age of Vauban*, p. 156. The quotation is a comment by the Chevalier du Theil in his 1778 treatise on the "uses of the new artillery."

[28] Duffy, *The Fortress in the Age of Vauban*, p. 157.

[29] Duffy, *Fire and Stone*, p.104.

[30] Donald D. Horward, *Napoleon and Iberia—The Twin Sieges of Ciudad Rodrigo and Almeida, 1810* (Tallahassee: University Presses of Florida, 1984). This study provides a fascinating account of two of the most important sieges of the war in the Peninsula in 1807–1814. One of the most interesting aspects is the classic way these sieges were conducted almost a century and a half after Vauban, and in almost the exact manner that he prescribed.

Fortification in the New World | 3

Introduction

By the eighteenth century, fortification was a mature science, reflecting a continuous growth in Europe of at least two centuries and more. The so-called Italian, Dutch, French, and German schools or systems of fortification had all been in the spotlight for a time, and had contributed substantially to the state of the art. A complex and sizeable technical vocabulary particular to fortification and the military sciences had developed, and at the same time had been disseminated widely throughout the Western world. The terminology of fortification and siegecraft, barely comprehensible to the average individual today, was as recognizable to the educated elite of the eighteenth century as the terminology of the computer is to modern man. Encyclopedias, manuals, and dictionaries (see Figure 3.1) commonly car-

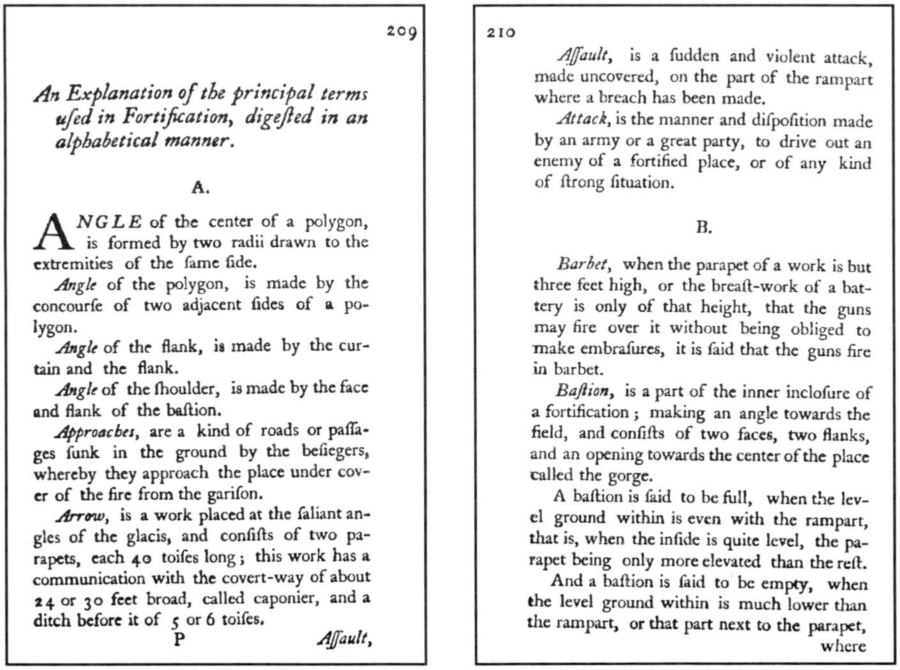

209

An Explanation of the principal terms used in Fortification, digested in an alphabetical manner.

A.

ANGLE of the center of a polygon, is formed by two radii drawn to the extremities of the same side.

Angle of the polygon, is made by the concourse of two adjacent sides of a polygon.

Angle of the flank, is made by the curtain and the flank.

Angle of the shoulder, is made by the face and flank of the bastion.

Approaches, are a kind of roads or passages funk in the ground by the besiegers, whereby they approach the place under cover of the fire from the garison.

Arrow, is a work placed at the saliant angles of the glacis, and consists of two parapets, each 40 toises long; this work has a communication with the covert-way of about 24 or 30 feet broad, called caponier, and a ditch before it of 5 or 6 toises.

P   *Assault,*

210

Assault, is a sudden and violent attack, made uncovered, on the part of the rampart where a breach has been made.

Attack, is the manner and disposition made by an army or a great party, to drive out an enemy of a fortified place, or of any kind of strong situation.

B.

Barbet, when the parapet of a work is but three feet high, or the breast-work of a battery is only of that height, that the guns may fire over it without being obliged to make embrasures, it is said that the guns fire in barbet.

Bastion, is a part of the inner inclosure of a fortification; making an angle towards the field, and consists of two faces, two flanks, and an opening towards the center of the place called the gorge.

A bastion is said to be full, when the level ground within is even with the rampart, that is, when the inside is quite level, the parapet being only more elevated than the rest.

And a bastion is said to be empty, when the level ground within is much lower than the rampart, or that part next to the parapet, where

Figure 3.1   Pages from John Muller, *A Treatise Containing the Elementary Part of Fortification (1746)*. A prime example of the spread of fortification manuals and literature throughout Europe and North America in the eighteenth century. A copy of Muller's book was owned by George Washington.

ried sections on the art and science of fortification and siegecraft, and were widely available and attractive to the educated classes of the time, not just to military professionals.[1] This was vital with respect to the transfer of the techniques of fortification to the New World. It meant that a knowledgeable audience, familiar with those concepts and ideas, had been developing for some time.

What accounted for the extensive spread of the ideas and vocabulary of fortification and siegecraft? Ultimately, a fairly complex process had made it possible for the public to acquire access to plans and maps of fortified places over the centuries. For example, when engineers were in training, or when fortresses were still in the design stage, techniques that made use of scale models, two-dimensional plans, relief profiles, and perspective drawings were commonly employed and then often published. (An exception was the collection of models in the *Galerie des Plans Reliefs* in Paris where the fortress designs were supposed to be guarded as state secrets.) Moreover, because of the immense cost of a fortification and its military importance, the usual procedure was for the senior engineer to draft a memorandum detailing its profile, expense, innovations, and dimensions, together with several sheets of scale plans. Eventually, copies of many of these plans found their way to publishing houses, which then disseminated them to interested readers throughout Europe.

It was also a general rule that a military engineer submit his plan for a fortification to his commander in chief for approval; if, however, the pressure of military events did not permit, the initial design stage might be skipped over entirely.[2] Because of this practice, numerous plans of various forts were drawn up, eventually finding their way into books and atlases. In addition, detailed plans were often required when a fortification was simply being inspected as to its readiness and general condition; as a result, more profiles of forts made their way into European consumption.[3] Finally, the completed attack or defense of a fortified place tended to produce a plethora of complex plans that depicted not only the general profile of the fortress, but also the disposition of the attacking forces (right down to individual regiments), as well as the topography of the place. Some of these demonstrated an almost textbook quality, and were studied as such by interested readers of the eighteenth century. The art and science of fortification thus spread widely through the general culture of the time. As has been pointed out:

> Not surprisingly, fortification plans were especially familiar to both amateur and professional students of the military sciences. Indeed, the extent to which they had permeated a wider culture is reflected by their appearance in both the art and the literature of the seventeenth and eighteenth centuries. A knowledge of fortification enhanced the education of a gentleman as well as that of a professional soldier. English travelers on the Grand Tour, for example, viewed the fortifications to the north of Venice as part of the "standard package." Atlases of fortification plans were published in several European countries in the seventeenth and eighteenth centuries and were sold to the libraries of laymen as well as military experts. . . . As everyday tools in the hands of military engineers and commanders, these plans had become fairly well standardized by the second half of the eighteenth century.[4]

Professional (or amateur) military engineers who possessed the requisite skills were increasingly in demand in the colonies as well as in Europe. These skills included the ability to choose a suitable site, to design plans depicting the fort and its dimensions, to apply the correct principles for designing a functional fort, and then to successfully carry through with the actual construction. In the early years of colonization, the mother country usually provided the engineers and the monies for fortifications. Eventually, however, as the colonies became more developed and populated, the educated elite began to acquaint itself with the literature and vocabulary of fortification and its related subjects. Would-be colonial engineers managed on occasion to train with engineer-soldiers from the mother country, and to participate now and then in the construction of colonial fortifications.

Thus, as far as the physical transfer of the traditions of military fortifications from Europe to North America was concerned, it quite logically followed the path of European colonization. The Spanish, French, and English who explored and settled the new territories carried with them well-established techniques of fortress building, and transplanted them efficiently wherever they deemed it necessary. By the beginning of the seventeenth century, numerous forts, though often crudely modified to fit the more uncivilized terrain, were appearing at strategic sites. Like their European counterparts before them, North American forts were closely tied to political and military developments. Indeed, colonial forts grew in size and complexity in direct relationship to the growth of rivalries and military activity in the New World. As competition between the European powers for control of more territories increased in intensity and eventually exploded in armed hostilities, the science of fortification also grew in importance.

The process of fortification in the New World fell into roughly three stages. The first was marked by the appearance of rather primitive colonial fortifications, built at strategic sites for the same reasons as in Europe centuries before: to control locations of obvious importance such as harbors, natural interior routes, the mouths of rivers that flowed into the Atlantic or the Gulf of Mexico, or the confluence of lakes and major rivers in the interior. These forts, generally thrown up hastily from the raw materials at hand, were basically designed to uphold colonial land claims, to limit the expansion of rival powers, and to help exert control within the territories already claimed.

The second stage represented a transitional period of fortification that occurred as rivalries among the various colonial powers heated up. Thus, the French-British-Indian wars in North America during the mid-eighteenth century witnessed the growth of better, more permanently constructed fortifications, as well as the appearance of actual sieges on a European model. These changes not only transformed military operations in the colonies into much more complex procedures, but also provided opportunities to apply the theories of military fortifications and siegecraft as already developed in Europe. This period culminated in wholesale introduction to America of the concepts of fortress warfare and siegecraft, especially during the Anglo-French colonial wars and the crucial years of the American Revolution.

The third and final period of fortification occurred roughly from the beginning of the nineteenth century until the American Civil War. During this time, the government and military establishment of the United States not only identified and institutionalized in the curricula of its military and engineering schools the then-prevalent theories of fortress building and siegecraft, but also attempted to apply them on a national scale in the course of pursuing domestic and foreign policies.

Colonial Fortification in North America

The Spanish Experience

Between the sixteenth and eighteenth centuries, forts of various types and permanence were becoming scattered over the different strategic areas of the North American continent.[5] (See Figure 3.2.) Most of the engineers who plied their trade in the colonies concentrated on a fortification style that, although simple, fell squarely into the mainstream of European tradition. The design most frequently used in America was the square, four-bastioned plan. Easily constructed in the wilderness from abundant timber, or from stones and brick in more accessible and settled locations, this type of fort was economical, flexible, and neatly adapted to the terrain. It was also easily defended by a small garrison, since the distance between the curtain and faces of the bastions in this design always adhered to the rule of not exceeding the range of musket fire. The application of this simple design was a vital component of the strategy of swift expansion. The instincts of the Spanish and French, in particular, led them to explore the vast new territories as swiftly as possible. By throwing up some sort of simple fortification at strategic points with the materials at hand, they attempted to both stake a claim and establish control.

The earliest builders of forts were, of course, the Spanish, who led the way in the colonization of the Americas. In California, Texas, New Mexico,

Figure 3.2   Locations of some principal colonial fortifications.

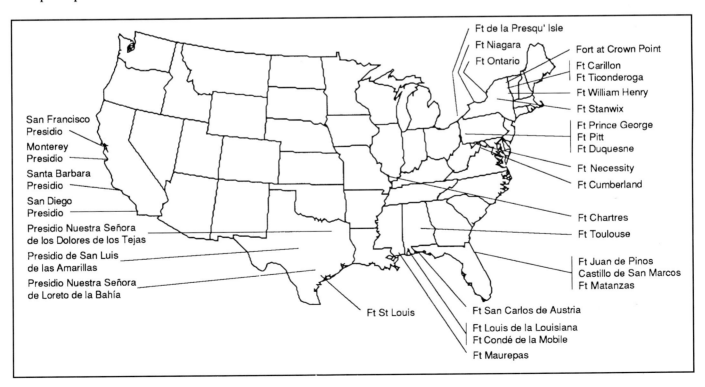

and Florida, they hastily erected various presidios to garrison soldiers, to provide support for religious missions, and to secure the territories from competing powers. Most of these small forts were initially unimpressive, primitive, and impermanent in nature, even though they reflected most of the basic principles of fort building. The Spanish did attempt to transform many of these early forts into more durable structures when competition with the other colonial powers heated up. These forts, which dotted California and Texas, became more orderly and were better constructed in the eighteenth century.[6]

While most Spanish forts and missions were unremarkable, one stood out because of its huge cost and complexity. Begun in 1672 and completed in 1756, the Castillo de San Marcos at Saint Augustine stood at the center of the Spanish system of defense in Florida. A square, four-bastioned fort of stone and stucco, with a wet ditch surrounding the enceinte, it also featured a ravelin to defend the gate, which in turn was safeguarded by a drawbridge and **portcullis** (a gate with an iron grating made to be raised or lowered). Interestingly, too, a series of outer defenses, generally lines of earthen outer works with palisading added to the fort between 1720 and 1730, in effect transformed Saint Augustine into a fortified town with the Castillo de San Marcos as its citadel.[7] (See Figure 3.3.) Additions to the Spanish system of

Figure 3.3   Castillo de San Marcos, Florida (1672–1756). Plan (1785); facsimile (1884) *National Archives, Washington, D.C.*

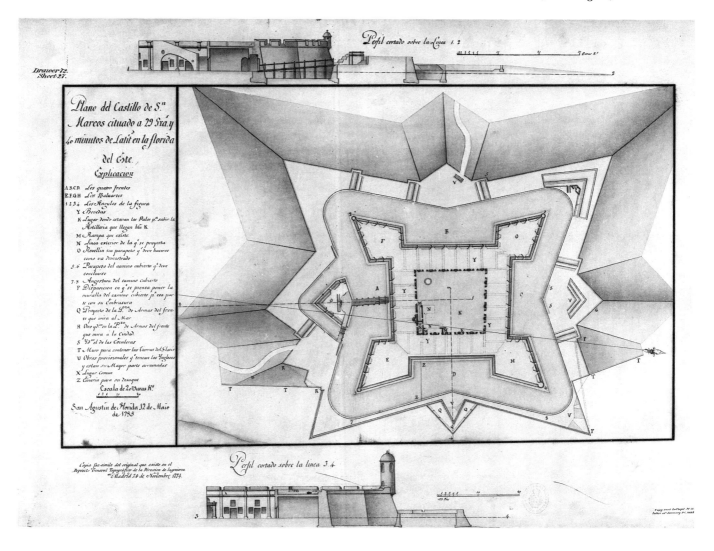

fortification in Florida were Fort Matanzas (1736) and Fort San Carlos de Austria (1698).

The true picture of Spanish power was, however, not really consistent with the immense territory that appeared to be controlled by these presidios and forts. Most of these fortifications were little more than enclosures of sun-dried brick, reinforced by small round or square towers, and furnished with a modicum of useful armament. Many of them were not even able to prevent Indian raids, especially from the swift, mobile attacks of the Apaches and Comanches in the Southwest. By the end of the eighteenth century, Spain had few settlers and even fewer funds to invest in her territories. Ultimately, the Spanish experience with fortification was shaped by the country's increasing exclusion from North America by the French and British. The less territory she could legitimately control, the less reason to pursue the construction of forts.

The French Experience

Although the Spanish were the earliest to build forts, it was French fortification that demonstrated a serious and strong commitment to colonization in North America during the eighteenth century. Swiftly fanning out over huge territories by means of the waterways, the French systematically threw up forts at every strategic site to stake their claim over the areas they had penetrated. It is likely that their fort-building during the early eighteenth century represented an interesting, if inchoate plan, to lock up routes of expansion that might be used by their colonial rivals. In short order, they strung out a series of forts aimed at denying access to any other powers also exploring these areas. To secure their claims to the lower Mississippi, the French built Fort Maurepas (1699) on the Bay of Biloxi, two forts in the Mobile Bay area, Fort Toulouse (French Louisiana), and, further north, Fort Chartres (Illinois). To complete a strategic link between their holdings on the St. Lawrence and the Mississippi, they also established a series of forts intended to secure control of the gateway to the Ohio country, and to check British expansion westward. In 1753, the Marquis de Duquesne sent an expedition of 2,000 colonial troops and 200 Indians to the southern shores of Lake Erie, where they built Fort Presqu'Ile and, 15 miles further inland, Fort Rivière au Boeuf. Most intriguingly, one of the best descriptions of this fort (a description that could have applied to so many other forts in the wilderness of eighteenth-century North America) was provided by Major George Washington who, in December 1753, delivered a message from the governor of Virginia demanding to know by what right the French had established themselves there:

> It is situated on the South, or West Fork of French Creek, near the Water, and is almost surrounded by the Creek, and a small Branch of it which forms a Kind of an Island; four Houses compose the Sides; and the Bastions are made of Piles driven into the Ground, and about 12 Feet above and sharp at Top, with Port-Holes cut for Cannon and Loop-Holes for the small Arms to fire through; and there are eight 6 lb. Pieces mounted, two in each Bastion, and one Piece of four Pound before the Gate; in the Bastions are a Guard-House, Chapel, Doctor's Lodging, and the Commander's private

Store round on which are laid Plat-Forms for the Cannon and Men to stand on: There are several Barracks without the Fort, for the Soldiers Dwelling, covered, some with Bark, and some with Boards, and made chiefly of Loggs: There are also several other Houses, such as Stables, Smiths Shops, & c.[8]

Perhaps spurred by reports of such French fort building, the colonial government in Virginia voted £10,000 in 1754 to build a four-bastioned fort at the confluence of the Monongahela and Ohio rivers (Fort Prince George). This attempt, however, was foiled by the French capture of the site, and the completion in its place of Fort Duquesne, seen in Figure 3.4, in the same year. Situated so as to take advantage of the protection from attack provided

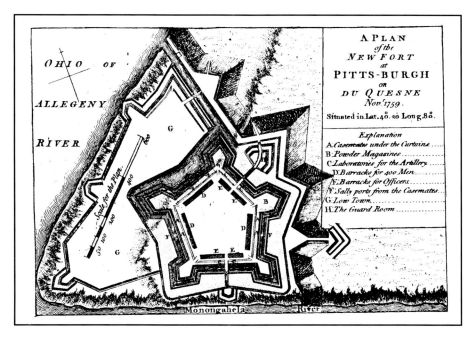

Figure 3.4   Plan of Fort Duquesne, Pennsylvania (1754), François le Mercier, engineer, and of Fort Pitt, Pennsylvania (1759–1765). Harry Gordon, engineer (Rocque, 1765).

by the rivers and a steep incline, the bastions in those directions were simple, loopholed stockades. Facing the land, the rest of the curtains and bastions were composed of two parallel walls, 10 1/2 feet apart, consisting of square-hewn logs laid horizontally. The walls were tied together by heavy cross timbers, and the space between was filled massively with earth. By far the most technically advanced and strongest fort built on the frontier to that point, Fort Duquesne with just 300 troops in residence was enough to persuade the Indians of the Ohio to join the French side. It also provided a formidable strategic link with Fort Chartres and the other posts in the Illinois territory. Despite the fort's relative complexity for North America, some French officers were correct in predicting that the fort was still too small and vulnerable to cannon fire from nearby heights. The French destroyed the fort themselves before retreating from what appeared an untenable position during the hostilities with the British in 1759.

The northern approaches to Canada from the 13 colonies were usually by way of the Hudson River, lakes George and Champlain, and the Richelieu River to the St. Lawrence. To secure this route, the French constructed Fort Saint-Frédéric (eventually renamed Fort Crown Point) on the western shore of Lake Champlain in 1731. To augment their control further, Fort Carillon—

better known as Fort Ticonderoga (see Figure 3.5) after its capture and reconstruction by the British in 1759—was built in 1755 on a rocky ridge on the southern end of Lake Champlain where Lake George flows into it. The engineer in charge was a Canadian, Michel Chartier, Sieur de Lotbinière, who was born in Quebec in 1723 and had been sent to France to study the techniques of military engineering. Despite graft and political intrigues, the basic outline of the fort was complete by the winter of 1756.[9] As at Fort Duquesne, the wooden walls of the main enclosure were two in number. The 10 feet of space between them was filled with earth to absorb cannon shot, and they were tied to each other with cross timbers dovetailed in place. The latter were composed of heavy oak timbers, 14 or 15 inches square, laid horizontally one on top of the other. A major problem was the continual rotting of the timbers, and so in 1757 an attempt was made to revet the timber scarp with a stone veneer in order to construct a more durable fort. It is no coincidence that by this time, serious military conflict had broken out between the French and British. As always, the demands of warfare acted as a spur to the art and science of fortification.

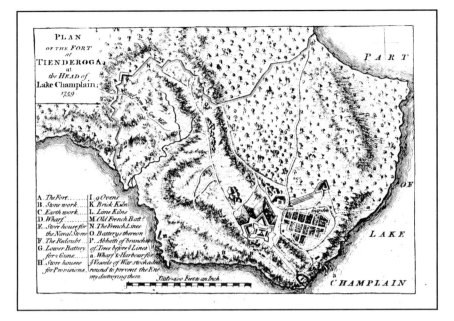

Figure 3.5   Plan of Fort Ticonderoga (Rocque, 1759).

Fort Niagara was also strengthened between 1750 and 1759 by the addition of new earthworks and batteries. The irregular design of this fort, seen in Figure 3.6, was a fine example of the skill of François Pouchot, a royal military engineer. Because this fort was tucked neatly into the peninsula at the juncture of the Niagara River and Lake Ontario, a siege was possible from only one direction. To counter that possibility, the earthen enceinte was built with modified **demibastions** (a bastion with only one face and one flank), and reinforced with a large ravelin, redoubts, and a ditch, all systematically laid out in the design.

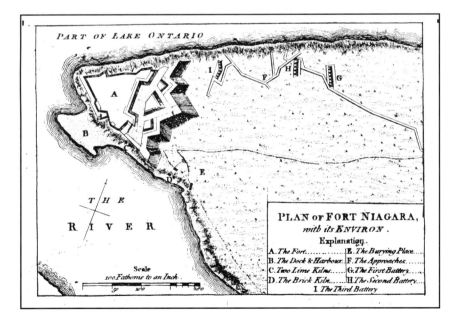

Figure 3.6   Plan of Fort Niagara, New York (1679, 1755), François Pouchot, engineer (Rocque, 1759).

Further north yet, the prolific French fortifiers had decided that they must also safeguard the seaward approaches to the Saint Lawrence. In 1721, under the direction of the chief engineer of Canada, Jean-François du Verger de Verville, work began on the new fortress of Louisbourg on

Cape Breton Island, which formed the southern shore of the entrance to the Gulf of St. Lawrence. The site of the fort, pictured in Figure 3.7, was strategically chosen to be on the east coast of the island at Havre à l'Anglais, a harbor that could shelter the French fleet and be used to trap any British ships that might venture into the St. Lawrence. Verville decided to erect his works up on a peninsula. There he constructed a bastion and redoubt in masonry, which were to contain a barracks for at least six companies and their officers, and were to be protected from surprise by a ditch and covered way. Other bastions were to be built on the two hills found between this point and the sea, with a demibastion guarding each of the seaward flanks. A heavy battery was to be established to command the upper part of the harbor. The Bastion du Roi, one of the full bastions, was in fact a miniature citadel with a gorge wall, barracks, governor's residence, and chapel. Because of Verville's insistence on using masonry despite the depredations of the climate on such building materials, Louisbourg was costly to build and to maintain.[10]

The British Experience

In contrast to the French, who were the beneficiaries of a fairly organized military engineering tradition with respect to fortifications, the British in the early eighteenth century gave very little thought to any systematic fortification in their colonies in North America. Most of the settlers in the 13 colonies were untutored in military engineering, did not have access to a skilled corps of engineers from the mother country, and had little desire or financial capability to set about building an elaborate system of defense. Those forts that existed were anything but formidable edifices—generally nothing more than storehouses surrounded by quickly thrown up stockades of timber. For example, Fort Necessity, built under the direction of 22-year-

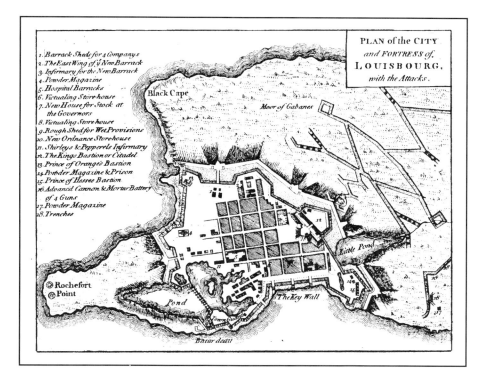

Figure 3.7   Plan of Louisburg (1721), Jean-François du Verger de Verville, engineer (Rocque, 1759).

old Lieutenant Colonel George Washington in May 1754, was described by an observer as a "small Stocado Fort made in a circular Form round a Small House that Stood in the Middle of it to keep our provisions and Ammunition in, And was Cover'd With Bark and some Skins, and might be about fourteen feet Square."[11] The circular shape made the fort indefensible from within, of course, since the walls could not be enfiladed, and not surprisingly, in July 1754, this hapless little fort was taken by the French.

Other early colonial forts had traces that allowed for variations required by the terrain and even sported bastions, but in general all were too weak to withstand a direct assault with cannon fire.[12] Their chief *raison d'être* was to protect colonial settlements as much as possible from surprise attacks by the French or Indians. Fort Oswego on the southern shore of Lake Ontario, built in 1724 by Governor William Burnet of New York, was an unprepossessing stone and earth work. Fort Cumberland (1754, Maryland), Fort William Henry (1755, New York), and Fort Stanwix (Fort Schuyler, New York, 1758) were all examples of rectangular, bastioned forts in the mid-eighteenth century, thrown up as quickly and as inexpensively as possible in the wilderness to secure strategic sites and to protect settlements in their vicinity (see Figure 3.8).

Thus, up to the the mid-eighteenth century or so, colonial forts were often little more than hastily built dots on the landscape, intended to mark commonly agreed upon strategic locations. And so they might have remained, for the comparative insignificance of colonial affairs was demonstrated by the fact that, although in 1755 there was armed conflict at every point where the French and English came into contact in America, war was not declared until fighting actually broke out in Europe in May 1756. The moment that colonial competition escalated into a more global military context, fortification in America experienced a major leap in complexity and scale. In comparison to what had gone on before, larger funds were

Figure 3.8   Plans of Fort William Henry, New York (1755).

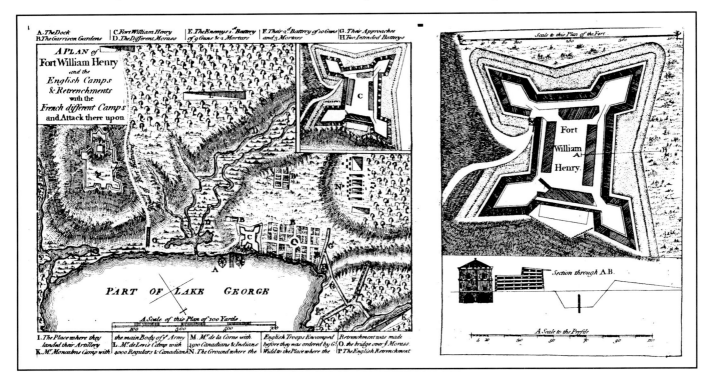

expended in rebuilding or refurbishing old forts, and in designing new ones. More significantly yet, as many more troops and cannon were shipped to the colonies to man these forts, the practice of gunnery and siegecraft on the frontier was fundamentally transformed. While colonial conflicts had previously been characterized by simple, small-scale raids, which had often used the Indians as cat's-paws, they now escalated into major military campaigns and sieges patterned on the European experience.

The Transition Period of Fortification

The Impact of the French and Indian Wars

Not surprisingly, the prospect of imminent hostilities between France and Britain proved to be the stimulus necessary for a strong and systematic renewal of fortification in North America, as did the war between Great Britain and her rebellious colonies some years later. The French, as has been noted, had left a strategic trail of forts in the wake of their explorations. Faced with a challenge from the French and their Indian allies who threatened to block any further English expansion past the Appalachians, the British now realized the necessity of financing the building and garrisoning of permanent fortifications. As the conflict exploded, significant work was undertaken at various times on forts Pitt, Ontario, and Crown Point—all of which occupied strategic locations with respect to the ongoing hostilities.

Fort Pitt (1759–1763) was the most extensive fortification undertaken by the British before the American Revolution. Constructed near the site of the former Fort Duquesne, its engineer, Harry Gordon, designed a pentagonal trace with bastions to conform to the triangular shape of the site defined by the Ohio and Monongahela rivers, and to provide more interior area for the fort. Built of earth and masonry, the ramparts on the landward side were strengthened by a 15-foot brick scarp; above and behind the scarp, earth was used to form the terreplein, banquette, and parapet. A place of arms, a ravelin, and a ditch further augmented the fort's defenses.

Fort Ontario (1759–1763) was also a five-bastioned, pentagonal fort, smaller than Fort Pitt, and designed to fit at the junction of the Oswego River and Lake Ontario (see Figure 3.9). Fort Crown Point (1759), a similar work, was also built of earth and logs, and was constructed to fit the irregular peninsula formed by a bay and the main body of water of Lake Champlain. Fort Beauséjour (New Brunswick) had the honor of being the first known pentagonal, five-bastioned fort in North America; its construction was begun by the French in 1751, but it was taken by the British in 1755. Logically turning to European military techniques, even when attacking forts in the wilderness, the British expedition followed standard siege pro-

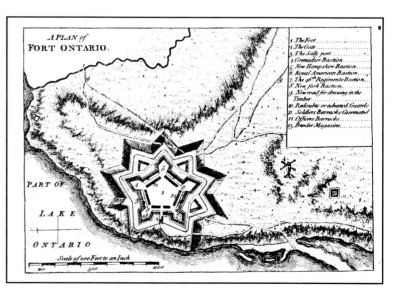

Figure 3.9 Plan of Fort Ontario (1759–1763).

cedures insofar as they were actually necessary. They isolated Beauséjour, brought up large mortars, successfully captured it, and subsequently renamed it Fort Cumberland.[13]

As the expeditions of George Washington and his small force of colonists moved not very successfully to counter the French in 1754, the alarmed English colonies threw up all sorts of official and "private" forts along the length of the Allegheny Mountains. Most were hardly a formidable barrier to the French and their Indian allies, as the debacle with Fort Necessity so unfortunately illustrated. By 1755, the British government answered the French challenge by dispatching Major General Braddock and two regiments of infantry. Despite initial major setbacks, including Braddock's disastrous defeat that same year, British naval superiority ultimately enabled them to control supply routes, and, by 1760, to muster about 60,000 troops in North America (including the colonists), outnumbering the 15,000 French and Canadian forces.

Indeed, the advent of the European regulars had perhaps the most impact on the progress of military fortifications in the New World. The creation of a primary theater of war, and the infusion of military professionals onto the scene, meant that other military traditions would follow, including the art of systematic and formal siegecraft hitherto not very common to the colonial terrain. The Marquis de Montcalm (1712–1759), a veteran of over 16 sieges in European campaigns, was placed in charge of French forces in 1756. He determined that instead of continuing the "scattered raids and hunting parties," which seemed to be, in his opinion, the amateurish and disorganized way the colonials waged war, operations would now be carried through a proper sequence.[14] Directed by the Marquis de Vaudreuil, the governor-general of New France, to take Fort Oswego in the summer of 1756, Montcalm successfully subjected the garrison to a formal siege. In short order, he also besieged the recently built Fort William Henry at the south end of Lake George, and captured a significant amount of supplies of gunpowder and rations. Shortly thereafter, Montcalm beat back a combined British and colonial attack on Fort Carillon, inflicting nearly 2,000 casualties on them in the process.

These French successes undoubtedly convinced the British that systematically planned advances, a proper use of artillery, and formal siege attacks could be as effective in colonial warfare as in Europe, and the renewed campaigns of 1758 began to reflect these axioms. Inexorably, the British and colonial troops struck back, employing these tactics singly or in combination, as necessary. For example, Lieutenant Colonel Bradstreet captured Fort Frontenac (renamed Fort Kingston) and made it difficult for the French to supply Duquesne and all the other posts beyond the southern shore of Lake Ontario. Brigadier John Forbes and Colonel Henry Bouquet pushed on from Pennsylvania to Duquesne, which they found burned and abandoned by the French, and claimed the site as Fort Pitt. By 1759 the British had laid formal siege to Fort Niagara, and with its capture isolated Canada from the southern lakes and the Ohio country. At the same time, when it became apparent that the new British commander in chief, Major General Amherst, was amassing enough men and artillery to besiege forts Carillon and Saint-Frédéric, the French fell back to the northern end of Lake Champlain. Changing his target, Amherst left Halifax in June 1758 with 4,000 British troops and 2,500 colonials, 10 engineers, 51 siege guns, and vast amounts of ammunition, and opened two trench attacks against Fort Louisbourg. Unlike the amateurish, if successful, colonial and British siege of Louisbourg in 1754, after some initial disorganization the British set up batteries that enfiladed the west front of the fort, and on July 25 opened a breaching fire that forced the French to surrender the next day.[15]

The following year saw the final British blows against the French strongholds of Quebec (see Figure 3.10) and Montreal. The landing on the heights above Quebec by the British under the command of Major General James Wolfe (1727–1759) led to the battle that resulted in both his and Montcalm's deaths, and in the town's capture. This event has been described as "the first regular engagement that was ever fought in North America," and as such perhaps neatly illustrates the transfer to the New World of European experiences in fortifications and siegecraft.[16] This siege, which lasted from May to mid-September of 1759, displayed few of the steps of a classic Vauban-style operation. Like so many of the colonial forts, Quebec at that time was far from being a proper fortress compared to the full-blown European model. To begin with, its walls were neither well designed nor well built. Although by 1749 Quebec was enclosed on the west by a single system of masonry defenses, even the French officers who had cause to survey it disdained the result. Louis-Antoine de Bougainville, one of Montcalm's officers, reported to Paris in 1758 that "Quebec is without fortifications and is not capable of being fortified; if we cannot hold the approaches to it there is nothing for it but to lay down our arms."[17] Montcalm himself wrote in his journal that the city's fortifications were "so ridiculous and so bad that it would be taken as soon as besieged," and acidly commented that the engineer who designed the fortification, notably Chaussegros de Léry, had "robbed the king, like the others."[18]

The difficulty was that Quebec appeared to have little with which to defend itself in case of siege: it boasted neither ditches, counterscarp, glacis, or covered way to slow down an assaulting force. And to make matters worse, the city was dominated by heights on which an enemy could erect batteries and

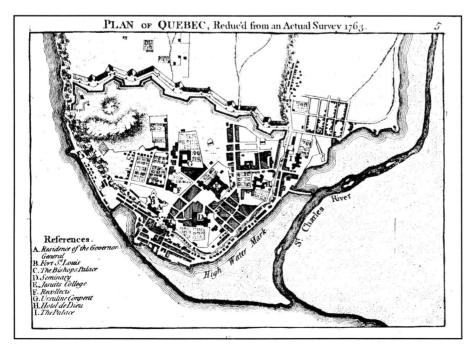

Figure 3.10   Plan of Quebec (1763).

make protected approaches. A mere wall was not of much use without the exterior works that were designed to protect a fortress from direct artillery fire and capture by escalade. Chaussegros de Léry apparently had little faith in the ability of a fortress to use its own artillery to counterattack against a besieging army—the very attitude that Montalembert and Carnot attempted to counter in their writings. No gun mounts had been provided in the faces of the bastions confronting the Plains of Abraham, and most of the embrasures were placed in the bastions' flanks for firing along the walls. An observer in 1759 wrote that although the western ramparts had 52 guns, ranging from 2-pounders to 12-pounders, "none of them can fire towards the open country; they all fire in flank and in enfilade, so they are only useful in case of the enemy trying a scaling attack."[19] Unspoken is the implied observation that by this stage in a siege, it is generally too late. After the British captured Quebec, embrasures in the bastion faces were quickly cut and cannon mounted.

The French engineers responsible for Quebec's defenses also failed to mount batteries at the south bend of the river opposite the city to command the nearby anchorages, or secure the heights directly above them. In fact, the Quebec fortress was not extended to the south shore of the river until 1865, when three forts were built there in fear that General Grant and an American army might invade. As a result, the British were able to occupy the Lévis heights and to set up batteries that brutally bombarded the city and facilitated the Royal Navy's passage past Quebec into the upper river.

Thus, four years after Braddock's little army had been decimated on the banks of the Monongahela, French weaknesses and shortsighted strategy permitted the experienced 8,500 British regulars to surround Quebec, isolate it as effectively as if it had been formally invested, and concentrate freely on taking the place. The result, then, was not a classic siege in the Vauban style, but a working siege nonetheless. Although as early as June 27 Wolfe began landing troops on the Isle d'Orléans from ships of the fleet, and continued to bombard the town from the Lévis heights, it was not until September 13 that he successfully gambled with the landing of troops and cannon at the Anse de Foulon. When Montcalm learned that the British troops had climbed the heights with cannon and were gathering on the Plains of Abraham—high ground that commanded sections of the city walls—he was forced to attack with the 4,500 men he had available (about half were militia), and hastened to the historically famous engagement. The capitulation of Quebec on September 18, 1759, was a traditional one: the garrison was allowed the honors of war, and it was agreed to transport the French troops as conveniently as possible to the first port in France.[20] Only the fortified town of Montreal remained a strategic danger for the British, until it, too, was invested by Amherst with over 17,000 men. In the end, Governor-General Vaudreuil surrendered Montreal and, in effect, the whole of French Canada.

Fortification and Siegecraft During the American Revolution

In a manner similar to European conflicts, the colonial theater of war during the 1750s had served to emphasize the importance of fortifying at strategic places, and the need for professional military engineers who understood and could implement the techniques of fortification and siegecraft. While the canvas these wars were acted out upon may have been less ornate and complex than in Europe, the principles of fortress warfare remained the same and were just as directly applied to the colonial terrain. The hostilities between France and England had also led to a quickening of the pace of fortifications and of the garrisoning of troops in North America. It was the large-scale importing of regular troops into North America during the crisis with France that had, as is well known, immense and unforeseen results in the decade that followed the peace treaty signed between the French and English in 1763. The cost of maintaining British troops and securing the huge tracts of territory west of the Appalachians with effective garrisons created a financial burden that the British government, not surprisingly, tried to pass on to the colonial assemblies. It seemed only fair to the British that the colonies match their commitment in North America. The British government's surprise and chagrin when the colonies found these demands for taxation to be offensive and an attack on their independence, was probably genuine. As matters worsened during the early 1770s, the British were aware that since they had fewer troops than the colonial militia, the forts already built and garrisoned would be of primary importance if rebellion were to break out on a large scale. In turn, the rebellious colonists were also becoming aware that they might have to quickly acquire the principles of defending or besieging those same forts, not to mention as much other practical military experience as possible.

In the final analysis, America's military success during the Revolutionary War astonished even the participants themselves. George Washington mused in 1783 that "it will not be believed that such a force as Great Britain has employed for eight years in this Country could be baffled in their plan for Subjugating it by numbers infinitely less, composed of Men oftentimes half starved; always in Rags, without pay, and experiencing at times every species of distress which human nature is capable of undergoing."[21] While many factors accounted for the ultimate American victory—French assistance, poor British strategy, British global distractions and responsibilities, the distance between Britain and the colonies, the vastness of the American theater of war, and sheer luck, to mention a few of the most obvious—the ability of the rebellious colonists to apply competently their theoretical knowledge of military affairs during real hostilities was an equally significant one.

The Americans owed their military competence, to an astonishingly large extent, to book learning. To be sure, some like George Washington were veterans of the French-Indian wars; others had acquired some experience by serving with local militia or British units.[22] Of the generals appointed to the Continental Army in 1775, only three could be described as professional soldiers—Charles Lee (1731–1782), Horatio Gates (c.1727–1806), and Richard Montgomery (c.1738–1775).[23] Most of the rest, however, owed their knowledge entirely to amateur interest in the books and treatises the eighteenth century offered with respect to military affairs in general, and fortification in particular. Henry Knox (1750–1806), Anthony Wayne (1745–1796), and Nathaniel Greene (1742–1786) came into the Continental Army directly from civilian life. What they knew about waging war derived entirely from their reading or from sporadic involvement with a local militia. Greene, for example, was a keen, self-taught student of military art, profiting especially from the works of de Saxe and Turenne.[24]

Henry Knox, Washington's chief of artillery, presented an even more striking example. He had learned his trade by reading the books of the masters of fortification and military science that he sold in his New London bookstore in Boston, and by chatting with British officers who passed through his establishment.[25] When asked by John Adams to list some of the foremost authorities, he easily named Pagan, Vauban, Belidor, and Coehoorn among others.[26] Knox, seen in Figure 3.11, conscientiously applied his entirely theoretical knowledge to the various campaigns he undertook, for his only practical training came from his membership in a militia company of artillery known as the "Train" under British command in the 1760s, and, just before the outbreak of the Revolution, in the militia grandiosely titled "The Boston Grenadier Corps." Yet, throughout most of his career with the Continental Army, Knox's military expertise was more than adequate. After Ethan Allen, Benedict Arnold, and the Green Mountain Boys captured Fort Ticonderoga from the British in May 1775, Knox organized, at General Washington's request, an extraordinary trek during the brutal winter months to bring back to Massachusetts a huge train of captured artillery. The commander in chief recognized the desperate need for such cannon in his orders, stating, "The want of them is so great that no trouble or expense must be spared to obtain them."[27] Once Knox had brought off this amazing logistical feat, he joined Washington and engineer Richard Gridley in setting up batteries in two new redoubts, built quickly and quietly during the night of March 4, 1776, on the Dorchester Heights overlooking Boston. Using the classic tools of entrenchment and fortification, stealthily hauling up fascines, timbers, barrels, and hay all night, the Americans successfully fortified the heights above Boston, and thus commanded the British forces who had fallen back into the city. It became impossible for the British to answer the American bombardment, and they were forced to evacuate. General Sir William Howe later reportedly remarked that "the rebels have done more in one night than my whole army would have done in a month."[28]

Figure 3.11   Henry Knox (1750–1806). *Courtesy of the West Point Museum Collections, United States MIlitary Academy, West Point, N.Y.*

Another occasion, however, revealed the negative side of relying upon skills and knowledge derived solely from book learning—that is, the almost comic-opera events at Chew House in Germantown, not far from Philadelphia, in the fall of 1777. When the Continental Army attack was momentarily held up by British fire from a strongly fortified old house, the decisions of a quickly held council of war were carried by Knox's advice. Quoting from some expert in strategy and tactics he had read about in his bookstore, Knox argued that one should never leave an occupied enemy stronghold behind one's lines. Knox convinced the others that they should hold things up until the artillery could demolish Chew House. Had the results not been so potentially serious, they would have been almost hilarious: several thunderous bombardments and a comically foiled attempt to burn the place down notwithstanding, the well-constructed stone walls of the house refused to crumble. Despite the fact that precious time was being wasted on reducing this single spot, and that nearly one-half of the Continental Army that should have been pushing rapidly on against the British lines was being held idle, Knox began another futile bombardment. Unfortunately, this time the heavy artillery fire convinced the forward American forces that they were being attacked in the rear, with the result that they broke and ran just as victory was in sight. Luckily for the

Americans, the British lines had also broken in disarray only a few minutes before, or the consequences of this fiasco might have been much more serious. The whole incident demonstrated the unfortunate possibilities inherent in getting experience solely from books.

Still, if theoretical knowledge was at times the only sort the colonists had to lean on, for the most part they accorded it the proper respect. Any kind of learning vis-à-vis military affairs was recognized as important at the outset by the American leadership. Washington himself was a firm believer in the value of military treatises and texts detailing the soldier's art. In fact, he attached so much importance to learning from military texts that, in 1777, he opened his "General Instruction for the Colonels and Commanding Officers of Regiments in the Continental Service" with the order: "As War is a Science, and a great deal of useful knowledge and instruction [is] to be drawn from Books, you are to cause your Officers to devote some part of their time to reading Military authors."[29] With respect to the subject of military engineering, Washington was no doubt even more aware of the immense amount of expertise it involved, and how important that might be to his fledgling army. As early as 1775, he recognized that treatises on engineering were one thing and practical experience quite another when he wrote to the president of Congress, "The Skill of those engineers we have . . . [is] very imperfect and confined to the mere manual exercise of cannon, whereas the war in which we are engaged, requires a Knowledge comprehending the Duties of the Field and Fortifications." He went on to lament that his forces suffered in particular from "a want of engineers to construct proper works and direct the men."[30] Charles Lee also complained sardonically, "There is not a man or officer in the Army, that knows the difference betwixt a Chevaux de Frise, and a Cabbage Garden."[31]

Perhaps Washington's own experiences in 1754 during the construction of the badly designed and untenable Fort Necessity in the wilderness, which paralleled Benjamin Franklin's supervision of the construction of Fort Allen in Pennsylvania in 1756, made him particularly aware that the art of fortification was indeed a science that required some expert help to master. Perhaps the added embarrassment of having to abandon Fort Ticonderoga in the summer of 1777, two years after its capture from the British, also underscored the colonists' practical inexperience. In spite of all their reading, they had committed the major blunder of neglecting to fortify nearby Mount Defiance, which commanded the fort. The British were not so negligent, and their newly installed batteries forced the Americans to give up Ticonderoga as untenable.

To be sure, there were a few homegrown engineers available to the Continental Army who either had been trained by the British before the Revolution, had managed to acquire an education in Europe, or had simply picked up their trade on the job. Richard Gridley (1710–1796), the first American chief of engineers who helped fortify the heights over Boston, had participated in the two sieges of Louisbourg, and had seen service during the siege of Quebec. His skills were acquired by studying under a British military engineer in America during the wars with France.[32] Dutch-born Bernard Romans (c.1720–c.1784) received his training as a military engineer in England until he was enlisted by Washington in 1775, and Colonel Rufus Putnam (1738–1824), a millwright by vocation, though entrusted with various fortification projects during the war, was largely self-taught. Moreover, he was considered by others to be too lacking in formal mathematics to be anything more than a competent land surveyor.[33] But helpful as these individuals were to the Revolutionary War effort, it was clear that their experience was not sophisticated enough, nor their numbers large enough, to turn the tide against the British.

Consequently, General Washington and Congress logically turned to France—America's ally and the home of the most rigorously organized and trained corps of engineers in the world. Benjamin Franklin and Silas Deane, the American commissioners to France, were authorized to recruit four military engineers to first help with the war effort, and ultimately to help build up an American corps of engineers. The arrival in 1777 of Louis Lebègue Duportail (1743–1802) as commandant (with the rank of brigadier general) of the newly formed corps of engineers, assisted by French engineers Louis de Shaix la Radière, the Chevalier du Laumoy (1750–1832), and Jean-Baptiste Gouvion (1747–1792), marked a milestone in the development of military engineering in America. With these men began the significant transfer into the ranks of the American Army of a group of officers trained in the traditional methods of the French masters, and in the scientific approach of the school at Mézières—a French connection that was to have enormous consequences during the American Revolution itself and for many years thereafter.[34] For the short term, this close link with France was to mean an energetic increase in fortification of places such as Valley Forge, Saratoga, West Point, Charleston, and Yorktown, to name a few works crucially affecting the outcome of the war. In the long term, it also meant a welcome infusion of skill and training into the ranks of the American Army that, despite a continuous undercurrent of grumbling about foreign mercenaries, took strong root and continued to flourish after the war.[35]

Others with similar backgrounds were also recruited, including the Pole Thaddeus Kosciuszko (1746–1817), Pierre-Charles L'Enfant (1754–1825), and Louis Antoine de Cambray (1751–1822). Duportail himself actively worked for the recruitment of competent sappers, engineers, surveyors, and draftsmen, even if their qualifications were theoretically below the standards of Mézières.[36] So important were foreign recruits to the American engineers that as late as April 1782, when the corps contained 14 officers, only one was an American—a Captain Niven of Huguenot extraction, who ranked thirteenth on the list.[37] The service of these engineers was to prove invaluable. They advised not only on the construction of many defenses, but also on the planning and directing of operations for besieging British fortified sites. In many cases their excellent work in strengthening strategic positions bought the Continental Army precious time by making the British overly cautious, or by deterring an attack outright.

Before examining these contributions, however, several aspects of the American Revolutionary War should be mentioned. It must be emphasized that despite the fact that the Continental Army was modeled on the conventional European infantry of its day, and that its leaders followed the tactics taken from the treatises of European experts, on the whole the campaigns of the war in America did not follow the usual European pattern of set, enormous battles. Nor was the lengthy and methodical investment of fortified places a routine event. Whether the forces involved wished it or not, it was a war of movement, shaped by the strategies involved. Once the British had decided upon a strategy of retaining all the 13 colonies, rather than settling merely for control of a few coastal strongholds, then constant movement of their forces over long distances was required. Their aim of controlling the Hudson Valley from New York to Canada, in order to isolate New England from the other colonies, also dictated the same strategy of rapid movement over long distances. In the South and other regional theaters of war, mobility was also the strategy adopted by the Americans and dictated by their needs. The essence of Major General Nathaniel Greene's tactics against Lord Cornwallis in the southern colonies lay in taking advantage of rugged and difficult terrain to evade major battles with the British forces—necessary when pitting tough regulars against the erratic performance of inexperienced and often halfhearted colonial troops. The key tactic was *petite guerre*: keeping the enemy off balance by harassing and skirmishing, but at all costs avoiding a major confrontation.[38] For Cornwallis, the frustrations lay in his knowledge that only the destruction of the American Army would win the South to the British side. For Greene, the imperative was to maintain an army, no matter how small or how battered, to keep the hope of independence alive. These strategies explain why, during the course of an eight-year war, with the exception of the sieges of Charleston and Yorktown, few classic European-style investments took place; or why, with perhaps the exception of West Point, most of the fortifications undertaken during the war were more correctly described as hastily constructed field fortifications, rather than carefully planned structures intended to be both permanent and strategic.

Nevertheless, the incorporation of the French engineers into the American forces allowed General Washington the luxury of dispersing them to construct, or augment, fortifications where it was deemed necessary. From 1777 to 1778, Duportail labored over the Valley Forge encampment, strengthening the naturally rugged location with entrenchments, redoubts, and brush obstacles. He did this so successfully that General Howe decided not to attack the camp because he feared its defenses were too strong.[39] Anticipating an English attack in 1780, French engineers also did their best to fortify Charleston, South Carolina, pictured in Figure 3.12. The Chevalier de Laumoy (1750–1832), L'Enfant, and Duportail all at various times hurriedly designed as many obstacles as possible to fortify the approaches to the town. Compared with the type of works that were used in classic permanent fortifications, the obstacles employed during the Revolutionary War to slow down a British attack were less elaborate. Outworks that were often laid to hamper the British included pickets; a row of palisades called **fraises**, which were planted obliquely in the ground at the edge of a ditch or other earthwork; **trous de loup**, which was an obstacle of pits, each of which was an inverted pyramid or cone with a pointed stake projecting from the bottom; and double **abatis**, or rows of obstacles made up of closely spaced trees with branches trimmed to points and interlaced. Ships were also sunk across the channel of the Cooper River in order

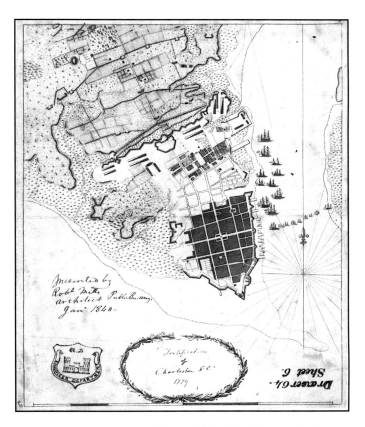

Figure 3.12   Charleston, South Carolina (1779). Plan drawn by Robert Mills. *National Archives, Washington, D.C.*

to close it to navigation. Despite all this effort, Charleston fell to a larger British force, but it was generally believed that this work of fortification permitted a weak garrison to resist for more than six weeks.[40] Unfortunately, Duportail, Laumoy, L'Enfant, and Cambray were all captured with the fall of Charleston, and while Duportail was exchanged in November 1780, the other three had to wait until nearly a year after the surrender of Yorktown for a formal release.

Fortifications at West Point

With respect to the most elaborate and permanent fortifications of the Revolutionary War, the work done at West Point is by far the most important and interesting. In one respect, the fortifications that were eventually constructed at West Point represented a paradox: although the site was deliberately chosen for strategic reasons, the completed works were the result of anything but a coherent plan. In actuality, the permanent fortifications established at West Point evolved often haphazardly from a welter of disparate plans, designs, compromises, and economies. Given the difficulties that plagued the project, ranging from the unrelenting demands of the war, the constant shortage of manpower and funds, and the chronic dissension among the engineers and commanders over every aspect of the job, it was amazing that the works at West Point ultimately emerged as a viable and innovative system of fortification.

The choice of the site was no accident. From the beginning of the American Revolution, it was apparent to both sides that control of the Hudson River and the Hudson Highlands was imperative. General Washington succinctly laid out the reasons why the Americans thought so in a letter to General Israel Putnam in December 1777:

> The importance of the Hudson River in the present contest, and the necessity of defending it, are subjects which have been so frequently and fully discussed, and are so well understood, that it is unnecessary to enlarge upon them. These facts at once appear, when it is considered that it [the river] runs through a whole State; that it is the only passage by which the enemy from New York, or any part of our coast, can ever hope to cooperate with an army from Canada; that the possession of it is indispensably essential to preserve the communication between the Eastern, Middle and Southern States; and further, that upon its security, in a great measure, depend our chief supplies of flour for the subsistence of such forces as we may have occasion for, in the course of the war, either in the Eastern or Northern Departments, or in the country lying high up on the west side of it [along the Mohawk].[41]

West Point, lying in the middle of this region, was considered of such strategic importance that Washington even called it the "key of America." It was one of the few places where the Hudson River was narrow enough to permit obstructions to be placed against a British fleet's advancing northward. Moreover, with its central location, West Point could also be crucial to any future operations against the enemy in the interior regions, given the British dominance on the water. Yet, despite this general recognition of the place's strategic possibilities, the first few years of the American

Revolution saw little progress in fortification specifically at West Point. Instead, dissension over which locations or designs were the most suitable erupted among the various engineers, civilians, and soldiers assigned to evaluate the defenses of the Highlands. Lack of a clear-cut chain of command also contributed to this dangerous indecisiveness that lasted until 1778.

Another explanation for the laggardness in focusing on West Point proper lay in the fact that the initial fortification undertaken in the Highlands was begun elsewhere. Although the Provincial Congress of New York had sent out Christopher Tappan and Colonel James Clinton to sail past the area for a quick evaluation in June 1775, the appointment of Bernard Romans in August represented the first serious attempt to begin actual construction of fortifications (see Figure 3.13). Romans, however, wanted to concentrate his defenses on Martalaer's Rock (present-day Constitution Island), despite the fact that the high, unfortified terrain across the river at West Point would command the works he planned on the island. Aware that this was a major flaw in the design, various representatives of the New York congress pressed

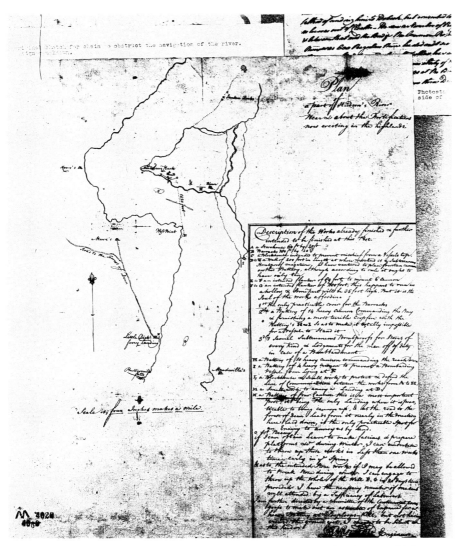

Figure 3.13   Bernard Romans, "Plan of a Part of Hudson's River" (1775). *USMA Library, West Point, N.Y.*

Transcription of copy from the map written in late Autumn 1775 by Bernard Romans .

Plan of a part of Hudson's River Near and about the Fortifications now erecting in the highlands
Description of the works already finished and further intended to be finished at this Post.
A a Storehouse 60 ft. by 20 ft.
B Barracks 100 ft. by 20 ft.
C a Blockhouse intended to prevent mischief from a vessels top
D to E a Wall of 200 foot in length at whose west end is a subterraneous bomb-proof magazine, I have ventured to place fourteen cannon on this battery although according to rule it ought to have only ten.
E to F an intended flanker of 69 foot to mount 6 cannon
F to G an intended flanker of 200 foot, this happens to run in a hollow & some part will be 35 foot high, But it is the soul of the work affording
1st the only practicable cover for the Barracks
2dly a Battery of 14 heavy cannon commanding the Bay and furnishing a most terrible crossfire with the Battery's H & I so as to make it totally impossible for a vessel to stand it. 3dly Several subterraneous bombproofs for stores of every kind & lodgements for the men off of duty in case of a Bombardment.
H a Battery of 10 heavy cannon commanding the reach down
I a Battery of 4 heavy cannon to prevent a Bombarding vessel from Lying at K.
L a Blockhouse & small work to protect & defend the Line of Communication between the works from A to H.
M a small work to annoy a Landing at D
N a Battery of four Cannon this a most important post, it being the only landing where it is practicable spot for an enemy to annoy us by land.
O a Beacon
If i can obtain leave to make facines and prepare platforms etc. during Winter, I can undertake to throw up those works in less than one weeks time early in ye Spring. And as to the intended stone works if I may be allowed to Break Stone during winter I can engage to throw up the whole of the wall F,G in 20 days times provided I have the necessary number of masons well attended by a sufficiency of labourers. I am further directed by a committee of the Continental Congress to make out an estimate of expence for a heavy Battery at Pooploops-Kill, but not having viewed the ground yet, I choose to be Silent on this head.[10]

Romans to change his site, setting off a protracted period of dissension and of very little progress.[42] Despite such pressure to focus on West Point, it still did not become the key point for the planned defenses. Instead, attention shifted further down the river to the Popolopen Creek-Anthony's Nose area.

Concerned about the lack of real progress in the Highlands, General Washington eventually decided to assume responsibility for the situation himself. Under his prodding, from May 1776 to the autumn of 1777 a number of hurried attempts were made to establish serious defenses in the area, after two years of dangerous delay. Under the direction of various officers of the Continental Army—Lord Stirling (also known as Brigadier General William Alexander), Colonel Rufus Putnam, the Continental Army's chief engineer, and the brothers George and James Clinton—a substantial fortification system was finally established in the ongoing attempt to deny the British the Hudson River. It comprised an outpost at Verplanck's Point, Fort Independence at Peekskill, the Fort Montgomery-Fort Clinton complex several miles south of West Point, and the fortifications at Constitution Island. Thomas Machin, a veteran artilleryman and engineer, also began work on a chain and boom to obstruct the Hudson at Fort Montgomery; he also established **chevaux-de-frise** (obstacles consisting of wooden shafts from which pointed staves projected) across the river from Plum Point to Pollopel Island, a wide, shallow area north of West Point.

Although General Washington correctly pointed out during an inspection of the entire region on November 11–12, 1776, that despite the existence of these forts along the river, a land attack from the rear would place them all in jeopardy, still nothing was immediately planned for West Point. In fact, it was the failed attempt by the British in 1777 to separate the colonies by sending three armies to meet in Albany—one army from Canada to Lake Champlain and the upper Hudson Valley, a second into the Mohawk Valley, and a third up the Hudson River—that finally provided the vital catalyst for fortifying West Point itself. Successfully attacking from the land side, the British captured and burned forts Montgomery and Clinton, cut Machin's chain, and sailed north, breaking through the chevaux-de-frise. Fortunately, Burgoyne's surrender at Saratoga kept Sir Henry Clinton from consolidating these successes. Fearful that if he advanced, his forces might be cut off from New York, Clinton destroyed the fortifications in the Highlands and withdrew. Nevertheless, the entire disaster convinced Washington that a complete re-evaluation of the fortifications in the Hudson Highlands was necessary, and that a professional engineer had to rectify matters swiftly.

Louis de Shaix la Radière, second in command to Duportail, was sent out to survey the area and to propose suitable fortifications. Unfortunately, Radière's arrival signalled another round of dissension, for a conflict promptly developed once again between the Frenchman and his commander, Major General Israel Putnam, over the question of the best site for concentrating the defenses. Envisaging defending his would-be fort in terms of a classic Vauban-style siege, Radière was convinced that rebuilding at the site of the ruins of Fort Clinton was by far the best plan.[43] Putnam and the two Clintons disagreed, convinced that West Point was the logical place to cluster defenses aimed at closing the river to the enemy. Putnam wrote testily to Washington about what he perceived as Radière's uncooperativeness and incompetence: "I have directed the Engineer to lay out the fort immediately—but he seems disgusted that everything does not go as he thinks proper, even if contrary to the judgment of every other person. In short he is an excellent paper Engineer and I think it would be as well for us if he was employed wholly that way. . . ."[44] It must have seemed to a weary Washington that the perpetual quarrels between the would-be fortifiers were never ending.

Finally, in 1778, a committee appointed by the New York legislature settled the matter. It definitively selected West Point over Fort Clinton as the most desirable location for constructing fortifications designed to prevent the British from launching another attempt in the Highlands, especially from a fleet sailing up the Hudson from New York. Early in 1778, determined not to be sidetracked by any other arguments, Putnam began construction on two water batteries—named Chain and Water respectively. These featured scarp walls of stone built higher than the gun platforms, and guns that fired through embrasures in the parapet. The parapet was constructed of gravel lined with timber or fascines.

With an attempt to control navigation on the river at West Point at last under way, Radière now recommended the construction of a fort to cover the batteries from the rear, and to place enemy ships under fire as they approached from the south. Designated as Fort Arnold in April 1778, it returned to its original name of Fort Clinton after Benedict Arnold's treason in 1780—not to be confused with the Fort Clinton at Popolopen Creek that was destroyed by the British in 1777. The design of this fort also became the subject of more controversy. Radière's plans, to Putnam's dismay, included masonry lining in the fort's western walls, a covered way, and a glacis, for he clearly intended to create a classic fortress defense in depth against a possible British siege. Dissension over these plans, which were considered too ambitious, costly, and time-consuming in wartime by Radierè's critics, brought work to a standstill. Disgruntled, Radière left West Point temporarily to join Washington at Valley Forge.

To complicate matters even further, Congress in turn decided to dispatch Thaddeus Kosciuszko to begin work at West Point in Radière's absence. This almost certainly guaranteed a conflict between the French engineer and the Pole, particularly since the two had been assigned to the same job, each by a different authority. In Radière's absence, Kosciuszko quickly added two more water batteries—Lanthorn (sometimes called Lantern Battery) and South (also known as the Knox Battery)—located, like the first two, on the western side of the Hudson River. However, after Radière's return, he and Kosciuszko had a falling out on whether to build redoubts or forts in the hills behind West Point. Well aware of the debacle at Fort Ticonderoga when the Americans had failed to ensure control of Mount Defiance overlooking the fort, Kosciuszko was most persistent about not leaving this high ground undefended. Finally, in April 1778, Washington settled the squabbling by reluctantly sending Radière back to Valley Forge, commenting, "As Col. La Radière and Col. Kosuisko will never agree, I think it will be best to order La Radière to return especially as Kosuisko is better adapted to the Genius and Temper of the people."[45]

With the chain of command at last regularized, substantial progress was made in the next few months under Kosciuszko's direction. Trained at Mézières, Kosciuszko (who seemed doomed to have his name perpetually mangled in the correspondence and dispatches of the time—for example,

Clinton managed "Kuziazke"; Washington, "Kosciousko" and "Koshiosko," among other attempts; and General Gates, "Kusiusco") had been commissioned an engineer colonel in the Continental Army in October 1776. He now devised a plan of fortification that centered works around Fort Arnold, and projected a series of forts and redoubts designed to protect West Point and its immediate vicinity. Forts Wyllys, Webb, and Meigs were proposed to protect Fort Arnold from an attack originating from the high ground along the river from the south, and Sherburne's Redoubt from infantry attack from due west.[46] Fort Arnold itself would not have the huge covered way planned by Radière, and would be built mainly of timber and earth instead of masonry. The south and west walls in particular, since they faced the hills from which an attack was most likely, reflected the most substantial part of the design: about 9 feet high, with a thickness of 20 feet at the top of the parapet, and less than that at the top of the bastion. In front of the walls stood a ditch 32 feet wide at the top and 24 feet on the bottom, with a glacis in front of it. Also planned were a storehouse, a powder magazine, a guardhouse, a commissary, and barracks capable of housing the garrison of 600 men.

On Crown Hill, looming high above all the others, Kosciuszko envisioned some sort of fortification. This was to become Fort Putnam. Built between 1778 and 1795, Putnam was second only to Fort Arnold in importance within the complex. None of the original plans or engineer drawings of Fort Putnam have survived, but it is clear that Fort Putnam represented the key to the defensive works at West Point, commanding as it did the entire site. Its location atop a rugged slope demanded a trace so irregular that its successful design and construction represented no small feat. In every sense, Fort Putnam provided the last link in a defensive chain that was quite amazing in its depth and mutual support:

> Both forts [Arnold and Putnam] were to withstand the enemy siege until the militia or Continental Army could arrive. Each was to maintain a ten-day supply of provisions at all times. The other works in the system were designed to deny the enemy the use of the most advantageous avenues of approach to the chain and water batteries, to prevent surprise, to delay the enemy and gain as much time as possible for the arrival of outside assistance, and to cover the infantry approaches to Fort Putnam and Fort Arnold. Sherburne's Redoubt, Forts Webb and Wyllys, and Fort Arnold would all protect the northern, eastern, and southern approaches to Putnam while the latter would reciprocate by denying the Plain to the enemy. In other words, the various positions would be mutually supporting and reinforcing by fire. . . .[47]

In addition, Thomas Machin was directed to design another, thicker "great chain" to create an obstruction in the river. It stretched from a small cove directly below Fort Arnold and in front of the battery that would be named after it to another small cove on Constitution Island. With this, the proposed fortifications were essentially complete in theory, if not in practice.

In September 1778, the chief engineer, Duportail, was requested to make an inspection of the works at West Point. His report as to the status and readiness of the fortifications provided a detailed picture of the work accomplished to date. While he felt that Fort Arnold appeared to be "pretty well situated and traced," he called for masonry and bricks to be used in contrast to Kosciuszko's advocacy of earth, and suggested that the sides be raised, a small covered way be added, and palisades at the front be established "to secure the body of the place against all surprise." Duportail felt that Fort Putnam, "the key to all the others," lacked only a larger bombproof and needed the raising of one of its sides "which looks toward the river" to be "rendered almost impregnable." He also suggested that palisades, chevaux-de-frise, and abatis be constructed in front. He disliked Fort Wyllys's position for a number of reasons, and suggested it be rebuilt altogether. Failing that, he offered a couple of quick remedies to improve its usefulness for the short term. The batteries below Fort Putnam, "extremely well placed for battering the Vessels which should approach the Chain," received suggestions for minor alterations to make them more secure, as did the redoubts and the chain itself, which he saw as needing strengthening in particular. Overall, he summarized the fortifications succinctly: "The Works which are in hand at West Point and some inconsiderable ones, which it is necessary to add to them, will, with the help of the chain, perfectly fulfill the object which is proposed,- that of hindering the enemy's remounting the North [Hudson] River."[48]

Clearly, West Point stood as the most ambitious project of fortification undertaken by the Continental Army up to that point (see Figure 3.14).

Figure 3.14   Plan of West Point:
this plan of the complete system of
defenses at West Point was copied
from the original map drawn in
1780 by the Chevalier de
Villefranche (1747–1784), a
topographical engineer serving in
the Continental Army. *USMA*
Library, West Point, N.Y.

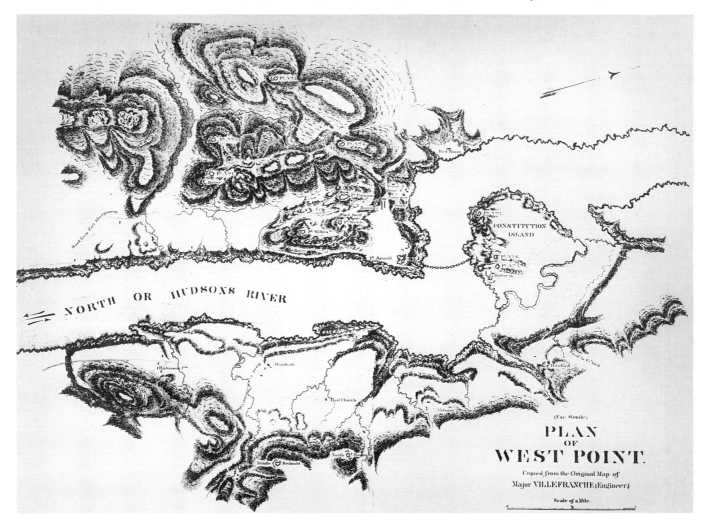

During 1779, some 2,500 troops toiled on further construction of the West Point complex. Redoubts were built atop Rocky Hill (located about one–half mile west of Fort Putnam and rising 200 feet higher), as well as on three additional high points to the south, to the southwest, and across the river. Duportail estimated it would require at least 1,800 troops to garrison West Point and to defend it adequately—a large number for an army whose constantly fluctuating numbers were of unceasing concern to the command.[49] By the fall of 1779, substantial construction had been completed, and the 16 proposed enclosed positions were either finished or under way. To some of the French engineers, the West Point defenses appeared too scattered, a violation of Mézière's traditional approach that invariably predicated a massive fortress on a single site, even though an iron adherence to this tradition too often ignored Vauban's repeated advice about the importance of always adapting to the terrain. Yet, the achievement in fortification at West Point presented an ultimate irony: despite the conflicting designs and suggestions of all the engineers, despite the lack of formal training of the American planners, and despite the constant lack of funds and personnel, the works at West Point appeared, in the final analysis—by means of luck and chance, foresight, and ingenuity—to have developed into a system of permanent fortification perfectly fitted for the strategic objectives originally intended. It permitted Washington and the Continental Army to defend the Hudson with minimal troops, even though the British controlled New York City, while shifting the main army to operations elsewhere—particularly to the south and to Yorktown in 1781. Indeed, insofar as deterring an attack was concerned, a primary factor in the building of any fortification, West Point appeared to have achieved its first strategic objective. The British never attempted to send a fleet past it up the Hudson; and perhaps only a historian might be callous enough to regret that its design as the first permanent fortification of the Revolutionary War was never tested in a siege.

The Siege at Yorktown

The reverse side of the art and science of fortification was, of course, that of siegecraft. At the same time that the French and American engineers were constructing works to strengthen specific strategic places they controlled, they still had to keep in mind the process involved in ousting the British from their strongholds. The difficulty in acquiring practice in siegecraft lay in the fact that, as mentioned earlier, few classic European-style sieges occurred during the Revolutionary War, primarily because the strategies adopted did not call for them. Nor were there in America any massive fortresses of such importance by European standards that neglecting to besiege them might decide the outcome of the war, or totally close off access to any particular territory. Naturally, the British built or repaired fortifications in areas under their control, but these differed very little from the sort of fort building they had practiced all during the eighteenth century.[50] In the same way, in 1781 when the British forces in the south found themselves pulled back into Yorktown, Virginia, as a matter of proper procedure, they undertook to strengthen the fortifications of the town.[51] On the heights above the York River, the British constructed a series of defensive lines consisting of abatis, fraises, and ditches. Situated in front of the ramparts were batteries, and beyond them a series of carefully spaced redoubts, all designed to keep the enemy well away from the town. Across the river, the British Colonel Tarleton held a smaller defensive perimeter at Gloucester Point, and between the two lay a small flotilla of British ships anchored there. Nevertheless, once a combination of events conspired to make General Washington decide to confront Cornwallis and his troops at Yorktown, what followed was the only truly classic European-style siege of the war. (See Figure 3. 15.) Admittedly, by European standards it was of no great magnitude. The total number of troops in all three armies barely exceeded 25,000 men, a number so small that Napoleon reportedly remarked sardonically that the fate of North America was decided with forces the size of a corporal's guard. [52]

Nonetheless, the siege at Yorktown produced an amazing number of contemporary journals, accounts, plans, and maps describing the events. There were probably several reasons for this interest. The siege was the only major engagement in which the Comte de Rochambeau's army participated, and for many of the French engineers, it represented a chance to put into practice what they had learned at Mézières. For their American counterparts, it was at last a chance to see theory translated into practice under actual combat conditions. More importantly, the siege and capitulation turned out to be the final, decisive confrontation of the war for American independence, although that was not immediately obvious. Once this became apparent, participants rushed to record their observations about the events at Yorktown.

Released from captivity at Charleston in time for this encounter, Duportail, along with Gouvion, vigorously directed the earthworks of the siege, and Henry Knox brilliantly organized the placement of artillery where it could do the most damage. By September 30, the investment of Yorktown was almost complete. Cornwallis had helped greatly by withdrawing his forces into the inner defensive perimeter after being assured by Sir Henry Clinton that a relieving force of men and ships was to be sent. Such a withdrawal enabled the allied forces to move into the abandoned positions, and coincidentally provided a more concentrated target for the American and French artillery. To the left were the French guns and troops; to the right the Americans; and to the rear, the artillery park of Knox, all of which faced the British positions northward. After some delays because of shortage of transport and because, as Washington reported, "both the Allied armies are assiduously employed in making fascines and gabions, and in transporting our heavy cannon, mortars and stores," the Allies were finally ready.[53] The "opening of the trench" on the evening of October 7 signalled the beginning of the excavation of the first parallel in the classic Vauban manner. (As a sort of happy coincidence, one of Vauban's grandnephews was present at Yorktown.[54]) Once begun, the work proceeded swiftly day and night, some troops digging the trenches, others building redoubts or working on the emplacement of the cannon. A journal kept by Gaspard de Gallatin, an officer in Rochambeau's first brigade, provided an almost textbook account of the process of the siege each night and day:

> From the 7th to the 8th [October]:
> Night workmen, 900 men.
> Last night 500 workmen were employed under the direction of engineers to begin the communications with the rear and on the left of the parallel to improve it, as well as the redoubt, and to make the zigzag communicating trenches to the batteries. The 400 other night

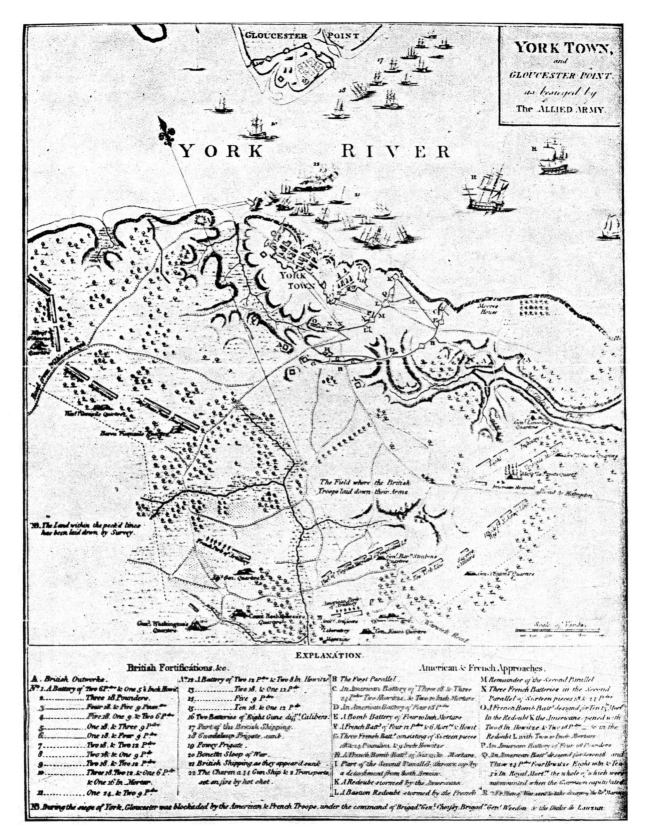

Figure 3.15   Plan of the siege at Yorktown.

workmen were employed, together with the artillerymen, in the construction of the batteries. For the offensive against the upper river we continued the construction of the battery which was found at daybreak, in condition to fire. We employed 400 day workers, taken from the trench battalions, to perfec' the works of the two preceding nights and to continue the construcuon of the batteries. For the American offensive, they began to construct batteries also. Wounded in the main offensive, six men.[55]

The first parallel was about 2,000 yards long, and was supported by four redoubts and five batteries about 500 yards from the British lines. The right half of the parallel was assigned to the American units, the left to the French. In order to command the British ships, the French also built a trench and battery between the York River and one of the branches of the creek to the west of the town. On the afternoon of October 9, after the first parallel had formed "a large ditch, broad enough for carriages to travel in, about four feet in depth, and covered with a rampart of gabions, or cylindrical baskets, fixed upon the ground by means of projecting stakes, filled and covered over with loose dirt, and forming a height of about seven feet on the side towards the town," General Washington ordered the first batteries to commence firing.[56] The damage from the bombardment immediately devastated men and materiel. Cornwallis was astounded to find that the enemy was equipped with heavy siege cannon, and no doubt irritated at being driven from his headquarters in the town to seek shelter in a cave in the side of the river bank.[57] Several nights later, the French unveiled the cannon that fired "hot shot"—that is, heated cannon balls grasped with tongs brought especially from France—and set fire to three British vessels, including the *Charon*, which burned all night while the other ships rushed to get out of range. By this time, counting cannon of all sizes, over 50 cannon, howitzers, and mortars were throwing shot and shells into Yorktown so fast that the spectators described the air as resounding with a continuous roar.[58]

With the British unable to move around to man their own batteries, Washington ordered on October 11 that the second parallel be opened halfway between the first one and the enemy lines. By the fourteenth, the allies had pushed this parallel to within striking distance of the two British redoubts that were the key to their defensive system. Two detachments of troops, one French and the other American (led by Alexander Hamilton), were assigned to seize the redoubts; and once incorporated into the allied lines, they served as a base for even more intense cannon fire. British cannon had dwindled to almost nothing, and their fortifications were visibly crumbling under the bombardment. On October15, Cornwallis sent a morose report on his situation to Clinton, reluctantly recommending that the latter not try to relieve him:

> Last evening the enemy carried my two advanced redoubts on the left by storm, and during the night have included them in their second parallel, which they are at present busy in perfecting. My situation now becomes very critical; we dare not shew a gun to their old batteries, and I expect that their new ones will open tomorrow morning; experience has shewn that our fresh earthen works do not resist their powerful artillery, so that we shall soon be exposed to an assault in ruined works, in a bad position, and with weakened numbers. The safety of the place is, therefore, so precarious, that I cannot recom-

mend that the fleet and army should run great risque in endeav-
ouring to save us.[59]

Cornwallis did order an obligatory, if futile, sortie to spike the allied cannon, and bad weather aborted an effort to evacuate his troops by boat across
the river to Gloucester. Finally, on the morning of October 17, a British
drummer appeared on the crumbling ramparts to beat a parley.

The siege had been conducted according to form, and the capitulation
more or less followed the classic pattern established in Europe. However,
still smarting over the terms of surrender that the British had imposed on
General Lincoln at Charleston over a year before, the American commissioner, Colonel Laurens, insisted on similar terms for Cornwallis's troops—
something less than "the full honors of war." The British were to parade
at the surrender with their colors cased, and to play one of their own tunes
instead of being allowed the compliment of saluting their opponents with
an enemy air. Usually punctilious about observing the proper etiquette of
war, the French apparently did not object to these terms, probably because
Cornwallis had failed to observe the traditional rule of a besieged garrison
commander: he had not waited until the ramparts had been breached before
surrendering. (Admittedly, as had been pointed out sardonically, over the
years many a breach in European sieges had to be enlarged by both sides
after a surrender so that the garrison troops could formally march through
it as good form demanded.[60]) In other respects, the proper decorum was
adhered to, especially during the actual ceremony of surrender on October
19. Indeed, Washington on that same evening gave a reception for all senior
officers, graciously including the British who were represented by their second in command, General O'Hara. The latter had performed the actual
ceremony of handing over his sword, since Cornwallis claimed to be ill. The
French, in their turn, entertained other British officers "with great deli-
cacy and forbearance."[61]

Although the Americans observed the proper etiquette during the ceremony of surrender, the entire event had some darker undercurrents running through it that many noticed, and that some among the French found
distasteful. During the ceremony of capitulation itself, many of the British
found it difficult to surrender to the American rebels as if they were an
equal army, and behaved sullenly.[62] One rather critical French observer
characterized the unpleasant overtones as being caused by the unwilling-
ness of the Americans to observe "the chivalrous manners that were owed
to defeated courage," whether in donning the proper clothing or in
demeanor.[63] For the Americans, the British surrender was a glorious
moment, long in coming and worth gloating over. If they exhibited a defi-
nite bitterness and less than delicate behavior toward their vanquished
enemy, the Americans felt it was deserved. Indeed, given the fact that the
war had begun as a rebellion, with many of the elements of a civil war pitting rebels against loyalists, it is not surprising that emotions ran high from
the beginning. Rumors and reports of British atrocities had long circulated,
including one at Yorktown that Cornwallis had sent slaves infected with
smallpox across the lines to spread the disease. The death of Colonel
Alexander Scammell, purportedly shot in the back after his surrender during a skirmish at the beginning of the siege, still rankled the Americans;
and the slaughter of the American garrison at New London, Connecticut,
by British forces led by Benedict Arnold, despite the fact that it had already

surrendered formally, was an added outrage. After six long years of brutal warfare, the American forces were not inclined to concern themselves over-much with the niceties of military chivalry and custom that the Europeans espoused. The French, on the other hand, were understandably more emo-tionally disengaged, and could afford to indulge in the luxury of criticism when they felt that the proper gallantries of military etiquette were not being followed.

Ironically, in vaguely perceiving that they and the Americans were not fighting the same sort of war, perhaps the French had begun to sense cer-tain changes in the air—changes that in a few short years would shatter the *ancien régime* as surely as they had shattered the eighteenth century rules of war. Gentlemanly adherence to the formalities that governed all aspects of a military campaign, especially among the aristocracy of the European offi-cer corps, was to become increasingly obsolete in an age of national armies and rampant nationalism. Bound to vanish as well was the easy mobility of soldiers who, sharing a similar code of war and military customs, had for many centuries been able to adapt smoothly to serving with one army or another in Europe. The model of a Lafayette or a Von Steuben, or of other aristocrats and officers offering their services efficiently and without cen-sure to a nation other than their own, would also become less common. The American Revolution represented a paradox: while on the one hand it was more or less fought like a classic European war of the eighteenth century, using European tactics, strategy, and military principles, on the other hand, it introduced new and more subversive elements to the eighteenth-century social and military order. By emerging as a war fought by a people rather than by an army, by making citizen militias equal to professional armies, and by emphasizing radical ideas about liberty and equality, the American rev-olutionary experience pointed the way to the warfare of the future.

Despite the natural ethnocentricity of those involved in the American Revolution, the events in the 13 colonies were really part of a worldwide struggle among the European powers for trade and territory. Britain's fail-ure to focus any more of its powerful naval resources on the American con-flict because of its preoccupation with events elsewhere was vital to American success. There is no question that the successful siege at Yorktown convinced the British government to cut its losses; and this same success must have bolstered the fledgling corps of engineers' confidence in their skills. In a few short years they had managed to transfer the collective military experience of eighteenth-century Europe to America, and apply it competently enough to the campaigns of the Revolutionary War. Perhaps Lord Cornwallis wryly summarized the events of the previous years the best, writing two years after the siege of Yorktown, "I am every day more and more convinced of the neces-sity of military reading."[64]

Notes

1. See John Muller, *A Treatise Containing the Elementary Part of Fortification, Regular and Irregular, With Remarks on the Constructions . . . of Marshal de Vauban and Baron Coehorn . . . For the Use of the Royal Academy of Artillery at Woolwich*, 3rd ed., (London: J. Nourse, 1774), pp. 218–240. Muller's work is a classic example of the effort to outline fortification termi-nology for the reader of the time. The title of the pages cited is "An explanation of the

principal terms used in Fortification, digested in an alphabetical manner." Besides this treatise by Muller, a copy of which was owned by George Washington, it is also interesting to note a few other titles on the subject of fortification in Washington's personal library, as cited in J. B. Harley, Barbara B. Petchenik, and Lawrence W. Towner, *Mapping the American Revolutionary War* (Chicago and London: University of Chicago, 1978), p. 66: for example, *The Field Engineer of M. le Chevalier de Clairac . . . With Observations and Remarks on Each Chapter . . .* trans. by John Muller; the two volumes of Le Blond's *The Military Engineer*; Count Saxe's *Plan for New-Modelling the French Army*; and Thomas Simes's *The Military Guide for Young Officers*, (London: 1772.)

2. Elizabeth S. Kite, *Brigadier-General Louis Lebègue Duportail: Commandant of Engineers in the Continental Army, 1777–1783* (Baltimore: John Hopkins Press, 1933). The omission of the design stage happened frequently during the American Revolution, but its unorthodoxy is revealed by the lament in May 1780 of Louis Duportail, Washington's chief engineer, that "M. de Laumoy and the engineers whom he has under his orders, have been so busy constructing the fortifications of Charlestown, both before and during the siege that there was no time to make a design of the plans- this deprives me of the satisfaction of sending them to Congress- supposing indeed the enemy would permit it." p. 175.

3. Harley, Petchenik, and Towner, *Mapping the American Revolutionary War*, p. 14. The authors cite a British engineer's orders during Burgoyne's campaign in 1776 and 1777, "to take such plans, and make such inspection of the works at Quebec, as may be necessary to form a report for the General."

4. Harley, Petchenik, and Towner, pp. 5–6.

5. See Willard B. Robinson, *American Forts: Architectural Form and Function* (Urbana, Illinois: University of Illinois Press, 1977). This extremely valuable work provides physical descriptions of nearly every fort of note in North America up to the Civil War.

6. Robinson, *American Forts*, p. 27. Included are excellent descriptions of the Presidio Nuestra Señora de los Dolores de los Tejas (1716), Presidio de Nuestra Señora del Pilár de los Adaes (1721), and the Presidio Nuestra Señora de Loreto de la Bahía (1722) in Texas, presented as examples of the Spanish style of fortification in colonial America; and a short description of the presidios at San Diego, Monterey, Santa Barbara, and San Francisco in California are also provided.

7. Robinson, *American Forts*, p. 17. Perhaps because of an unsuccessful siege by the English in 1702, the Castillo continued to be strengthened until expenditures on it reached a staggering sum of $30 million, causing the King of Spain to wonder sarcastically if its curtains and bastions were made of solid silver.

8. William A. Hunter, *Forts on the Pennsylvania Frontier, 1753–1758* (Harrisburg, Pennsylvania: Pennsylvania Historical and Museum Commission, 1960), pp. 87–88.

9. Edward P. Hamilton, *Fort Ticonderoga, Key to a Continent* (Boston: Little, Brown and Co., 1964), pp. 36–53.

10. John S. McLennan, *Louisbourg: from its foundation to its fall* (Nova Scotia: Fortress Press, 1969), pp. 51–52.

11. Hamilton, *Ticonderoga*, p. 57.

12. Robinson, *American Forts*, pp. 35–36.

13. J. Mackay Hitsman, *Safeguarding Canada, 1763–1871* (Toronto: University of Toronto Press, 1968), p. 9.

14. Charles P. Stacey, *Quebec, 1759, The Siege and the Battle* (Toronto: University of Toronto Press, 1959) pp.13–14.

15. McClennan, *Louisbourg*, pp. 264–285. An excellent description of this second siege of Louisbourg, including the traditional aspects of a formal surrender, is provided. The previous, rather disorganized siege of 1754, led by the merchant William Pepperell and a combined force of New England colonists and British regulars, is also described in detail, pp.147–166.

16. Stacey, p. 153.

17. Stacey, p. 31.

18. Stacey, p. 31.

19. Stacey, p. 33.

20. Stacey, p. 160.

21. George A. Billias, ed., *George Washington's Generals* (New York: W. Morrow and Co., 1964), p. xi.

22. John F. C. Fuller, *British Light Infantry in the Eighteenth Century* (London: I. Nicholson and Watson, 1925), pp. 97–99. The Royal American Regiment, founded as a light infantry unit by the Duke of Cumberland after Braddock's defeat, contributed greatly toward transplanting European military techniques to colonial North America. Its first lieutenant colonels—Henry Bouquet and Frederick Haldimand—were Swiss officers who

had served with the Prince of Orange. Ultimately, the regiment boasted 40 German officers in its ranks. During the American Revolution, members of the regiment supported both sides of the conflict.

[23.] Billias, *George Washington's Generals*, p. xiii. The author points out that while all three had seen service in the French war, and Lee had also served in Central Europe and the Balkans with foreign armies, their experience with command was limited. Of the three, only Gates was still with the Continental Army at the end of the Revolution. Montgomery was killed in the first year of the war, and Lee had ruined his career by 1778.

[24.] Theodore Thayer, *Nathaniel Greene, Strategist of the American Revolution* (New York: Twayne Publishers 1960) pp. 23–24.

[25.] North Callahan, *Henry Knox: General Washington's General* (New York: Rinehart and Co., 1958), p. 25.

[26.] Callahan, pp. 35–36.

[27.] Callahan, p. 38.

[28.] Callahan, p. 58. Howe estimated that it must have been the work of at least 12,000 men. In fact, the night's labors required 2,000 men and 400 oxen. See also Kite, *Louis Lebègue Duportail*, p. 30.

[29.] John C. Fitzpatrick, ed. *The Writings of George Washington from the Original Manuscript Sources, 1745–1799* (Washington, D. C.: U. S. Government Printing Office, 1931–1944), X, p. 238.

[30.] Robinson, *American Forts*, p. 50; Paul K. Walker, *Engineers of Independence, A Documentary History of the Army Engineers in the American Revolution, 1775–1783* (Washington, D.C. : Historical Division, Office of Administrative Services, Office of the Chief of Engineers, 1981), p. 1.

[31.] Walker, *Engineers of Independence*, p. 12.

[32.] Mark Mayo Boatner III, *Encyclopedia of the American Revolution* (New York: D. McKay Co., 1974), s. v. Gridley, Richard.

[33.] Boatner, *Encyclopedia*, s. v. Putnam, Rufus.

[34.] Elizabeth S. Kite, *Louis Lebègue Duportail*, p. 1. During the summer of 1776, before his recruitment by the Americans, Duportail had been asked to prepare a new set of rules for the corps of engineers of France, the *Génie*, at Mézières. This honor underlined the fact that he was not just a graduate of the school, but was also considered to be a theoretician who understood, *au fond*, its methods and techniques.

[35.] This theme of anti-French or anti-foreign bias appears constantly in the correspondence and speeches of the time, almost as a counterpoint to the French alliance and recruitment of French volunteers. Kite, in *Louis Lebègue Duportail*, for example, mentions the factions in Congress squabbling over the granting of commissions sought by the French volunteers, and includes a letter from Duportail to Congress trying to defuse the issue: "We beg the leave to observe to you that as Engineers we do not belong to any Regiment, consequently we cannot hurt the rank of any officer in the army, and it is most certainly quite indifferent to them what rank the honorable Congress will be pleased to grant us," pp. 27–28. After the Revolutionary War, the resentment against foreigners in general, and Frenchmen in particular, especially within the Corps of Engineers, persisted. See also a letter in 1816 from Christopher Van Deventer, a graduate of West Point and a life-long friend of Sylvanus Thayer, on the hiring of the French engineer Simon Bernard to oversee the work of American fortification: "One would suppose our Government would profit by experience—and recuring to the events of the Revolutionary War would determine against the employment of exotic talent. At that period it naturally looked to our allies for the means to supply the deficiency—and what with a sense of our weakness and gratitude to France for her profer of aid, we were almost frantic in our . . . for & admiration of French Eng's, and the French soldiery,—how greviously were they disappointed! . . . Their object was power and aggrandisement . . . [to] exalt themselves by supplanting native worth." Christopher Van Deventer to Sylvanus Thayer, June 4, 1816. *Thayer Papers, 1808–1872*, II, United States Military Academy Library, West Point. Another revealing comment came in 1803 from Secretary of War Henry Dearborn, who spoke of founding a military academy for the training of engineers "so that we may avoid the unpleasant necessity of employing Foreigners as Engineers." Emanuel R. Lewis, *Seacoast Fortifications of the United States: an Introductory History* (Annapolis: Leeward Publications, 1970), p. 25n.

[36.] See Kite, *Louis Lebègue Duportail*, pp. 47–50, for a memorandum written by Duportail that dealt with the the organization of companies of sappers whom he recognized as essential to any work of fortification or siege. Shortly thereafter, he asked for the recruitment of the Chevalier de Villefranche, who later did significant work at the fortifications at West Point. Duportail did not describe de Villefranche as an engineer "because he was not in that character in France and has no such pretensions himself—but he studies with a view to become a member of the Corps—he has studied Geometry, understands surveying and Drawing, and therefore ought to be very useful to us." Kite, p. 50. Duportail also asked for the recruitment of Jean Bernard de Murnan, who for various reasons did not enter the French Corps of Engineers despite successfully completing the course of study, but who, according to Duportail, possessed "sufficient theoretical knowledge to make him an exceedingly good Engineer." Kite, p. 52.

[37] Kite, p. 245.

[38] Billias, *George Washington's Generals*, pp. 122–130.

[39] Howe, from his headquarters in Philadelphia during the winter of 1778, defended his earlier decision not to attack Valley Forge: "Having good information in the spring that the enemy had strengthened his camp by additional works and being certain of moving him from thence when the campaign opened, I dropped all thought of attack." Kite, *Duportail*, p. 46.

[40] Kite, *Duportail*, p. 174. Part of Duportail's report on the events that led to the surrender of Charleston includes the following sarcastic, if somewhat ungrammatical, appraisal of the British siege, and by implication, praise for the garrison's defense: "To remain forty two days in open trenches before a Town of an immense extent fortified by sandy intrenchements raised in two months without covered way, without our works, open in several places on the water side, exposed every where to attacks and defended by a Garrison which was not sufficient by half of what was necessary, before such a place I say and display all the appearance of a regular siege, is nothing very glorious."

[41] Fitzpatrick, *Writings of Washington*, X, pp.129–133. Duportail also recognized the importance of West Point in a memorandum he wrote for Congress in 1779: "It [West Point] is the Key of the North River, and if the enemy is once master of its navigation, the Communication between New England and the other States is entirely cut off; this Communication is however necessary to our Army, which cannot even subsist without it on either side of the River. . . . Thus the loss of West Point must necessarily expose a part of the Country to be without Troops for its defence, and perhaps, as I have already said, the whole Continent. . . . I have no doubt, that when the English receive sufficient reinforcements, to come out of New York and open the Campaign, their first Operations will be against Fort West Point as it is the only Way for them to do anything decisive. It should then be our care to put it in a proper state of defence." Kite, *Duportail*, p. 129.

[42] For a detailed discussion of Romans's plans and designs for Fort Constitution, see Charles E. Miller, Jr., Donald V. Lockey, and Joseph Visconti, Jr., *Highland Fortress: The Fortification of West Point During the American Revolution 1775–1783*, (West Point, New York: Department of History, United States Military Academy, 1979), pp. 15–32.

[43] Kite, *Duportail*, includes a letter from Radière in which he lays out his objections to fortifying West Point instead of Fort Clinton, pp. 86–87.

[44] Kite, p. 85.

[45] Kite, pp. 94–95.

[46] Miller, Lockey and Visconti, *Highland Fortress*, pp. 90ff., provide a detailed account of the designs planned for the various forts, redoubts, and water batteries at West Point, as well as of the historical analysis that went into proving that *Captain Champion's Plan of the Highlands*-ca. 1778 in the Manuscript Division, Special Collections, USMA Library, West Point, was prepared by Kosciuszko himself. See also the meticulous reconstruction accomplished by John H. Mead, *Archeological Survey of Fort Putnam and other Revolutionary Fortifications at West Point, New York*, 1967–68 (West Point: an unpublished study for the West Point Museum Fund, 1968) pp. 76–79.

[47] *Highland Fortress*, p.109.

[48] Kite, *Duportail*, pp. 96–100.

[49] Kite, p. 100.

[50] See Robinson, *American Forts*, pp. 59–61, for a brief description of British works during the war. Among the fortifications built were: Mud Fort (later known as Fort Mifflin), Pennsylvania, 1771–1777, designed by John Montrésor, chief engineer of the British forces in America; Stony Point overlooking the Hudson; Paulus Hook in New Jersey; and Fort Mackinac, Michigan.

[51] See the relevant chapters in Theodore Thayer, *Yorktown: Campaign of Strategic Options*, Harold M. Hyman, ed. (Philadelphia: Lippincott, 1975), for an account of the events that led up to the siege of Yorktown.

[52] Lee Kennett, *The French Forces in America, 1780–1783* (Connecticut: Greenwood Press, 1977), p. 143. Pointing out Britain's global interests and problems during 1781, the author contrasts some statistics of the siege of Gibraltar, which was conducted at the same time as Yorktown: at Gibraltar, the besiegers alone had 40,000 troops and 50 ships of the line; the siege lasted for three and a half years, cost five times the 400 allied

casualties at Yorktown, and was unsuccessful.

[53.] Kite, *Duportail*, p. 212, from a letter from George Washington to the president of the U. S. Congress.

[54.] Kennett, *French Forces in America*, p. 142.

[55.] Gaspard de Gallatin, *Journal of the Siege of Yorktown*: unpublished journal of the siege of Yorktown in 1781, as recorded in the hand of Gaspard de Gallatin and trans. by the French Department of the College of William and Mary, (Washington: U. S. Government Printing Office, 1931), p. 5.

[56.] Abbé Robin, *New Travels Through North America* (Philadelphia, 1783); reprinted (New York: New York Times, 1969), p. 57.

[57.] Kennett, *French Forces in America*, pp. 144–145, lists the copious firepower the allies had at Yorktown: Knox had three 24-pounder siege guns, and twenty 16–pounders; Rochambeau's forces had twelve 24-pounders, and eight 16-pounders. In addition, the batteries of the French fleet under De Grasse had more than 2,000 cannon.

[58.] Callahan, *Henry Knox*, p. 187.

[59.] Thayer, *Yorktown*, p. 126.

[60.] Kennett, *French Forces in America*, p.150.

[61.] Thomas J. Fleming, *Beat the Last Drum: the Siege of Yorktown, 1781* (New York: St. Martin's Press, 1963), p. 333.

[62.] Most of the accounts of the events of that day, whether eyewitness or later versions, describe various incidents that revealed the depths of enmity and bitterness between the British and Americans. These incidents include: the initial effort (intentional or not) of General O'Hara, sent in place of Cornwallis, to surrender his sword to Rochambeau rather than to Washington; the British troops' effort while marching to keep "eyes right" toward the French, as if to blot out the existence of the Americans on the other side of the road; their attempts to damage their muskets by flinging them down with force until stopped by General Lincoln; and the emotional outbursts of many of the British during the ceremony of surrender. To quote Abbé Robin, "After the surrender, the English behaved with the same overbearing insolence as if they had been conquerors, the Scots wept bitterly, while the Germans only conducted themselves decently, and in a manner becoming Prisoners. With a meanness always attendant upon vanquished insolence, the English servilely cringed to the French, vainly attempting to screen the disgrace of being conquered by those that had so often denominated American rebels, and republicans." *New Travels Through North America*, p. 64.

[63.] Kennett, *French Forces in America*, p. 151.

[64.] Callahan, *Henry Knox*, p. 188.

Fortification and the American Experience | *4*

Introduction

In the years immediately following the American Revolution, most of the previous concern about the location and condition of military fortifications in America—inland or coastal—diminished with the cessation of hostilities. Winning material support from Congress for the Continental Army and its needs had always been one of General Washington's most pressing problems during the war. Not surprisingly then, once the war was over, a natural weariness with the human and financial demands of so many years of conflict made many in the U.S. Congress and the government even more reluctant to consider the whole question of national defense, especially if heavy expenditures were involved. Convinced that it was not feasible to strain the finances of the fledgling nation with the undeniable expense of new fortifications, members of Congress tended to ignore the entire issue of defense. Indeed, with the danger of imminent invasion by the British over, the individual states were reluctant to spend money even to repair old fortifications, much less to build new ones. Unfortunately, all these forts also required maintaining large garrisons to defend them, a most unpopular proposition after the Revolutionary War. Ultimately, whatever public debate over the question of fortifications lingered after the end of the war became rather loosely focused on two general questions. Should a coherent plan of fortifications be undertaken by a corps of engineers for the defense of the new nation? And if the answer were in the affirmative, how could all the knowledge and experience that had been so painfully acquired with respect to the art and science of fortifications be maintained and efficiently disseminated to such a corps?

That these two problems were inextricably linked had been obvious from the start to those who cared about the question of fortifications. General Washington and his officers had discovered the need for fortifications during the war and, concomitantly, that their successful construction required the services of skilled and trained engineers. During the American Revolution, it had been apparent that some sort of corps of engineers, most likely modeled on its distinguished counterpart in the French Army, should be established to take responsibility for fortification and related engineering projects in America. The first awkward steps to achieve this end, as described in a previous section, had been taken by General Washington and Congress under the goad of wartime demands. However, the second problem—that of somehow institutionalizing the skills required by competent military engineers—was far from being thoroughly analyzed, much less solved. Should there be an American equivalent of the famed French Ecole du Corps Royal du Génie at Mézières, or after the French Revolution, of the Ecole Polytechnique? If so, how was it to be organized and who would direct it, given the few Americans who possessed the requisite skills? What was to be its curriculum, and who was qualified to organize it? A rather odd attempt by Congress in 1777 had led to the authorization of the "Corps of Invalids," whose duty it was to include "a military school for young gentlemen previous to their being appointed to marching regiments," but the lack of funds and the pressures of war had led to its abandonment.[1]

In fact, toward the end of the Revolution, a somewhat tepid consideration of the status of post-war defenses and the military establishment had taken place. The Congressional Committee on Peace Arrangements, including Alexander Hamilton and James Madison as members, had requested the views of some of the senior officers of the Continental Army as to what sort of peacetime policies should be adopted. Major General Duportail, as chief engineer, had taken the time to write a memorandum on September 30, 1783, for General Washington's use in which he expressed his belief in the importance and common sense of uniting the engineers and artillery under one head. Arguing that their "preliminary knowledge" and training with respect to fortifications was identical, and that such a combination would not only be economical, but also help to remove the rivalry between the two corps, Duportail recommended the creation of a post-war force of two regiments of artillerists and engineers. He added a warning, however, that "if the United States are to have fortified harbors, what I am proposing will be insufficient."[2] He further commented on the necessity for some sort of military academy to teach the skills required by the corps of engineers, especially with respect to the art and science of fortification.[3] The obvious relationship between fortification and the teaching of its techniques to engineers was recognized from the beginning, especially by French engineers like Duportail who prided themselves on the value of the training they had received at Mézières.

Henry Knox, as chief of artillery, also gave some thought to the post-war organization of the military, and to the requirements of national defense. Besides recommending the establishment of a national militia, Knox focused his interest on West Point where he had served as post commander during the last period of the war. Re-emphasizing its importance as "the key to America," Knox argued adamantly that West Point be fortified and maintained at all cost. In addition, without specifically designating a site for it, he suggested that a "complete system of military education which would embrace the whole theory of the art of war" be set up. He suggested that it be composed of two military academies, one for the Army and one for the Navy, each with about 40 pupils a year under the direction of a superintendent.[4] Knox's most likely model, due to his reading of classic texts as a bookstore owner, was probably the British academy at Woolwich, but he had no prejudices against the French school at Mézières, which he recognized as providing much of the curriculum and theory for the entire art and science of fortification.[5] That Alexander Hamilton also saw the need for a national military academy was borne out by a report he wrote years later in 1799, proposing such a plan in detail. Moreover, some years earlier Hamilton had written the first draft of a speech for George Washington in which he stated, "A military academy instituted on proper principles, would serve to secure to our country . . . a solid fund of military information, which would always be ready for national emergencies, and would facilitate the diffusion of military knowledge as those emergencies might require."[6] For the moment, however, although the committee endorsed the idea of a consolidated body to be called the Corps of Engineers, anything else was considered too much of a strain on post-war finances, and these various recommendations were allowed to lapse into obscurity.

It was to take several decades after the American Revolution, much political and military blundering, and a good deal of trial and error on the part of various Presidents, members of Congress, and secretaries of war before the two tangential problems of a corps of engineers and a school to train its members were solved. Nonetheless, by the second decade after the American Revolution, progress in fortifications came to revolve around the establishment, growth, and eventual success of two institutions: the United States Corps of Engineers and the U. S. Military Academy at West Point. The latter would strive to evolve the curriculum to teach, including among other things, the theories and skills of military fortification, and to graduate competent engineers; the former would oversee the direction of these engineer-officers and send them out across America to design, construct, and maintain such fortifications as were deemed necessary for the national defense. Without the training, organization, and drive provided by West Point and the Corps of Engineers, there would have been virtually no defense policy, nor the development of personnel capable of implementing it. The history of fortification in America prior to the Civil War revolved around these two institutions, prospering or stagnating in direct proportion to their success or failure during this period.

The Development of the First System, 1794–1799

By 1794, the situation in America with respect to any sort of defense policy was everywhere dismal. Not only was there a lack of a coherent defense policy, but there barely existed a regular army capable of defending the nation.[7] Moreover, much of the technical knowledge on fortifying, so painstakingly acquired during the American Revolution, was being frittered away.[8] The physical status of specific fortifications around the nation was not much better. What forts still remained functional, particularly the ones on the seacoast or those guarding important harbors, had in fact been built primarily with colonial resources. Later, very little assistance had come from the Continental Congress, even during the Revolution itself. Many of these fortifications, such as those at Boston, Newport, Philadelphia, and Charleston, actually dated from early colonial days. However, they had very little work done on them after the fall of Quebec in 1759, since no further threat from the French was feared. During the Revolutionary War, forts—including coastal ones—naturally became more numerous, as works that had been long deteriorating were refurbished, and new ones constructed to meet the British threat. These forts had been designed to protect inland locations, lines of communication, and seaports. However, there was no real pattern or coherent national design in their construction, and they varied tremendously in style. Earth, timber, and stone were the materials commonly available and, thus, the most commonly used. The variety of cannon found in them was also haphazard. Whatever was available, regardless of type, caliber, or age, was impressed into service as long as it was functional. After 1783, although any number of these fortifications remained in existence, they were allowed to deteriorate badly for the next decade, since so few of the individual states cared to maintain them. In fact, when the first national effort to refortify the harbors was undertaken in the 1790s, only three locations—Castle Island (Boston), Goat Island (Newport), and Mud Island (Philadelphia)—were found to have forts sufficiently worth repairing, rather than having new ones built on the same site.[9]

This dismal state of affairs could continue only as long as the nation was able to enjoy the luxury of indifference to the state of its fortifications. In 1794, that situation changed drastically as an international crisis once again raised the specter of invasion. It also pushed to the forefront the abysmal condition of national fortifications and the perennial problem of the lack of skilled engineers. The threat in 1794 came from Great Britain, deeply embroiled in her war against revolutionary France. Her maritime policy of seizing all neutral shipping destined for ports under French control caught up more than 250 American ships and crews in 1793, enraging American ship owners and uniting the states along the seaboard in demands for retaliation.[10] However, if war against Britain were to be declared, the American government knew that more raids by the Royal Navy, and possibly a full-scale invasion, were a strong possibility. A new look at the status of fortifications—particularly of those on the seacoast—was deemed immediately necessary; and on January 20, 1794, Congress appointed a committee to investigate as quickly as possible the state of fortifications at the principal harbors on the Atlantic seaboard, and the problems involved in repairing them or building new ones.

That the first resurgence of concern about fortifications should focus almost exclusively on those guarding the seacoast was not surprising. Historically, these fortifications were often the oldest and most sophisticated to be found in North America. Many of the colonies with important harbors and strategic locations had thrown up fortifications that were primitive or modest in the beginning, but which became increasingly more complex as time went by, especially after the outbreak of the Anglo-French rivalry in the first half of the eighteenth century.[11] The theory that underlay their construction was a two-fold one: first, that any threat to the colonies would come from the sea, and second, that fortifications at strategic seacoast locations could deter such a threat.[12] As a result, during the American Revolution, the French engineers under Duportail had labored especially energetically to fortify the most important places on the Atlantic seaboard, fully aware that any invasion would be launched primarily from the ships of the Royal Navy.

Because of this French influence on fortification, most American forts, whether seacoast or inland, reflected Vauban's basic design concepts—bastioned, with outworks and glacis, offering that basically horizontal profile that aimed at providing on all sides the least possible target to enemy artillery. Forts protecting the seacoast or important rivers generally featured a two-tier artillery set-up: external batteries of guns known as water batteries, placed behind earthen embankments close to the shore and designed to provide heavy close-in fire (often with hot shot); and the larger guns of the main fort to engage the enemy ships at long range. (In later years, as will be seen, the theories of René Montalembert were to strongly affect the design of the coastal forts and the emplacement of cannon.) Earth, properly sloped to fit the Vauban design, and then sodded or seeded with binding knotgrass, was the most important material used by engineers of the time, since it was expected to absorb shot with little damage.[13] A few forts, usually those on small islands where any land attack was unlikely, were more simply designed as "star forts," with no bastions. But overall, although all these forts were dramatically simple compared to the vast and elaborate European models, many of those American forts that stood on the seacoast, or in the vicinity of harbor entrances to guard the more populous cities like Boston, New York, and Baltimore, would evolve in complexity and importance in the course of time. Despite their state of general disrepair in 1794, the seacoast fortifications would be seen as the first line of defense when danger threatened. As a result, when funds were finally appropriated by Congress to meet a possible British threat, they were earmarked for the coastal fortifications without much debate.

The congressional committee's report on the state of coastal fortification in 1794 was sobering. It reported that at least 16 harbors and ports required immediate fortifications so that they might at least be protected "against surprise by naval armaments," if not against full-scale invasion. Since time was too short for anything elaborate, the committee recommended that the parapets of the batteries and redoubts be formed of earth. The various states were urged to cede the land in question to the federal government, and it was suggested that funds be provided to purchase land where necessary from private citizens. After discussing the need for magazines and blockhouses for the garrison troops, the report estimated that the 16 sites for fortification would require a total of 445 guns to be manned by 26 officers and 670 men. It also itemized the location of the cannon, as well as authorizing the casting of 200 more at appropriate foundries. Although the committee did suggest that the fortifications to be built should be garrisoned by "troops in the pay of the United States" rather than maintained by the individual states—an implicit acknowledgment of the principle that a national corps of engineers and artillerists was needed—the question of manpower, given the woefully small size of the regular army, was not really properly addressed. One of the committee's rather lame suggestions was that "some artillery officers in service might be used on the present occasion, and that part of the infantry officers might be chosen for the purpose, who would soon acquire a tolerable degree of knowledge in the use of cannon."[14]

After some debate over these recommendations and the addition of five more sites to the list, "an Act to provide for the Defence of certain Ports and harbors in the United States" was passed by both houses and signed into law by the President on March 20, 1794, along with the necessary appropriations to start the process.[15] To Henry Knox, then secretary of war, fell the task of preparing detailed plans for the proposed works and assigning the appropriate engineers to construct them. His first rude awakening was the discovery that, once again, only foreigners—primarily Frenchmen—were available and qualified to do the job. Appointments as "temporary engineers" were offered to seven of them, and each was designated the responsibility for an individual section of the coastline.[16] Each also received detailed instructions from Secretary Knox on dealing with the governors of the states involved, a copy of the congressional committee report, and a sense of the amount of funds available.[17] With the urgency of their mission explicitly emphasized, they were dispatched to their assigned areas in the summer of 1794 (see Figure 4.1). Their work on the seacoast fortifications would subsequently be known as the "First System."[18]

As a model for what was accomplished by these engineers in 1794, it is perhaps useful to examine briefly the work of Stephen Rochefontaine (1755–1814), who had shrewdly anglicized his name, no doubt aware of the lingering prejudice against foreign engineers. Assigned to cover the area from Portland, Maine, to New London, Connecticut, Rochefontaine's decisions about rebuilding or repairing fortifications provide a comprehensive picture of the state of national defenses after nearly a decade of neglect. Much of his initial effort, like that of the six other engineers, revolved around locating the sites designated by Congress, assessing their condition, submitting plans and costs for their repair, proffering designs for new forts, and, where necessary, negotiating with the local governments to sell or cede to the federal government the land on which the fortifications stood.

Rochefontaine moved with impressive speed from north to south, tracing the congressional directive as to the chosen sites. In Portland, after purchasing for $68 the four acres containing the ruins of old Fort Allen, built in 1776 and renamed Fort Sumner after 1797, he submitted plans to rebuild the fort as an enclosed work. It was to include parapets supported by stone walls and earth, brick barracks with a bombproof powder magazine beneath, and a covered way connected to a water battery at the harbor edge. The cannon in the water battery were to be comprised of 10 heavy guns mounted

Figure 4.1 Locations of some principal fortifications of the First System, 1794–1801.

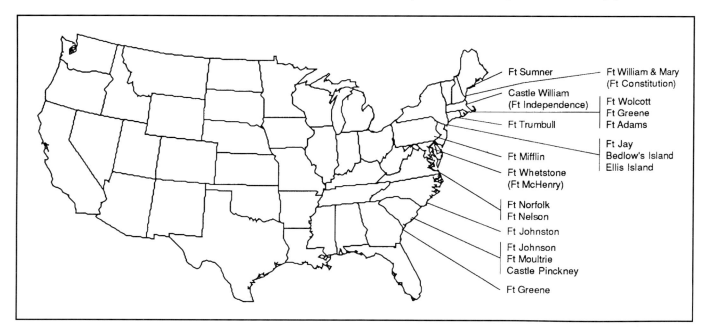

Ft Sumner

Castle William (Ft Independence)

Ft Trumbull

Ft Mifflin

Ft Whetstone (Ft McHenry)

Ft Norfolk
Ft Nelson

Ft Johnston

Ft Johnson
Ft Moultrie
Castle Pinckney

Ft Greene

Ft William & Mary (Ft Constitution)

Ft Wolcott
Ft Greene
Ft Adams

Ft Jay
Bedlow's Island
Ellis Island

on seacoast carriages, while the main fort would have only a few 6- and 12-pounders mounted on "travelling carriages," in case their mobility was required to defend other positions.[19] At Portsmouth in New Hampshire, an old colonial ruin on New Castle Island in the harbor, known locally as Fort William and Mary, was rebuilt with masonry and sod, with the addition of a small citadel which was to hold seven heavy guns on seacoast carriages.[20]

The three selected sites on the Massachusetts coast, all of which already sported some fortification ruins from colonial days, were Cape Ann, Salem, and Marblehead. Little was done to rebuild the ruins of Fort Point at the head of Gloucester harbor, despite the fact that Rochefontaine produced plans to refortify the site. However, after a town meeting in Salem, Rochefontaine decided to work on Fort William on the west side of the harbor entrance; at the same time the site was ceded to the United States. Rebuilt with masonry and sod, it too featured a brick citadel and magazine, and was expected to hold six guns on seacoast carriages and four light guns on travelling carriages. Boston had been pinpointed by Congress as a vital harbor requiring a major fortification effort, and over $9,000 had been appropriated to do the job. Fortunately, the area boasted two fortifications dating from colonial days in fairly good condition. Castle William (later renamed Fort Independence), a work of brick cemented with mortar made of burnt oyster shells and featuring over 100 guns, was located on Castle Island. Prior to the American Revolution, Castle William had been considered the second most powerful seacoast fortress after Louisbourg. The other was Fort Warren on Governor's Island, for which Rochefontaine prescribed more cannon and some refurbishing. Here, however, the Commonwealth of Massachusetts refused to cede the islands to the federal government for various reasons, and after some controversy, the War Department disbursed only $2,000 for repairs to the two works, turning the whole business over to the local authorities.[21]

Fort Washington (Fort Wolcott after 1798) on Goat Island in the harbor of Newport, had been heavily fortified during the American Revolution, especially after 1781. Rochefontaine and Knox agreed upon heavier guns for the works, and the former set up a battery at Howland's Ferry at the north end of Rhode Island to add more firepower. As for the fortifications at New London, the local government had already made an attempt to repair Fort Trumbull, described by Knox as a "citadel surrounded with Batteries and Glacis, to cover it from the direct fire of Ships of War and to scour the entrance of the harbour and the neighbourhood of the citadel with Cannon and Musketry."[22]

The other French engineers, responsible for areas ranging down the coast as far as Georgia according to Knox's instructions, also accomplished a good deal. They repaired or refurbished forts and batteries at most of the sites laid out by the congressional committee at such places as Fort Jay, Fort Mifflin, Fort Whetstone (on the site subsequently occupied by Fort McHenry), Fort Moultrie, Fort Pinckney, Fort Mechanic, and Fort Greene, to name a few. However, although their work represented a giant stride forward after the neglect of a decade, it was unlikely that simply repairing or remodeling previously fortified sites would provide an impregnable seacoast defense. The funds Congress provided, usually at the prodding of the President or secretary of war, were modest and erratic. Without a constant infusion of more money for repairs and upkeep, these fortifications too easily fell into disrepair again. All through the period prior to 1812, a specific pattern was discernible: regardless of which faction was in power, Federalist or Jeffersonian Democrat, fortifications were generally neglected until some international crisis pushed them into the forefront. However, as soon as the danger subsided, so did interest in appropriating funds or in the state of national defenses. Secretary of War James McHenry noted with exasperation the false economy of constructing impermanent works too cheaply, and on a piecemeal basis, every time there appeared to be a crisis: "A regard to ultimate economy will require, that such of the fortifications as may be always important to the general defence should be constructed . . . of the most durable materials."[23]

Four years later in 1798, this pattern was again repeated. Although the previous threat from Great Britain had suddenly dissipated, one from France had taken its place. By sufficiently modifying the orders in council in mid-1794 to allow American shipping to resume its lucrative trade with the British West Indies, and by promptly compensating American ship owners for their previous losses, the British government had successfully mollified the American public. Relations with revolutionary France, on the contrary, began to worsen in the next few years, fuelled in 1799 by French attacks on American shipping headed for British ports, as well as by the notorious incident of diplomatic bribery, the XYZ Affair.[24] Prodded by President Adams and Secretary of War McHenry, Congress appropriated $250,000, a larger sum than any other proposed thus far for coastal defense. Essentially the same list of seacoast fortifications cited in 1794 was designated for attention once again.[25] For the next few years efforts were made to use masonry, especially for revetment, in some of the works. By 1801, however, a general deterioration of these fortifications was common again, with the exception of one or two of the major works, such as Fort Mifflin and Fort McHenry.

Perhaps Fort Mifflin near Philadelphia (see Figure 4.2), and Fort McHenry in Baltimore best illustrated the greatest degree of permanence that was achieved with the fortifications of the First System, given the up and down nature of the pattern just described. Fort Mifflin, constructed between 1798 and 1803 for the defense of Philadelphia, was located on Mud Island at the confluence of the Schuylkill and the Delaware River on a site originally laid out by the British in the 1770s. Although original plans for the fort, drawn in 1794 by Pierre Charles L'Enfant (architect of the city plans for Washington, D.C., in 1791) were lost, another French engineer, Louis de Tousard, was instructed in 1798 to proceed along the lines started by L'Enfant. Built on an unusual plan that had features of both star and bastion designs, the fort was later described by Jonathan Williams, a future chief engineer, with great interest:

> The first part is formed of four redans defending the river on the south & East. The Walls generally eleven & a quarter feet high are of large stones perfectly cut and put together. . . . The second part of the works, viz; that which has been added on the north and West side is composed of two redans toward the West & of a regular front towards the North or land side: that front consists of a casemated Bastion. N.E. a Curtain of ninety six yards & a full half bastion N.W. forming thus a kind of horn work. The wall all round has a good brick revetment, with handsome white Stone Cordon.[26]

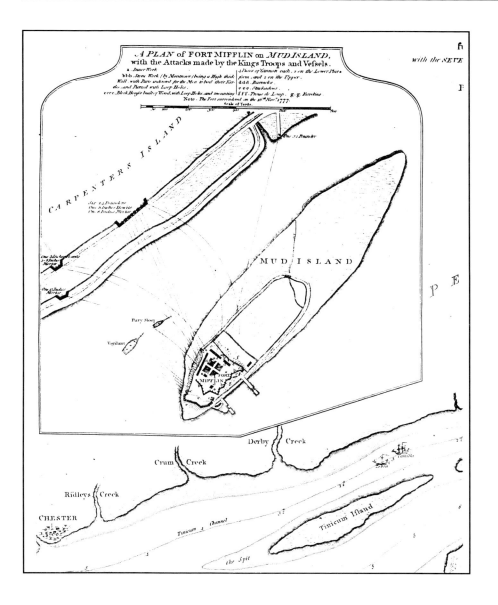

Figure 4.2 A plan of Fort Mifflin (originally Mud Fort), Pennsylvania; Captain John Montrésor of the British Army was the first engineer to design a fortification on the site.

Fort McHenry, built between 1798 and 1800 to guard the harbor of Baltimore on the site of old Fort Whetstone (1776), was the result of the labor of several engineers—notably John Jacob Ulrich Rivardi, Louis de Tousard, Alexander de Leyritz, and Jean Foncin.[27] By the time the fort, seen in figures 4.3 and 4.4 (page 124), was bombarded by the British in 1814 (the event that inspired Francis Scott Key's poem), it stood as a pentagonal, bastioned fort with a regular trace. The scarp was revetted with brick, and it boasted a ravelin first constructed in 1813 and then replaced in 1837.[28] Given the federal government's reliance upon French engineers, it is not surprising that Fort McHenry featured the basic Vauban bastion design that predicated attacks from the land, even though the fort guarded only a narrow land approach on the northwest. Both forts were efficiently redesigned by the engineers of the First System, and were considered vital to the defense of Philadelphia and Baltimore in future years.

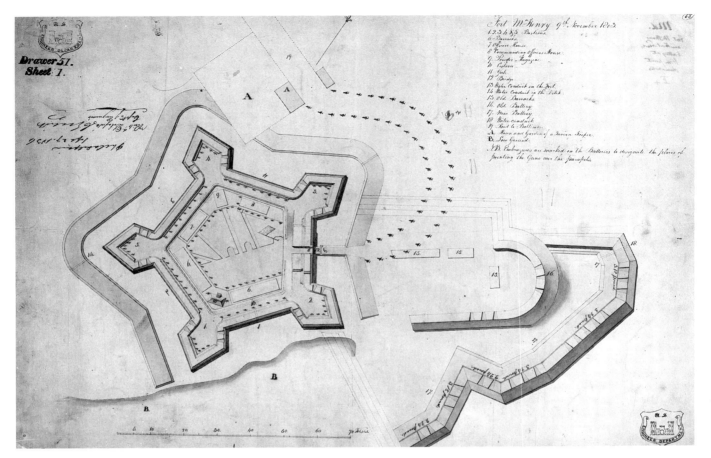

Figure 4.3 Fort McHenry, Maryland (1798). Jean Foncin, engineer. Plan (1803). *National Archives, Washington, D.C.*

Figure 4.4 Fort McHenry: the "star fort." *Courtesy of the Smithsonian Institution.*

The Corps of Engineers and West Point: The Formative Years, 1794–1812

The twofold situation with respect to fortifications that had persisted since the end of the American Revolution—namely, the construction of sporadic and makeshift fortifications provoked by recurring international crises, and the need to depend on foreign engineers—began to be subtly altered after 1800. Although no new federal construction of any consequence was undertaken after that date, with the exception of some work done by individual states such as New York and Massachusetts on their harbor defenses, certain changes fundamental to the progress of future fortifications were actually taking place. Despite the fact that the Jeffersonian Administration came into office in 1801 determined to cut the size of the military establishment to the bone, legislative reforms in 1801–1802 finally succeeded in establishing viable infrastructures in two important areas: the creation of a separate corps of engineers and of a functioning military academy at West Point. Neither of these institutions found its path in the first few years to be smooth or simple. Nevertheless, their very existence fundamentally changed the course of fortifications in America. It meant that although foreign sources, particularly the French, would still be heavily drawn upon, the faculty and curriculum at West Point would finally achieve the goal of a corps of trained, native-born engineers, capable of undertaking the missions assigned to them without having to depend on outside forces for help.

This process actually began in May 1794 when, in response to the need for troops to man the seacoast fortifications and for engineers to work on them, Congress finally passed the legislation to create the Corps of Artillerists and Engineers. To Secretary of War Timothy Pickering fell the task of finding qualified officers for the new corps. However, like his predecessor Henry Knox, Pickering found to his chagrin that very little had changed despite the founding of the Corps of Artillerists and Engineers. In the final analysis, there was still no American soldier-engineer suitable to command the entire corps.[29] The only viable candidates were once again Frenchmen and other foreigners. Ultimately, Stephen Rochefontaine was chosen to be commander of the Corps of Artillerists and Engineers. He had served as a captain with the engineers under Duportail, most notably at Yorktown after which he received a promotion to brevet major. Commissioned as majors in the new Corps were J. J. Ulrich Rivardi, a Swiss who had been doing excellent work on the fortifications at Baltimore and Norfolk, and Louis Tousard (1749–1821), an artilleryman who was a veteran of the Continental Army.[30]

The corps' relationship with West Point was closely established when the latter was designated as headquarters. West Point, was chosen for a number of reasons. First, it had already emerged as the place to assemble all those recruits who were not assigned outright to other fortifications, primarily because it had a large supply of military stores left over from the Revolutionary War and was the usual supply point for newly raised companies. Second, since various individuals, ranging from Presidents Washington and Adams to their two secretaries of war, had already grasped the necessity of training the officers, cadets, and soldiers of the newly established Corps in the theory and practice of engineering and fortification—that is, of setting up some sort of school of instruction—West Point appeared a convenient site (see Figure 4.5) to accomplish this end. Secretary Pickering wrote in 1796:

> The corps of artillerists and engineers appears to be an important establishment. To become skilful in either branch of their profession, will require long attention, study, and practice; and because they can now acquire the knowledge of these arts advantageously only from the foreign officers, who have been appointed with a special reference to this object, it will be important to keep the corps together for the present. . . . Its principal station [West Point] may then become a school for the purpose. . . . [31]

And finally, Fort Putnam and Fort Clinton (formerly Fort Arnold), built to provide a defense of the Hudson River, were seen as useful for training troops in the required techniques of fortification.

Despite this flurry of activity, nothing was done at West Point in the way of instruction from 1794–1795, primarily because the three "foreign officers" were still busy ranging up and down the seacoast, repairing the fortifications of the First System they had already contracted to survey.[32] Tousard arrived at West Point at the end of 1795 to find that only about half of the assigned officers, and three of the thirty-two cadets authorized to the new Corps had reported in. Indeed, the largest functional unit at West Point in 1795 turned out to be the garrison band, which boasted twenty members.[33] When Lieutenant Colonel Stephen Rochefontaine finally

Figure 4.5   West Point, New York (1778).   Plan (1818) drawn by George W. Whistler. *National Archives, Washington, D.C.*

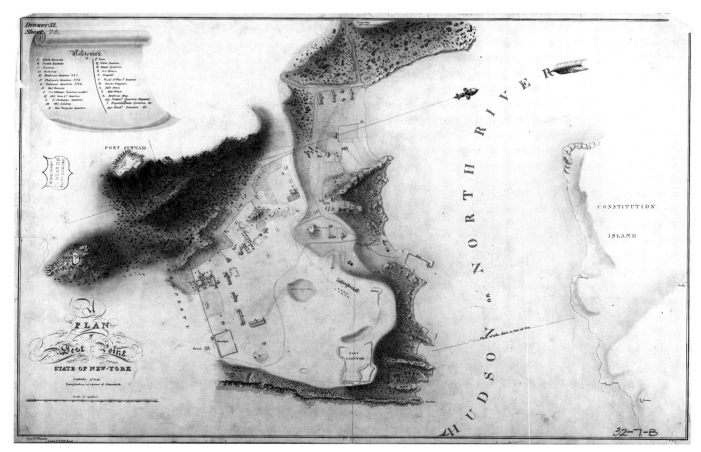

reported to West Point in January 1796 to assume command of the Corps of Artillerists and Engineers and the garrison, the events that ensued unfortunately proved that achieving a school of instruction in engineering, fortification, and gunnery would be anything but simple. Within a short time the entire organization at West Point collapsed in a welter of conflicts caused by personality clashes at the command level, by the lack of a clear-cut curriculum and trained instructors, and even by the lack of the students' comprehension of the nature of their role in the school.

The situation at West Point degenerated into absenteeism of a high order as the officers and cadets evaded classes wherever possible, resentful at being forced to attend classes they thought were useless, and delivered in thick French accents to boot. While Joseph Warin was supposed to be lecturing on fortification theory and drawing, Major Rivardi recorded that at times Rochefontaine was the only officer present. A suspicious fire eventually destroyed the officers' barracks that contained the hated classroom. Rochefontaine persisted in his efforts despite the ill feeling toward him, constructing a parapet for artillery practice and a wooden model of a bastioned fort for instruction. Unfortunately, Rochefontaine and Tousard also developed a nasty rivalry, fed by the general dislike of Rochefontaine, as well as by Rochefontaine's fear that his command was being undermined. A "duel" between Rochefontaine and a Lieutenant William Wilson, each sporting two loaded pistols and a sword, was perhaps the lowest point of this whole period; and Rochefontaine's account of the events is unintentionally comical:

> The first fire went off almost at the same time on both sides—my second Pistol went off unaware and I remained against my antagonist who had yet a loaded pistol against me. He came up to me within three steps and missed fire. It is a general rule in such occasions to lose the chance when the pistol has not gone off, yet my adversary cocked up and missed his fire a second time. In order to prevent his firing a third time, I fell on him to try to prevent him from cocking his piece, but he did it notwithstanding, and his pistol missed fire again, the muzzle touching my breast. The two witnesses came up then and separated us. My noble adversary, enraged at not assassinating me on the spot, was furiously asking powder of his second, to kill said he that Son of a Bitch. This was his noble expression on that occasion. [34]

This totally unworkable situation ended in 1797 with a dismal court of inquiry agreed to by Pickering's successor as secretary of war, James McHenry. Classroom instruction by that time was probably pointless. As has been pointed out, "The basic failure to found an academy in 1796–98 lay in the fact that no American officers *were* qualified to instruct in engineering and gunnery—and at the same time they were unwilling to accept instruction from foreigners who were qualified."[35] Thus, by the end of 1798, despite efforts to establish an organized and efficient Corps of Engineers and Artillerists with a school of instruction at West Point, the situation was, in fact, embarrassingly deficient. The seacoast fortifications still required foreign engineers to construct them, they were manned by troops who had minimum expertise in gunnery, most of the officers of the Corps were off serving at territorial forts, and the garrison at West Point had dwindled to one sergeant, one corporal, and five privates.[36] The first efforts to achieve a situation that would alter this state of affairs had been an embarrassing failure.

A few more attempts to rethink or restructure a school of instruction or military academy were made in the next two years. Toward the end of 1799, Alexander Hamilton, then the active head of the so-called Provisional Army (with the title of inspector general), approached Secretary McHenry with a far-ranging proposal concerning the need for an efficient military academy:

> One which I have always thought of primary importance, is a military academy. This object has repeatedly engaged the favorable attention of the administration, and some steps toward it have been taken. But these, as yet, are very inadequate. . . . Since it is agreed that we are not to keep on foot numerous forces, instructed and disciplined, military science in its various branches ought to be cultivated . . . so that there may always exist a sufficient body of it ready to be imparted and diffused, and a competent number of persons qualified to act as instructors to the additional troops which events may successively require to be raised. . . .
>
> To avoid great evils, [the government] must either have a respectable force prepared for service, or the means of preparing such a force with expedition. The latter, most agreeable to the genius of our government and nation, is the object of a military academy. I propose that this academy shall consist of five schools—one to be called "The Fundamental School"; another, "The School of Engineers and Artillerists"; another, "The School of Cavalry"; another, "The School of Infantry"; and a fifth, "The School of the Navy." . . . The cadets of the army, and young persons who are destined for military and naval service, ought to study for two years in the Fundamental School; and if destined for the corps of engineers and artillerists, or for the navy, two years more in the appropriate school.[37]

In fact, Hamilton's plan basically presaged what was to become the modern system of service academies and branch technical schools, but the political mood for such far-reaching changes was hostile. Except for the doubling of the numbers of artillerists and engineers, the Army was returned to the strength it displayed in 1796, and Hamilton himself was discharged from service in 1800.

Toward the end of his administration, President John Adams had also turned some attention to the idea of a military academy.[38] He was, in fact, prepared to appoint the 64 cadets authorized for schooling in the Corps of Artillerists and Engineers, as well as engineers and teachers to instruct them. Adams suggested to the secretary of war that Captain William A. Barron, a skilled mathematics tutor and a Harvard classmate of his son, John Quincy Adams, be appointed to teach mathematics to the 2d Regiment of Artillerists and Engineers. Although Adams went on to mention a French engineer in New York as a possible instructor, he added, "I have an invincible aversion to the appointment of foreigners, if it can be avoided. It mortifies the honest pride of our officers, and damps their ardor and ambition."[39] In the pressure of events surrounding the 1800 election, Adams's interest in this issue was perforce swept aside. However, just before he left office, he appointed nine new cadets who, together with Joseph G. Swift, would become the first "academy cadets."[40]

Ironically, the most significant developments toward a functional mili-

tary academy occurred during the administration least likely to be sympathetic to such an outcome. The inauguration of Thomas Jefferson as President
on March 4, 1801, began ominously for the military establishment and the
future of military fortifications. The incoming Democratic-Republicans had
made it clear that they were planning heavy financial retrenchments, and
the decentralization of federal authority to achieve more reliance on state
militias than on the standing army. The new secretary of war, Henry
Dearborn, targeted the seacoast fortifications almost immediately as the
first area to undergo belt-tightening. In a flurry of directives, he began by
directing Louis Tousard, who had been working at Newport, to stop and take
up his new position as inspector of artillery. Dearborn stated bluntly, "It is
with the approbation of the President of the United States that I now direct
a suspension of all expenditures of public money as far as relates to fortifications in the harbour of Rhode Island."[41] Orders were even sent out urging
all construction be performed by troops rather than by laborers under private contracts as another cost-cutting measure.

Despite his avowed intention to cut costs, Dearborn cautiously began to
move in the direction of regularizing the situation of a military academy, or
school of instruction, specifically at West Point. In April 1801 he wrote to the
commanding officer at West Point, "It is in contemplation to establish a
Military school at West Point, and also to consider that place as the permanent residence of the Inspector[s] of Artillery and Fortifications."[42] Toward
this end, Colonel Tousard, author of *American Artillerist's Companion* (see Figure
4.6), was finally confirmed in his appointment as inspector of artillery and
assigned to West Point with some specific duties connected to the academy.
Yet, despite being ordered to West Point, Tousard was still expected to supervise the commanders of 18 army posts as to the condition of all ordnance in
their keeping, and to inspect cannon being cast at various foundries. Working
with the plans of the previous administration, Dearborn consulted President
Jefferson as to his opinion on the appointment of an inspector of fortifications. Jefferson, in fact, respected the need for some scientific schooling for
officers, if for no other reason than to end the much disliked reliance on foreigners. There was an added inducement in the fact that the leading candi-
date for inspector of fortifications was Jefferson's fellow member of the United
States Military Philosophical Society, Major Jonathan Williams (1750–1815),
a man with a great deal of theoretical knowledge of fortifications who was
at that time supervising the repairs at Fort Niagara. Significantly, Dearborn's
message announcing the assignment of inspector of fortifications connected
the position intimately with West Point: "The President having decided in
favor of the immediate establishment of a Military School at West Point, and
also on the appointment of Major Jonathan Williams as Inspector of
Fortifications, it becomes necessary for the Major to be at West Point as soon
as possible, for the purpose of directing the necessary arrangements at that
place for the commencement of the school."[43]

Despite this encouraging activity, the ensuing events at West Point itself
during these administrative changes were almost a repetition of the troubles of 1796. Tousard was resentful, feeling that he deserved total command
of the military academy. Too many officers still felt it was beneath them to
attend classes, and a lack of coherent direction in the teaching staff and curriculum led to clashes and quarrels that greatly irritated the secretary of
war. Finally, Dearborn decided that some clarification as to who was actually

Figure 4.6   Frontispiece, Louis de Tousard, *American Artillerist's Companion.*

Figure 4.7 Jonathan Williams (1750–1815), first superintendent of USMA.

in charge at West Point was necessary. Even though Tousard was the best qualified to direct instruction in engineering and gunnery, the secretary showed his reluctance to assign foreign officers to key positions.[44] Dearborn decided to hand the direction of the military academy he envisaged to Major Jonathan Williams (pictured in Figure 4.7), although the title of "superintendent" was not yet spelled out: "The President is pleased to appoint and you are hereby appointed Inspector of Fortifications, under the Act of Congress of March 3, 1799. You will . . . repair to West Point, in the state of New York, and take upon yourself the superintendence of the Military School at that post, until you shall receive further instructions."[45] Thus, although the legislation formally enacting the U. S. Military Academy did not occur until March 1802, by the end of 1801 much of its framework had already been erected.

The legislation that was signed by President Jefferson on March 16, 1802, signified a sharp reduction in the size of the Army. It provided in general terms that "the military peace establishment of the United States . . . shall be composed of one regiment of artillerists and two regiments of infantry, with such officers, military agents and engineers, as are hereinafter mentioned."[46] The decision to combine the two previous regiments of artillerists and engineers into a single regiment of artillerists, and to establish the tiny Corps of Engineers, created an unhappy personnel problem. Of the two previous lieutenant colonel commandants of the old regiments—Louis de Tousard and Henry Burbeck—only one would be promoted to colonel and given command of the regiment of artillerists. Plainly unpopular because of their French birth, both Tousard and Major J. J. Ulrich Rivardi, although highly qualified, generally unassuming, and very much needed, were nonetheless sent polite letters of "derangement," suggesting they retire from service. In the end, the native-born and senior officer, Henry Burbeck, was promoted to colonel of the regiment.[47] Major Jonathan Williams was transferred to head the new Corps of Engineers. He now had assumed a triple assignment: inspector of fortifications, head of the tiny Corps of Engineers, and *de facto* superintendent of the military school located at West Point.

As far as the U. S. Military Academy's relationship to the Corps of Engineers was concerned, the wording of the 1802 legislation was very vague. In some senses, the wording suggested that the Corps *was* the Military Academy, as well as an organization that was to be independent and separate from the line of the Army.[48] The Corps of Engineers had no troops, but was allocated a small number of officers and cadets, namely 20. However, 40 additional cadets (2 being allowed for each company of artillerists) were soon perceived as being eligible for instruction at West Point. Throughout 1802, Secretary Dearborn kept shuffling various elements around, trying to stabilize the situation *vis-à-vis* the Corps of Engineers and West Point. His first appointments to the Corps besides Williams were Captain William A. Barron, Lieutenant Peter A. Dransy, Lieutenant James Wilson, and Captain Jared Mansfield, who was a civilian, Yale graduate, and well-known mathematician.[49] Shortly thereafter, Williams was promoted to lieutenant colonel, Major Decius Wadsworth of the artillerist regiment was transferred in grade to the Corps of Engineers, and Second Lieutenant Alexander Macomb, Jr., of the 2d Infantry Regiment was promoted to first lieutenant and transferred as well, beginning a brilliant career that culminated in his becoming eventual head of the Corps and the entire Army.

In March of 1802, the tiny Corps of Cadets, as it was to be known, listed nine cadets as present for duty at West Point. However, the only faculty member actually in place at that time was Captain Barron, since Major Williams was on leave, Captain Mansfield had not yet reported, and Lieutenant Wilson had been detailed to act as judge advocate for a court-martial at Fort Mifflin in Philadelphia. Ironically, on the same day in October that Macomb was transferred, Secretary Dearborn informed cadets Joseph G. Swift and Simon M. Levy that they were appointed second lieutenants in the Corps of Engineers. In effect, the "Class of 1802" had "graduated," and since Swift, pictured in Figure 4.8, had been senior as a service cadet to Levy, he thus became the first "graduate" of the U. S. Military Academy, only seven months after the official establishment of the institution.[50] In 1802 as well, 16-year-old Joseph Gilbert Totten, seen in Figure 4.9, was appointed as an academy cadet, beginning a distinguished career as a future chief of the Corps of Engineers and an expert on seacoast fortifications.[51]

The next few years, however, continued to be unsettled ones for both the engineers and the Military Academy. To begin with, the question of command at West Point, which had repeatedly cropped up at various times since 1794, again emerged as a source of conflict in 1802. Part of the problem was a financial one—the post commander automatically drew double rations—and part of it lay in the natural desire of the officers involved to enjoy the prerogative of command. At West Point the problem arose because the Corps of Engineers, consisting only of officers and cadets, shared the post with a garrison of artillerists commanded by Captain George Izard. According to the 1801 orders, this artillery company was intended to act as support for the Military Academy and Izard was clearly designated as the post commander. Given the larger number of troops he commanded and his specific appointment, as well as his military expertise (like Williams, he came from a prominent family and had received European schooling in military art), Izard understandably felt that West Point was his post and that everyone residing in it should be under his authority. As chief engineer and superintendent, Lieutenant Colonel Jonathan Williams, on the other hand, clearly felt that he should have command, given his office and seniority. The result was a growing clash between the two men that simmered on throughout 1803, producing Williams's growing disenchantment with the situation as it existed. This particular situation was *de facto* resolved when Izard resigned rather than accept orders to move his company to an isolated frontier post in Tennessee.

The next issue that plagued the Corps of Engineers, and indirectly the Academy, was that of line command—that is, Dearborn's adamant refusal to allow any officer of the Corps of Engineers to command officers or troops of another unit—an issue that was to emerge even more controversially on the eve of war in 1812. In June 1803, Williams submitted his resignation, ostensibly citing as his primary reason his disagreement with the engineer command decision. A more likely cause, however, was his growing frustration with the cavalier way Secretary Dearborn kept interfering with the personnel of the Corps and, by inference, with its mission of achieving a workable curriculum of instruction. Tiny as the Corps of Engineers was, it kept losing officers to other assignments. For example, in 1802, Major Decius Wadsworth, the second-ranking officer of the Corps, had been ordered to Norfolk to supervise the fortifications there, and in 1803, he was sent even farther to Fort Adams in the Mississippi Territory. Lieutenant James Wilson, finally back

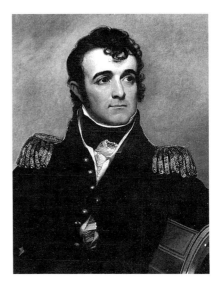

Figure 4.8   Joseph J. Swift (1783–1865). *Courtesy of the West Point Museum Collections, USMA, West Point, N.Y.*

Figure 4.9   Joseph G. Totten (?–1864). *Courtesy of the West Point Museum Collections, USMA, West Point, N.Y.*

at West Point after performing as judge advocate, had to be sent back to Norfolk to replace Wadsworth. The last straw for Williams was, most likely, Dearborn's order in 1803 that he personally report to Fort Johnston in North Carolina to inspect the work done there under an old contract. It was all too evident to Williams that Dearborn was not interested in allowing the Corps to settle in and become sufficiently organized to start up an efficient curriculum for the Military Academy, and his resignation was in the nature of a protest over all these factors. Williams's vacancy was not filled officially until his return to service nearly two years later.

With Williams's departure, the Corps of Engineers and the small U. S. Military Academy fell into a period of stagnation and neglect. Captain William A. Barron, now the senior engineer officer at West Point, supervised the instruction of a mere 11 cadets and an increasingly absent faculty.[52] In 1804, Major Wadsworth reported back to West Point, and assumed command of the post and the superintendence of the Military Academy. He did not long remain in the position for a number of reasons, and when Dearborn decided to assign him to New Orleans, Wadsworth submitted his resignation.[53] After some quiet negotiations, Williams was reappointed to the Corps of Engineers in April 1805, and ordered to return to West Point to take command of the Corps and the U. S. Military Academy. (There being no officers at West Point but the engineers, the issue of command over which he had ostensibly resigned two years before remained dormant.) In effect, his return signalled a resurgence of energy and morale at West Point. Having been depleted by resignations, extended furloughs, and detached service, the hard-pressed Corps of Engineers was stimulated by the news of several promotions and the arrival of several new cadets. Barron and the absent Mansfield were promoted to the rank of major, Wilson and Macomb to captain, and Joseph Swift and Walker K. Armistead to first lieutenants. By 1806, although the fledgling Academy had produced only six lieutenants for the Corps of Engineers—it seems to have been generally accepted after 1802 that the only source of new engineer officers would be graduates of the Military Academy—it was significant that despite all the difficulties, and all the organizational stumbling and controversies, the nation had finally begun to achieve its aim of producing a corps of American-born, trained fortifications engineers. Indeed, their abilities were to be called into play almost immediately, as tensions with Great Britain mounted, and forced the question of national defense and fortifications once more into prominence.

The Second System, 1802–1812

Jonathan Williams's return to West Point coincided with a quickening of interest in the questions of coastal fortifications and national defense. After a period of calm, warfare had resumed in Europe with a concomitant threat to neutral shipping, a situation almost identical to the pattern of 1794 and 1799. President Jefferson succinctly described America's position in a message to Congress in December 1805:

> Since our last meeting the aspect of our foreign relations has considerably changed. Our coasts have been infested and our harbors

watched by private armed vessels. . . . They have captured in the very entrance of our harbors, as well as on the high seas, not only the vessels of our friends coming to trade with us, but our own also. . . . The first object is to place our seaport towns out of the danger of insult. Measures have already been taken for furnishing them with heavy cannon for the service of such land batteries as may make a part of their defense against armed vessels approaching them. . . .[54]

Secretary of War Dearborn forwarded to Congress in February 1806 a complete summary of the status of fortifications of the First System, supposedly in place. It essentially described a picture of incomplete works, plagued by design and construction problems and inadequate funds. The works at Portland, Portsmouth, Cape Ann, and Salem badly needed repairs to be effective, although Boston's Fort Independence was in relatively good shape, having had over $186,195 expended on it since 1794. At Newport, Fort Adams and Fort Wolcott were still incomplete, and, in the final analysis, were seen as unfortunately protecting "only one of the three open and convenient passages by which Rhode Island may be approached." New York harbor represented a particularly vexing problem, Dearborn reported. Even though works had started on Governor's, Bedlow's, and Ellis islands in the inner harbor, and off the Battery at the tip of Manhattan Island, engineers hired by the state in 1801 had produced a cost estimate of over $3 million to complete a coherent project of fortification, an impossibly prohibitive sum to most legislators in New York. Dearborn added that after he had directed Lieutenant Colonel Williams of the Corps of Engineers to make a personal survey of the harbor, the following conclusions were reached:

> The harbor of New York is not susceptible of such defence as ought to be relied upon by permanent or fixed batteries . . . and consequently, that some other system ought to be adopted. This, it is presumed, should consist of at least one regular enclosed work, capable of being defended against a sudden assault, together with such fixed batteries as may most effectually annoy ships of war on their approach to the city . . . and also of a suitable weight of moving batteries . . . mounted on travelling carriages, and placed in the city, together with a sufficient number of well constructed gun boats. . . .[55]

Fort Mifflin and Fort McHenry were basically in good shape, but defenses for Annapolis and Alexandria needed extensive work. Elsewhere, down the coast from North Carolina to the newly acquired territory of New Orleans, the various fortifications were in poor condition, due to difficulties with local contractors, quarrels over land rights, and a hurricane in 1804.

In response to this report, Dearborn named New York, Charleston, and New Orleans as the sites requiring priority attention. In all cases, the Corps of Engineers was directed to take responsibility, the first overt realization that, at last, a construction project of the first magnitude could be planned and carried out by American-born and American-trained engineers. Williams himself was assigned to take charge of New York harbor, and Alexander Macomb was sent to supervise the fortifications in the harbor at Charleston, where he was aided by Charles Gratiot who had been at West Point for two years, and had graduated in October 1806.

This major work proposed by the United States government, begun in 1807 and well advanced by the outbreak of the War of 1812, became known as the Second System. The works of the Second System were more elaborate than those of the First, although they continued to lack an all-encompassing plan or a consistent style of fortification. However, in addition to open batteries and masonry-faced earth forts, the Second System reflected the development of all-masonry forts, perhaps a major turning point in the progress of American military architecture. This type of fort, when combined with the adoption of the casemated gun emplacement, led to the development of high, vertical-walled harbor defenses in America. It allowed for the mounting of seacoast cannon within a fort, rather than on top of its exterior walls. In effect, this represented a new adaptation of the theories of René Montalembert, as well as the continuation of the tried and true designs of Vauban.

The growing interest in new theories of seacoast fortification was entirely attributable to the impact of Jonathan Williams and his brain child, the United States Military Philosophical Society. In November 1802, Williams had established a professional society that he hoped would spread its influence throughout the Army. Its objectives were to preserve previous military knowledge and experience, to stimulate scientific military thinking, and to facilitate the exchange of new ideas in the various fields of military art.[56] Elected president of the society, Williams had cleverly solicited President Jefferson's patronage and proceeded to sponsor a series of meetings, usually composed of officers and cadets of the Corps of Engineers, and later of interested and distinguished individuals. The society itself collapsed during Williams's period of absence from West Point, but upon his return to duty, he was determined to revive its influence. That he succeeded admirably is evident from the scope of the meetings and exchanges that were held between 1806 and 1809.[57] Although the discussions ranged over the field of the military art, many topics were directly related to the specific function of the Corps of Engineers at the time, namely the design and construction of fortifications. Under Williams's prodding, the general theories of René Montalembert, never officially accepted in his native country of France, diffused rapidly through American military ranks.[58]

The works of the First System, as already noted, were heavily dependent on Vauban's techniques and theories, primarily because until 1802, no other system was available to challenge his bastioned, horizontal fortress design. In addition, the French military engineers who had supervised most of the construction of the First System, such as Rochefontaine, Tousard, Vincent, Foncin, and L'Enfant, were students and products of the traditions of Mézières, which acknowledged no other system except Vauban's. Montalembert's theories, published in his 11-volume work, *La Fortification perpendiculaire*, appeared in 1778 to face an uphill battle in his own country, but made rapid inroads in Prussia, Austria, and America. Like Vauban, Montalembert was concerned primarily with the design of the huge, land-based European fortresses. However, for American engineers, the most important elements of Montalembert's work were those they regarded as uniquely adaptable to American concerns— namely, his attempt to increase the firepower of a fortress and the "perpendicular" aspect of his design. Montalembert accomplished the first element by designing circular towers, generally three stories high, with 24 to 36 guns placed to exploit their maximum effective range and deliver the most concentrated and heavy firepower over a short time; by raising his caponnière— covered ways for communication—to three stories so that more guns could be massed there; and by reviving the idea of casemates and galleries within the thick walls, so that each gun was protected inside a casemate while firing through a slitlike embrasure.

The second element of Montalembert's designs that was so attractive to American engineers—his "perpendicular concept"—meant that his fortifications stood boldly upright, often with soaring lighthouse-type towers, to exchange gunfire with the enemy. In contrast, Vauban's horizontal fortress was designed so that enemy fire would ricochet harmlessly over the walls. The perpendicular innovation was regarded as useful in seacoast fortification where fire with enemy ships had to be exchanged in straightforward volleys against a moving target, and where a massive number of guns in tiers protected by covered casemates would offer a much needed advantage to the fort. Montalembert's concept of a "polygonal trace" was also attractive to American engineers, particularly when a fort was susceptible to attack from land as well as from the sea. The landward side of a seacoast fortification could be constructed with simple bastions and curtains, but the seaward side could now be rounded and built in tiers to ensure maximum cannon fire on enemy ships.[59]

While these new concepts in fortification theory excited many in the Corps of Engineers, events in 1805 conspired to bring them to the fore on a larger stage than the meetings of the United States Military Philosophical Society. That year witnessed Napoleon's victories at Ulm and Austerlitz, as well as Nelson's victory at Trafalgar. The heating up of the conflict between Great Britain and France brought on the announced British blockade of all shipping designated to French ports, a move once again destined to hit at vital American interests, and to enrage public opinion. This British policy culminated in the *H.M.S. Leopard* incident in which a British squadron, hovering near the Chesapeake Bay entrance for over eight months to block shipping, forcibly captured an American vessel and impressed members of the crew. The unpleasant prospect of a war with England once again produced a quickening of concern about fortifications. During the next few years, President Jefferson, the Congress, Secretary of War Dearborn, and the Corps of Engineers all bent their energies to identifying the sites needing repairs, squeezing out the appropriations, and organizing the assignment of the small group of engineers to the proper locations. After much congressional debate, an astonishing sum of one million dollars was voted for gunboats and essential fortifications.[60]

Jonathan Williams, at that time in Washington, turned his energies to persuading the secretary of war to approve promotions within the Corps of Engineers, and to organizing a meeting in the capital of the United States Military Philosophical Society.[61] At the same time, Williams and Dearborn ironed out the details organizing the dispersal and direction of the engineer officers to various areas, creating the engineer "districts" as they came to be known:

> I shall proceed . . . to distribute the Officers of Engineers in the most convenient way. We are but sixteen in the whole of which two [Mansfield and Alden Partridge] are fixed for special duties, one being Surveyor General in the western country and the other a Professor at West Point. I have thought it best to have four fixed Points as the head Quarters of the four detachments into which I have divided my Strength. . . .
> I have left New Orleans out of the question, presuming on your arrangements with Col. Foncin; and I must take an occasional view

of Philadelphia [Williams's home] myself for I have no Officer to send there; its River is so long and difficult, that I suppose by resorting to obstructions as formerly it may in conjunction with Fort Mifflin be defended. . . .

> Distribution of the Corps of Engineers, and Assistant Engineers who may be employed for Special Purposes.

1. The River Mississippi & the Coast to be put under the Care of M. Foncin.
2. All the Ports in Georgia & the two Carolinas to be under the direction of Major Macomb who is to take post in Charleston & to be assisted by Capt McRee, Capt Gratiot, and Lieut W. Partridge.
3. All the Ports in Virginia & Maryland to be under the direction of Capt Armistead who is to take post at Norfolk & be assisted by Capt Bomford & Lieut E.D. Wood.
4. The River Delaware and New York Harbour will be taken charge of by Col. Williams whose station will be in the latter place, assisted by Lieuts Totten, Babcock and Buck with such cadets as may be taken from the military academy.
5. All the Ports in Connecticut, Rhode Island, Massachusetts & New Hampshire to be under the direction of Major Swift who will take post at Boston & be assisted by Lieuts Willard and Thayer with such Cadets as can be drawn from the military academy.[62]

The U. S. Military Academy at West Point was given only some cursory attention by both Williams and Jefferson, who suggested a few proposals to strengthen the faculty and curriculum, but in the end things remained unchanged during this crisis, perhaps because the congressional committee appointed to study them was hostile to extensive changes.[63] In fact, only Lieutenant Alden Partridge and three civilians comprised the entire faculty of the six-year-old institution. By 1810, so few cadets had been admitted that there was no graduating class that year.

As for the fortifications of the Second System that were undertaken by the Corps of Engineers, their locations extended from Portland to New Orleans, as shown in Figure 4.10. In some places the engineers simply refurbished the forts already in place, adding batteries and more guns where necessary to the Vauban-type designs. Fort Columbus (later Fort Jay) on Governor's Island in New York harbor, for example, had four bastions and a ravelin. It was designed for 104 heavy guns, of which 50 had been mounted by the end of 1809. In other locations, they built star forts, despite some grumbling about this style of fortification. Joseph G. Swift grudgingly constructed Fort McClary at Kittery, Maine, in this manner, under direct orders from Washington, D.C., where many were by no means convinced to abandon the old ideas for Montalembert's.[64] However, when they were given their freedom, the engineers often opted to try out the new theories. In New York harbor, Williams himself was able to incorporate Montalembert's designs in three locations within the harbor—on the west part of Governor's Island, off the tip of Manhattan Island, and in the Hudson River off the foot of Hubert Street. Castle Williams, the fortification constructed on Governor's

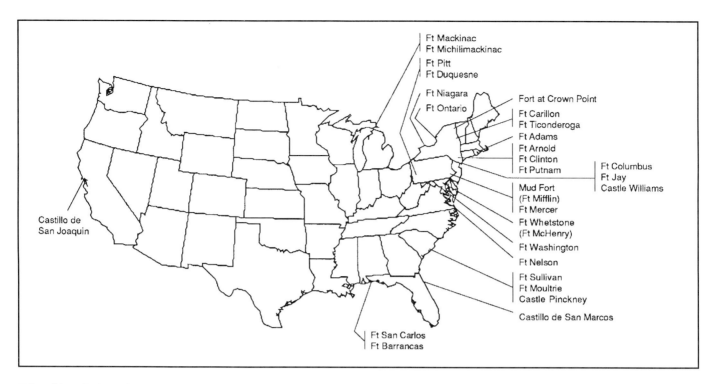

Ft Mackinac
Ft Michilimackinac
Ft Pitt
Ft Duquesne
Ft Niagara
Ft Ontario
Fort at Crown Point
Ft Carillon
Ft Ticonderoga
Ft Adams
Ft Arnold
Ft Clinton
Ft Putnam
Ft Columbus
Ft Jay
Castle Williams
Mud Fort
(Ft Mifflin)
Ft Mercer
Ft Whetstone
(Ft McHenry)
Ft Washington
Ft Nelson
Ft Sullivan
Ft Moultrie
Castle Pinckney
Castillo de San Marcos
Castillo de San Joaquin
Ft San Carlos
Ft Barrancas

Island in 1810 and named after the chief engineer, dramatically introduced into American military architecture the casemate emplacement for heavy guns in multiple tiers. Its walls of red sandstone, 40 feet high and 7–9 feet thick, became the prototype of the major seacoast forts built in America prior to the Civil War. (See figures 4.11 and 4.12.)

The Madison Administration, which took office in March 1809 with William Eustis as secretary of war, did not represent any great change with respect to national objectives on fortification. Even as relations with Great Britain worsened, Eustis's report to Congress on the status of seacoast defenses and on the appropriations needed sounded familiar. As before, New York and Charleston would require the most money. About $83,000 was needed in New York harbor, of which some $56,000 would be earmarked for completion of

Figure 4.10   Locations of some principal fortifications of the Second System, 1807–1813.

Figure 4.11   Castle Williams (Governor's Island, New York), named for its designer, Jonathan Williams, who incorporated many of Montalembert's ideas into this seacoast fort. *Courtesy U.S. Army Military History Institite*

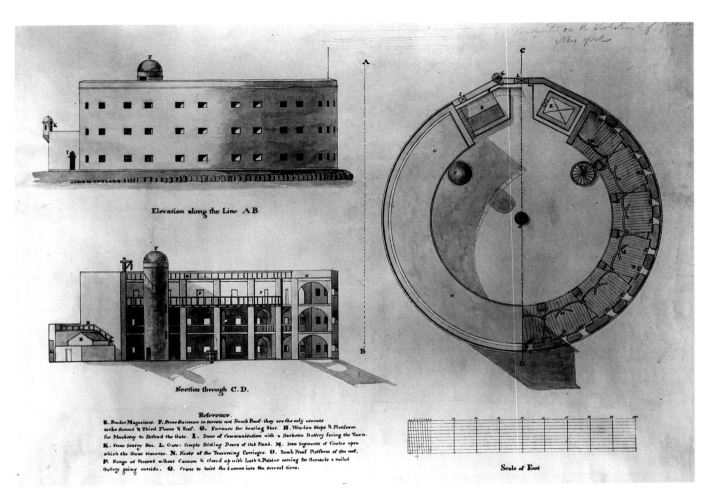

Elevation along the Line A B

Section through C.D.

Reference.

Figure 4.12 Plan, section, and elevation of Castle Williams, constructed on the west point of Governor's Island, N.Y. (1808). *Courtesy of the New-York Historical Society, N.Y.C.*

the works off the tip of Manhattan for two tiers of 56 guns; about $19,000 to complete the work on Bedlow's Island, and a mere $8,000 to finish Castle Williams. For South Carolina and Georgia, Eustis asked for $55,000, the bulk of which was to go to Charleston. Only $10,000 was requested for Newport and the difficult defenses of Narragansett Bay, clearly an inadequate sum.[65] For the small Corps of Engineers, the change of administration meant little. Work continued up and down the coast, guided by the organizational structure that Williams had created. One event that had an indirect impact on the Corps, however, was the legislation expanding the size of the Army, passed by Congress in January 1812 on the eve of war with Great Britain. It stimulated some of the senior officers of the Corps of Engineers to hope that they might profit by these changes by receiving higher promotions, and perhaps even command on the line—leading to just such an attempt by Jonathan Williams with dire results.

As for the U. S. Military Academy, a bill in April had a much more significant impact on the school. Resulting from congressional fears about military unpreparedness, the bill slightly increased the engineers by 7 officers and 112 enlisted men and corrected many of the fundamental problems that had been crippling the Academy. The most important changes included:

- an increase in the maximum number of cadets from 156 to 250
- a reaffirmation of the entrance requirements

- authorization for new professorships in natural and experimental philosophy, mathematics, and engineering
- a mandate for the superintendent to draw up a set of regulations for the cadets, to organize them into companies, and to establish a three-month encampment during which the cadets could get practical experience in soldiering.
- a requirement that each graduating cadet "receive a regular degree from an academic staff"

This last item, along with the newly created professorships, eventually led to the establishment of an Academic Board, which would provide the element constantly missing up to this point—a much needed guide in establishing a coherent curriculum.[66] Such then was the status of the Corps of Engineers and the U. S. Military Academy when war with Great Britain finally arrived in June 1812.

The Impact of the War of 1812

The three-year conflict with Britain carried a certain significance in that it tested under fire both the mettle of the officers of the Corps of Engineers, and the value of their fortifications work. A sharp controversy over the question of command in the line with respect to the Corps of Engineers had to be dealt with less than a week after the declaration of war with Great Britain. Secretary Eustis, in contradiction to the regulation upon which the Corps had been founded, wrote to all the district commanders that "whenever the Exigencies of the Service may require the talents & knowledge of the Officers of the Corps of Engineers beyond the line of their immediate profession, you may assign to those under your Command such duties in the Line of the Army, as may comport with their Rank."[67] For Colonel Jonathan Williams this was the much desired end to a situation he found increasingly intolerable in New York, where he was simply the supervising engineer at a project that was, for all intents and purposes, completed. Angrily he wrote to President Madison to complain about the situation, and, in effect, to suggest that the best solution was to give him command of New York harbor:

> While the Peace establishment alone existed I had but 3 Superior Officers (Genl Wilkinson, Colonels Burbeck and Cushing), I have now 14 Superiors, and while I cannot assume the command of a Subaltern, I am expected to perform professional duties where a Subaltern commands. War now being declared, my Situation in this Harbor becomes humiliating to the last degree. Works that have been constructed by me become inhabited and commanded by my inferiors, while I appear to be mainly a Spectator, for in military command I have not the authority of a Serjeant.
>
> I pray you Sir to relieve me from this unpleasant Situation, and by a Special order . . . to place me in that, which my nominal rank naturally points out, and which my honour requires. I indulge a hope that . . . I shall be placed in a command consistent with my Character, and such as I hope, also, is not unmerited by the public Services I have performed.[68]

Word of the change of policy had begun to circulate among the officers of the harbor garrisons, however, and the reaction of many of them was to send a "remonstrance" to their commanders objecting to the prospect of "encroachment upon our military rights" by officers who had already been promoted more rapidly than they had because of the small size of the Corps of Engineers.[69] It seemed that their grievances about this rapid promotion within the Corps could be suppressed as long as the engineers remained principally a detached unit of technical specialists, as originally described in the act of Congress of April 1806: "The functions of the engineers being generally confined to the most elevated branch of military science, they are not to assume, nor are they subject to be ordered on any duty beyond the line of their immediate profession, except by special order of the President. . . ."[70] The prospect of these young officers being placed in command positions over the officers of the harbor garrisons was not to be tolerated, and the possible appointment of 62-year-old Williams was simply regarded as the opening wedge. Probably unwilling to allow any further deterioration of morale, General Bloomfield in New York suspended the decision to give Williams command; and when the latter threatened to resign, President Madison took him at his word. For the second and final time, Jonathan Williams left the United States Army.[71] At the age of 28, the newly promoted Lieutenant Colonel Joseph G. Swift was once again promoted immediately to colonel, and named chief engineer and superintendent of the U. S. Military Academy at West Point to replace Williams.

Once the issue of command was out of the way, the engineers dispersed to their various assignments across the country. Swift was assigned as chief engineer of the 9th Military District in northern New York, along with Major McRee, Captain Totten, and First Lieutenant Sylvanus Thayer. Other engineers were sent to Maryland and Virginia, the Carolinas, and Georgia while Captain Alden Partridge remained in charge of the Military Academy with a faculty of three professors and two teachers. In fact, by the end of 1813 there were 99 cadets on the rolls; only a single cadet was graduated in 1813, 30 graduated in 1814, and another 40 in the first months of 1815, virtually exhausting the supply of cadets. There was no class of 1816.[72] It was significant that a number of engineer officers, and West Point graduates rendered particularly distinguished service during the war, and received brevet promotions.[73] The general competence and bravery they displayed during the conflict reflected well on their training and on the U. S. Military Academy, and served as a bulwark against critics in later years who would have preferred to abolish the school completely.

As for the First and Second systems of seacoast defense, what did the impact of the War of 1812 reveal about them? The fortifications built between 1794 and 1812 had been undertaken in the hope that they would deter enemy attack and possible invasion. In 1812 the worst-case-scenario had arrived, namely a conflict with the greatest naval power in the world. Yet, ultimately, only a small number of seacoast fortifications came under fire during the War of 1812—notably Fort Washington on the Potomac, Fort McHenry at Baltimore, Fort Bowyer on the eastern point of Mobile Bay, and Fort St. Philip at Placquemines, guarding the Mississippi about 70 miles below New Orleans—with results ranging from brilliant defense to abject surrender. The strong defenses at Boston, New York, and Charleston were not attacked, and, thus, the most elaborate works of the

First and Second systems were never tested as to their effectiveness. Whether their imposing appearance actually deterred the British from attacking, thus fulfilling a major objective of their design, can only be a matter for speculation. Of the two major fortifications designs of the time, the three Vauban-type works of Fort McHenry, Fort Bowyer, and Fort St. Philip stood up well to bombardment and attack. Unfortunately, those designs that reflected Montalembert's theories were never fired upon by the British (although Castle Williams had stood up nicely to a test-firing by two American frigates, the *President* and the *Essex*, in April 1812). Nonetheless, it was concluded by contemporaries that the casemated multitiered fortifications had achieved their objective of deterrence, and they subsequently became the model for all major fortifications after 1816 during the period of construction known as the Third System.

Notes

[1.] Sidney Forman, "Why the United States Military Academy was Established in 1802," *Military Affairs*, XXIX, 1 (Spring 1965), p. 19.

[2.] Kite, Duportail, p. 265.

[3.] Kite, pp. 268–269.

[4.] Callahan, *Henry Knox*, p. 203.

[5.] Callahan, p. 73. Knox wrote to a congressional committee in 1776 recommending, "An Academy established on a liberal plan . . . where the whole theory and practice of fortifications and gunnery should be taught; to be nearly on the same plan as that of Woolwich." E.D.J. Waugh, *West Point* (New York: The Macmillan Co., 1944), p. 43.

[6.] John C. Hamilton, ed., *The Works of Alexander Hamilton* (New York: Joint Committee of the Library of Congress, 1851), VII, p. 613.

[7.] Arthur P. Wade, "Artillerists and Engineers: The Beginnings of American Seacoast Fortifications, 1794–1815" (Unpublished Ph.D. dissertation, Kansas State University, 1977), pp. 6–7. The author gives a succinct summary of the doleful state of the Army after 1784, tracing the history of the initially understrength First American Regiment, and the slow changes that were stimulated by internal troubles such as Shays Rebellion in Massachusetts, and various Indian incursions. The impact of these events led to the legislation of 1792 that set up "The Legion of the United States" to include infantry, riflemen, dragoons, and artillery.

[8.] Wade, p. 14. During the international crisis with Britain in 1794, and on numerous other occasions after that, Secretary of War Knox discovered, as had been the case during the American Revolution itself, that no native American engineers were qualified for the fortification project Congress had mandated.

[9.] *American State Papers, Military Affairs* (Washington, D. C., 1832–1861), I, pp. 61–63. Hereafter cited as ASP, MA.

[10.] For the diplomatic and political history of this crisis with Great Britain, see Thomas A. Bailey, *A Diplomatic History of the American People* (New York: Appleton-Century-Crofts, 1958), pp. 72–73; and John C. Miller, *The Federalist Era* (New York: Harper & Row, 1960), pp. 140–141.

[11.] See, for example, Robert Arthur, "Coast Forts of Colonial Massachusetts," *Coast Artillery Journal*, Vol. 58, No. 2 (February 1923), p. 105. This historical tendency to "fortify" a harbor and strategic location was evidenced as early as the Pilgrim colony, which erected a "platform" to support its artillery on a convenient hill, shortly after the landing at Plymouth in December 1620. At the other extreme, of course, lay the much more complex colonial fortifications built up during the eighteenth century to guard the important harbors—such as those at Louisbourg, Boston, Newport, New York, and Charleston.

[12.] In 1821, the board of engineers emphasized this continuing tradition of deterrence when it described the function of coastal fortifications as one that would "render an enemy more backward in risking his expeditions, so we shall not only therefore be better able to resist attack, but . . . we shall be less frequently menaced with invasion." *ASP, MA*, II, p. 309.

[13] Emanuel R. Lewis, *Seacoast Fortifications of the United States: An Introductory History* (Annapolis, Leeward Publications Inc., 1979), p. 21.

[14] *ASP, MA*, I, pp. 62–64. The sites listed by Congress in 1794 were as follows: Portland, Maine; Portsmouth, New Hampshire; Cape Ann, Massachusetts; Salem, Massachusetts; Marblehead, Massachusetts; Boston, Massachusetts; Newport, Rhode Island; New London, Connecticut; New York City; Philadelphia, Pennsylvania; Baltimore, Maryland; Norfolk, Virginia; Oracoke Inlet, North Carolina; Wilmington, North Carolina; Charleston, South Carolina; Savannah, Georgia.

The fortifications that were subsequently chosen for construction and/or repair were: Fort Allen (Portland); Fort William and Mary (Portsmouth); Fort Point, Fort William, Fort Sewall, and Castle William (Gloucester, Salem, Marblehead, and Boston respectively); Fort Washington on Goat Island (Newport); Fort Trumbull (New London); Fort Jay on Governors Island, Bedlow's Island, and Oyster (later Ellis) Island, (New York); Fort Mud [later Fort Mifflin] (Philadelphia); Whetstone Fort [later Fort McHenry] (Baltimore); Fort Nelson and Fort Norfolk (Norfolk); Fort Johnston (Wilmington); Fort Johnson (Charleston); and Fort Greene (Savannah). As part of the repairs of New York fortifications, the French engineer Charles Vincent also undertook repairs to forts Putnam and Clinton at West Point.

[15] *Statutes at Large and Treaties of the United States of America, 1789–1873* (Boston: Little, Brown and Co.,1845–1873), I, p. 345. The five other sites included Wilmington, Delaware; Alexandria, Virginia; Georgetown, South Carolina; St. Mary's, Georgia; and Annapolis, Maryland. The amounts appropriated by Congress included $76,000 for construction of fortifications and purchase of land, $96,000 for the purchase of guns and ammunition, and a supplemental appropriation of $30,000 to cover higher than expected costs. Wade, "Artillerists and Engineers," p. 13.

[16] The foreign engineers chosen by Knox to undertake the seacoast fortifications in the following areas were: Etienne Bechet de Rochefontaine (New England); Charles Vincent (New York City); Pierre Charles L'Enfant (Philadelphia and Wilmington, Delaware); John Jacob Ulrich Rivardi (Baltimore and Norfolk); John Vermonnet (Annapolis and Alexandria); Nicholas Francis Martinon (North Carolina); and Paul Hyacinthe Perreault (South Carolina and Georgia). Most of them had served as engineer or artillery officers with either Rochambeau's forces, or in the Continental Army, and had fled to or remained in the United States to escape the turmoil of revolutionary France.

[17] It is interesting that Knox decided not to incorporate these engineers into the military at that time. He wrote to Rochefontaine that "it is explicitly to be understood by you, that the employment is only temporary, and not conferring or involving any military rank whatever." Most likely Knox hoped to ward off the criticism bound to come with the realization that once more, exclusively foreign engineers had to be hired. *ASP, MA*, I, pp. 72–74.

[18] The progress made by these men in designing and repairing the seacoast fortifications assigned to them is traceable only indirectly, since the War Department records were destroyed in a fire in November 1800. Fortunately, the congressional copies were preserved, including two excellent reports prepared by Knox just before he left office at the end of 1794.

[19] *ASP, MA*, I, pp. 75–76. The guns available at this time, from 6-pounders to 24-pounders—designated by the weight of their solid shot—were considered too light for coastal defense. Part of the fortification project of the "First System" was to arrange the casting of larger guns, especially 36-pounders, at private foundries as soon as possible. Because iron was plentiful and of good quality, it replaced brass (actually what was later known as "bronze") as the standard for heavy seacoast cannon in America. By 1801 an inspector of artillery had been designated, with the task of certifying all cannon cast for public use and dealing with all the foundries involved with production of cannon for the military. See Wade, "Artillerists and Engineers," p. 11–12.

[20] *ASP, MA*, I, p. 77.

[21] *ASP, MA*, I, pp. 71–72.

[22] *ASP, MA*, I, p. 74.

[23] *ASP, MA*, I, p. 120.

[24] For the political and diplomatic background of the crisis with France, see William Stinchcombe, *The XYZ Affair* (Connecticut: Greenwood Press, 1980), pp. 3–11; and Alexander De Conde, *The Quasi-War: The Politics and Diplomacy of the Undeclared War with France, 1797–1801* (New York: Scribner, 1966), pp. 3–17.

[25] Wade, "Artillerists and Engineers," pp. 88–95.

[26] Robinson, *American Forts*, p. 67.

27. Harold I. Lessem and George C. Mackenzie, *Fort McHenry* (Washington, D. C.: U. S. National Park Service; 1950), pp. 1–4.

28. Robinson, *American Forts*, p. 71.

29. Wade, "Artillerists and Engineers," p. 32. Henry Burbeck, the most qualified American and a good field artillerist, lacked the degree of engineering skill required for the position.

30. Wade, pp. 33–35. Little is known about Rivardi's background, beyond the fact that he appeared to be a Swiss who had served in Russia, and who had probably simply emigrated to America. At some point he came to the attention of Henry Knox who offered him an appointment as temporary engineer in 1794. For an account of the career of Louis de Tousard, see N.B. Wilkinson, "The Forgotten 'Founder' of West Point," *Military Affairs*, XXIV, (Winter, 1960–1961), pp. 177–188. Louis de Tousard was not an engineer, but rather a former artillery officer who had been recruited to join the Continental Army by the Franklin-Deane mission to France in 1777. Caught up in the various intrigues of the French Revolution in Santo Domingo in 1792, Tousard was able to escape imprisonment and settle in Delaware with his family, where he too came to the attention of Henry Knox in 1794.

31. Pickering to the U. S. Congress, February 3, 1796. *ASP, MA*, I, p. 113.

32. Richard C. Knopf, ed., *Anthony Wayne, A Name in Arms* (Pittsburgh: University of Pittsburgh Press, 1960), p. 429. This letter of June 27, 1795, from Pickering to Wayne referred quite bluntly to the Frenchmen as "foreign officers," while at the same time pointing out the need to employ them: "You expressed your wish in a former letter that the artillerists from the seaports should be marched to reinforce your army, but it had been previously thought necessary to collect them together at West Point that both officers and men might be instructed: for both being generally perfect strangers to the service, and their detached situations having prevented their acquiring under new officers any knowledge of discipline, without such instruction they could be of little use. The Instruction they will now receive from the foreign officers, whose education have been wholly military, will, it is expected, fit them for any service. . . . The whole will therefore be assembled at West Point, where a part are already arrived."

33. Wade, "Artillerists and Engineers," p. 43.

34. Wade, pp. 48–54.

35. Wade, p. 115.

36. Wade, p. 68. To add to this dismal litany, Rochefontaine was also dismissed from the Army on May 7, 1798, after a series of enquiries about alleged financial irregularities on his part. In fact, Rochefontaine was probably correct when he wrote Secretary Pickering in April 1798, "I conceive that the Executive of the U. States must wish that I had never been appointed to the command of this Corps. Nothing could surmount the jealousy, ill will and stupid animosity of some, and it is in general very difficult to impress upon the generality, the idea that a man born upon another hemisphere can be qualified to step forth and command over them." Wade, p. 77.

37. Henry Cabot Lodge, *Works of Alexander Hamilton* (New York: G. P. Putnam's Sons, 1904), VII, pp. 179–180.

38. In 1799, he wrote to Secretary McHenry about an offer he had made to Count Rumford (Benjamin Thompson), a royalist expatriate from Massachusetts, to head a proposed military academy in America, but Rumford apparently declined. See Wade, "Artillerists and Engineers," p. 116.

39. Charles Francis Adams, *The Works of John Adams* (Boston: Little, Brown and Co., 1853), IX, pp. 65–66.

40. The term "service cadet" was used about 1802–1805 to distinguish those serving with companies from the "academy cadets" who were appointed to West Point for actual instruction. The first service cadet to become an academy cadet was Joseph Gardner Swift. Swift had already served as a junior officer under Tousard at Fort Wolcott, and then with a company that was completing the construction of Fort Adams.

41. Wade, "Artillerists and Engineers," p. 113.

42. Wade, p. 119.

43. Wade, p. 121.

44. Ironically, while working at Fort Mifflin in 1798, Tousard had submitted a well-thought-out plan for a military academy to Secretary McHenry, recommending a complete course in the basic sciences, practical field instruction, a well-trained faculty, and rigid discipline. Wilkinson," The Forgotten 'Founder' of West Point," pp. 177–180. However, Tousard's being French-born no doubt worked against him. In a letter to Decius Wadsworth on June 21, 1803, Dearborn, for one, described the organization of a military academy in 1802 as the means by which "we may avoid the unpleasant necessity of employing

Foreigners as Engineers." Lewis, *Seacoast Fortifications*, p. 25.

[45.] Wade, "Artillerists and Engineers," p. 124.

[46.] Act of March 16, 1802, *Statutes at Large and Treaties of the United States of America*, 1789–1873 , II, p. 132.

[47.] The later careers of these men, after their varied service in America, were also interesting. Rivardi died apparently in Martinique in 1808, while Tousard briefly served in Santo Domingo until his return to France. In 1805, he was appointed to the French consulate in New Orleans, and ultimately became the French vice-consul in Philadelphia. During these years, Tousard finished the work he had begun at George Washington's behest in 1795, the two volumes of *The American Artillerist's Companion*, which included plates drawn by his own hand—a book that was adopted as a text book at the U. S. Military Academy in 1816, and became generally very popular during the nineteenth century. Tousard died in France in 1817 at the age of 68. See Wilkinson, "The Forgotten 'Founder' of West Point," *passim*.

[48.] Because it had no troops, and such a small number of officers and cadets, the Corps of Engineers was soon thought of by the rest of the Army as a unit of technical specialists, tolerated as long as its relationship to line officers remained remote. That Williams relished the independent status of the Corps is revealed by his effort to provide a special dress uniform for his officers, with an entirely different system of designating their rank from the rest of the Army. Secretary Dearborn tartly instructed that their epaulettes remain the same as the rest of the officer corps.

[49.] Stephen E. Ambrose, *Duty, Honor, Country: A History of West Point* (Baltimore: John Hopkins Press, 1966), pp. 25–27. In 1803, Francis de Masson, an immigrant from Santo Domingo, joined the faculty to teach French and military art. The only two military titles apparently available as text books were Vauban's *Traité de fortifications*, and H. O. Scheel's *Treatise of Artillery*, translated by Jonathan Williams. It is interesting that Dransy, however, declined his appointment. Despite seven years of service and a great deal of experience acquired helping Tousard with the fortifications at Newport, he probably felt that foreign-born officers might suffer short-lived careers in the future.

[50.] Class of 1802, *Register of Graduates and Former Cadets of the United States Military Academy*, 1802–1980 (Chicago: R. H. Donnelly and Sons Co., 1980). Swift would become chief engineer within ten years, but his skills were not really attributable to the education he received at West Point; in fact, he had gotten an eminently practical training in fortification engineering under the tutelage of Louis de Tousard and Peter Dransy at the difficult works at Narragansett Bay.

[51.] William A. Ganoe, "Joseph Gilbert Totten," *Dictionary of American Biography* (New York: Scribner's & Sons, 1936), XVIII, pp. 598–599.

[52.] In January 1804, Captain Jared Mansfield was appointed as surveyor general of the Northwest Territory by President Jefferson, but he was allowed to retain his commission in the Corps of Engineers and be eligible for promotion as if he were on duty with the Corps. While this decision guaranteed the retention of Mansfield's services, it also meant that there would be a permanently unfillable vacancy in the Engineers. When an ailing Second Lieutenant Simon Levy was given permission to convalesce in Georgia, Second Lieutenant Samuel Gates of the Artillerists, who had graduated in 1804, was allowed to replace him at West Point as a sort of combination post-graduate student and instructor. See Wade, "Artillerists and Engineers," pp.169–170.

[53.] Wade, pp. 171–172. Wadsworth had made a career out of being dissatisfied during his assignments, particularly during 1796 when Rochefontaine had presided over the disastrous effort to get an academy going at West Point; and despite the fact that he was in charge this time, Wadsworth's attitude probably was responsible for so much insubordination that he felt he had to convene a series of courts-martial and complain to Dearborn that the whole Military Academy be moved elsewhere.

[54.] James D. Richardson, *A Compilation of the Messages and Papers of the Presidents*, 1789–1902 (Washington D.C., U. S. Government Printing Office, 1905), pp. 383–384.

[55.] *ASP, MA*, I, pp. 192–6.

[56.] Jonathan Williams, "Report of the Superintendent of the U.S. Military Academy, 1810," in George W. Cullum, *Biographical Register of the Officers and Graduates of the United States Military Academy* (Boston: Houghton, Mifflin & Co., 1891), III, pp. 549–550.

[57.] See Sidney Forman, "The United States Military Philosophical Society, 1803–1813, *William and Mary Quarterly*, 3d. Ser., II, 3 (July 1945); and the Society's record in print, *Extracts from the Minutes of Stated and Occasional Meetings*, U.S.M.A. Library, West Point. The three major meetings reported most comprehensively are those of October 6, 1806, at West Point; January 30, 1808, in Washington, D. C; and December 28, 1809, in New York. By 1812, the Society listed among its members some of the most distinguished names in the American military, the government, and the scientific community. Unfortunately, the Society did not survive the disruption of the War of 1812.

[58.] Historians suspect that Montalembert's ideas were directly introduced to America by Jonathan Williams. Williams had been an American commercial agent in the 1770s at Nantes, the heavily fortified coastal city near the Ile d'Oléron where Montalembert had worked as governor. It is not known if he met Montalembert in person, but as a relative of Benjamin Franklin he certainly travelled in the right social circles to merit an introduction. In any case, at least 10 volumes of *La Fortification Perpendiculaire*, the only set in America, were in the library of the United States Military Philosophical Society prior to 1806. Forman, "The United States Military Philosophical Society," p. 282.

[59.] Lewis, *Seacoast Fortifications*, p. 28. Another innovation in the design of fortifications during the Second System that should be mentioned is the Martello tower, named after a small round tower in the Bay of Martello, Corsica, that, in 1794, beat off with a single gun the British warships *Fortitude* and *Juno*, which boasted 106 guns between them. This one incident led to the conclusion that a well-mounted and protected battery on land had an advantage over shipboard guns that were constantly moving. As a result, Martello towers were built at several points along the American seaboard during the War of 1812, implicitly running counter to Montalembert's theory of massed, heavy gunfire.

[60.] *The Debates and Proceedings in the Congress of the United States. . . . 1789–1824*, (Washington: Gales and Seaton, 1834–1856), XV, (10th Congress, 1st Sess.), pp. 992–994. Short title: *Annals of Congress*. The debates over the committee report on the status of seacoast fortifications were lively, with a great many members of Congress arguing that fortifications and gunboats would be expensive and perhaps useless against the British Navy and an invasion.

[61.] Promoted to colonel, Jonathan Williams; to lieutenant colonel, the still-absent Jared Mansfield; to major, Alexander Macomb and Joseph G. Swift; to captain, George Bomford, William McRee, and Charles Gratiot; to first lieutenant, Eleazer D. Wood, William Partridge, and Prentiss Willard. At the same time Joseph G. Totten, who had resigned in 1806 to join his uncle, Jared Mansfield, as surveyor, was reappointed a second lieutenant, along with three cadets, including Sylvanus Thayer. Alden Partridge remained a senior first lieutenant.

[62.] Wade, "Artillerists and Engineers," pp. 212–213.

[63.] Jefferson's recommendations are in *ASP, MA*, I, pp. 228–230. A committee of the House in 1834 described its counterpart that received these proposals to improve the Military Academy in 1808 as "identified with republican principles," and, as such, hostile to what they perceived as Federalist in origin. *ASP, MA*, V, p. 348.

[64.] Joseph G. Swift, *The Memoirs of Gen. Joseph Gardner Swift, U.S.A.* (Worcester, Mass: F. S. Blanchard & Co., 1890), p. 77. Wrote Swift, "I received from the War Department several plans of a species of Star Fort, contrived at Washington, too small for any flank defense, and too complicated for a mere battery, unsuited to the positions for which they had been devised. . . . I presume these plans to have emanated from some Revolutionary worthy near the War Department—probably Col. Burbeck. Evidently they were adopted in preference to the plans of us young officers who had given our opinion in favor of a more appropriate form and extent."

[65.] *ASP, MA*, I, pp. 296–297.

[66.] Act of 29 April 1812, *Statutes at Large*, II, p. 720.

[67.] Wade, "Artillerists and Engineers," p. 281.

[68.] Wade, p. 281.

[69.] Wade, p. 282. Captain George Armistead of the Artillerists, who was one of the signatories of the letter of protest, could have pointed out, for example, that he was still a captain after 13 years' service, while Joseph G. Swift of the Engineers was a lieutenant colonel after less than 10.

[70.] *Annals of Congress*, XV (9th Cong.), pp. 1246–1247.

[71.] Williams was almost immediately appointed a brigadier general in the New York militia, and set to work as a consulting engineer for the state fortifications being built at the Narrows. When they were complete and turned over to the Federal government, Williams returned home to Philadelphia. There he ran for Congress in 1814, but died in May 1815 at age 64.

[72.] *Register of Graduates*, USMA, pp. 207–209.

[73.] Ensign George Ronan, class of 1811, was the first West Pointer to die in battle, killed while fighting an overwhelming force of Indians and British at Fort Chicago. Alexander J. Williams, son of Jonathan Williams, died on the ramparts of Fort Erie; Lieutenant William Partridge was well-remembered for breaking his sword and flinging it at his commander, Hull, in protest over the latter's surrender to Brock at Detroit. Even then ill with fever, Partridge died several weeks later as a prisoner. As for some of the engineers mentioned so far, Swift was brevetted to brigadier general in early 1814 for meritorious service; Major Bomford was brevetted to lieutenant colonel for meritorious service at the end of 1814, and promoted to lieutenant colonel of ordnance at the end of the war. Major McRee was brevetted twice, to lieutenant colonel for gallant conduct at Niagara, and to colonel for his role in the defense of Fort Erie. Captain Wood was brevetted twice, and eventually killed leading a sortie from Fort Erie in 1814. Captain Totten was brevetted to major and lieutenant colonel for his services at Fort George and Plattsburgh, while Captain Sylvanus Thayer was brevetted to major for his services in the defense of Norfolk in 1814. Waugh, *West Point*, pp. 54–55; and Wade, "Artillerists and Engineers," p. 285.

The Golden Age of Fortification in America | *5*

Introduction

Although it appeared on the surface that the pressures of the War of 1812 had created a chaotic and draining situation at the U. S. Military Academy at West Point (in July 1812 there was only one cadet in attendance, and Alden Partridge was the only officer), in the long term the War, in fact, provided an impetus that rapidly carried West Point beyond its original design as an adjunct to the Corps of Engineers. The change arising from the expansion of the Army on the eve of war in 1812 was of great importance. It increased the authorization of the number of cadets to 250, and stated that they were no longer required to be attached to particular companies of the staff or line. At the same time, it created the framework of the organizational changes upon which others could build.

Moreover, as the war with Britain sputtered to an end in 1815, significant changes with respect to the future of the Military Academy occurred. First, President Madison separated West Point from the Corps of Engineers and made the position of superintendent full time and permanent. The chief of the Corps of Engineers now became inspector of the U. S. Military Academy, and served as the link between the superintendent and the secretary of war. For General Joseph G. Swift this change meant freedom to devote himself to engineer projects and issues without the encumbrance of having to constantly interrupt his duties with the problems of the Military Academy. He was quite content to have Partridge take up the official position of superintendent, since the latter, for all intents and purposes, had been in charge at the Academy since 1812.[1] For West Point, these changes meant sufficient organizational reforms had taken place to enable an energetic and progressive superintendent to radically alter and energize the Academy, if the opportunity arose and the will were there. Second, another event occurred that was to have a great deal of significance for the Military Academy: the dispatch of Major Sylvanus Thayer (1785–1887) to Europe to advance his military education and indulge his intellectual curiosity. It was fortuitous that Thayer asked Swift for permission to take a leave of absence to visit Europe for his "professional improvement" just as President Madison and Secretary of War James Monroe concluded that more information on

European military education and engineering would be useful in revitalizing the Military Academy. They were, in fact, pondering the question of whether West Point should be merely a training school for Army engineers, or a school for educating officers in the military profession on the European model.[2] Thayer so impressed Secretary Monroe that he decided to give him and the man who would accompany him, the brilliant engineer Lieutenant Colonel William McRee, an official commission:

> In consideration of the advantages which the United States may derive from the increased experience and scientific improvements of its officers, the President is pleased to afford you an opportunity for professional improvement.
>
> You will proceed to the Continent and prosecute inquiries and examination, calculated for your improvement in the military art. The military Schools and work-shops and arsenals, the canals and harbors, the fortifications, especially those for maritime defense, will claim your particular attention. You will be provided with funds for the collection of such books, maps and instruments for the Military Academy as may hereafter be directed by the War Department or the commander of the corps of engineers.[3]

The coming together of these two strands—the reforms to tighten up and reorganize the structure of the Military Academy, and the appearance of an intelligent and disciplined educator who would eventually become superintendent—were to have far-reaching implications for the curriculum of West Point, and, indirectly, for the future of all military engineering in America.

In the years that followed, up to the outbreak of the Civil War, the U. S. Military Academy and its graduates who filled the ranks of the Corps of Engineers were able to achieve, in a splendid fashion, the goal that had so long evaded the preceding generation. A cadre of trained and competent military engineers was not only able to build elaborate fortifications under what came to be known as the Third System (1812–1860), but was also able to undertake engineering projects that admirably served the developing nation. Successfully entrusted to the Corps and the Academy's graduates in the decades after 1815 were projects such as the construction of roads, bridges, canals, and railroads; the improvement of harbors; and the surveying and exploration of the territories. In fact, the General Survey Act passed by Congress in 1824 specifically authorized the President to use officers from the Army to make surveys for roads and canals considered of national importance. Indeed, the civil engineering curriculum at West Point, well organized, greatly expanded, and coherently taught, became the model for the nation and for civilian schools.[4]

The part of the military engineering curriculum that dealt with the art and science of fortification, however, remained entirely unique to West Point. Fortification engineers—except for a few rare imports—were invariably graduates of the Military Academy's curriculum and instruction. Without their services, the United States would have had virtually no defense policy with respect to its own shores. The building of forts, whether land-based or coastal as defined under the Third System, remained the basic cornerstone of America's defense up to the Civil War. This period represented the golden age of fortification in America, one during which West Point taught the theory, and the Corps of Engineers provided the concrete results.

In addition to the development of a successful curriculum at West Point, a stable balance appeared to have been achieved technologically between offensive and defensive weaponry during these years, making the building of forts seem both useful and functional for American defense. Ironically, these productive years also represented the last great period of innovative fortification, since beneath the surface scientific changes were stirring that would ultimately render the great fortresses obsolete. Still, while it lasted, the Third System produced the most elaborate and, historically, most interesting forts of American history. In every way, it fulfilled all the hopes of the previous generation.

The Role of the United States Military Academy in Fortification Theory and Practice

The dispatch of Sylvanus Thayer and William McRee to France represented a significant moment for the future of the United States Military Academy. Long fascinated by the career of Napoleon Bonaparte and French military traditions, Thayer was intensely keen to visit France, especially since Bonaparte had escaped from Elba just before Thayer's departure for France in June 1815. Much of Thayer's engineering education had come from French sources, and he was extremely interested in studying the institutions and techniques that had made French military art and science so formidable. Thayer, pictured in Figure 5.1, and McRee managed to spend two years abroad despite, as he wrote to Swift, "insurmountable obstacles to the pursuit of the principal objects of our tour." With Paris under Allied occupation (to Thayer's intense disappointment, his ship docked after the battle of Waterloo), many of the schools they had come to inspect were closed, many of the fortifications inaccessible, and at all times they were short of money:

> France is in every respect a conquered country & rigourously so treated. The Military Schools are suspended & their buildings occupied as Barracks. The Allies possess all the depots, arsenals & military workshops which have not been destroyed & occupy all the fortresses not in a state of siege or blockade. . . . Our money affairs are by no means flourishing altho we received at Flushing our advanced pay up to the 1st July 1816- Our expenses whether traveling or stationary far exceed all our previous calculations & a stranger cannot avoid being cheated let him be so vigilant. . . . We have not been able to find a single practical treatise on permanent fortifications other than the Science of Engineers of which there has been published a new edition. . . .[5]

Yet, despite all these problems, Thayer and McRee assiduously turned their trip into a successful mission. They studied the structure of the Ecole Polytechnique, the new training ground of the French corps of engineers, and met members of the faculty, most notably Claude Crozet whom Thayer would later recommend as a professor of engineering at West Point, and

Figure 5.1   Sylvanus Thayer (1785–1887). *Courtesy of the West Point Museum Collections, USMA, West Point, N.Y.*

Simon Bernard, who would eventually join the United States Corps of Engineers (the last foreign appointee to ruffle the feathers of the American engineers). They also purchased hundreds of texts, maps, charts, and technical treatises for future use at West Point, reporting to Swift:

> You will find in the collection several works of which we have procured, ten or a dozen copies. They are properly textbooks, of which a copy, should be in the possession of each officer of the Corps . . . besides two copies to remain in the library. . . . A number of works have doubtless, been purchased, that are to be found in the library. . . . In several instances, however, we conceived, one or more copies to be necessary, in addition to the one, that is at the Academy.- Such as Vauban & Bousinard; - or Belidor, in the case of a later or improved edition.[6]

After a great deal of effort and string-pulling, they were given permission to visit the School of Application for Engineers and Artillery at Metz. Afterward they attempted to reconstruct the courses as taught there for the U. S. Military Academy curriculum. Despite Commissioner Albert Gallatin's efforts on their behalf, Thayer and McRee were denied permission to inspect the fortresses of Metz, Brest, Cherbourg, and Lille, but they did manage to study the relief plans of all four in Les Invalides. In essence, Thayer absorbed what he considered most brilliant about the French traditions of military engineering, fortification, and education, and actively attempted to transfer them to the U. S. Military Academy once he was appointed superintendent in 1817, shortly after his return.

The events that led to the dismissal of Alden Partridge from the superintendence of the Military Academy and to his eventual court-martial are well known.[7] On July 17, 1817, Thayer received orders to assume the superintendence of the U. S. Military Academy. The challenge he faced was enormous, since the controversy and rancor generated by Partridge had exposed West Point and all its weaknesses to the general public, not to mention the fact that Partridge devoted the rest of his life to vilifying the place. However, since Thayer did not hold the office as the chief of engineers, as had Williams and Swift, he could devote all his attention to West Point; and during his tenure as superintendent from 1817 until 1825, he was supported fully by Secretary of War John C. Calhoun.

An able administrator and strict disciplinarian, Thayer established a sense of structure and order at the U. S. Military Academy. Most of his reforms were basically attempts to establish a viable curriculum and a workable administrative structure that could properly train and graduate the cadets in his charge.[8] His admiration for the French approach of a prescribed curriculum, with a heavy emphasis on science, was adapted as efficiently as possible to the curriculum already in existence at the Military Academy. The texts adopted during the 1820s at West Point, thanks to a stocking of the library with the purchases from the Thayer-McRee trip, reveal his respect for the French traditions. These included *Traité de la science de la guerre et de la fortification des places* by Guy de Vernon (translated for the Academy by Captain John M. O'Connor); Hachette's *Traité des machines*; Lacroix's *Traité du Calcul différentiel et intégral* and his *Eléments d'algèbre*; Biot's *Essai de géometrie analytique*; and Francoeur's *Traité de mécanique*.[9] Since it was obvious that cadets would need instruction in French, Thayer was delighted to find Claudius Bérard, a man who had translated his own texts for use in his courses, already on the faculty. The addition of Claude Crozet as professor of engineering in 1816 also produced translations of his two treatises on mathematics, and translations of engineering texts for later use at West Point.[10]

Two innovations among all Thayer's changes were perhaps most closely modeled on what he had observed and admired at the Ecole Polytechnique. Thayer established the Academic Board "under the presidency of the Superintendent, whose duty it should be to fix and improve the system of studies and instruction, to conduct and decide upon all examinations, and to specify in detail the duties of the several instructors." He also instituted the subdivision of classes into small sections to be graded daily on the basis of cadets' recitations. Thayer perceived the Academic Board as equivalent to the Conseil de Perfectionnement of the Ecole Polytechnique, established to supervise and improve the system of instruction, and any alterations in the curriculum and examinations.[11] The institution of small sections of cadets allowed Thayer and the faculty to keep abreast of the progress of each cadet and shift students from section to section according to their standing. This provided an even more disciplined sense of order in the curriculum, but it forced Thayer to make up for a formal lack of instructors by employing brilliant cadets as assistant professors when possible. Such an individual was Dennis Hart Mahan (1802–1871), who was appointed to the Military Academy in 1820. (See Figure 5.2.) His aptitude in mathematics captured Thayer's attention, and in his second year he was appointed assistant professor of mathematics, grappling with his own studies all the while. Mahan graduated first in his class in 1824, and Thayer kept him at West Point as principal assistant professor of engineering.

When Calhoun left the War Department in 1825, Thayer lost his valuable ally in Washington at a time of rising antimilitary and anti-West-Point feeling. Soon his insistence on enforcing the regulations governing the conduct of cadets without regard to partisan politics created a conflict with the Jackson Administration. After a long-drawn-out struggle over the dismissal of a cadet with powerful political connections, Thayer resigned in the summer of 1833.[12] Known as "the father of the U. S. Military Academy," Thayer and his general contributions to West Point have been detailed brilliantly by historians. His legacy to the history of military fortification, though, lay in the invaluable material he amassed from France, in the work he did to regularize the military engineering curriculum, and in the standards he set for the graduates who entered the Corps of Engineers.

Dennis Hart Mahan's effect upon the curriculum and history of West Point was as profound, perhaps, as Thayer's, if for no other reason than the length of his tenure at West Point—41 years from 1830 to 1871, during one of the most formative periods in the history of the United States Army. At the Military Academy, he formulated and taught the important subjects of civil engineering, military fortifications, and the science of war. His influence upon the engineers who went out to design and construct the fortifications

Figure 5.2   Dennis Hart Mahan (1802–1871).

of the Third System prior to the Civil War was widespread.[13] Frail and diffident as a cadet, Mahan's poor health persisted even after graduation and influenced Thayer to send him to Europe to rest, regain his health, and study. Mahan's inclinations toward engineering, military science, and fortification theory reinforced his own partiality to French traditions and Napoleonic history, and built an enthusiasm in him to spend his time in France. His trip was given official approval by Chief Engineer Alexander Macomb in 1826, and a letter authorizing his leave suggested some specific goals:

> Your request for a furlough and permission to travel in Europe . . . was granted unconditionally. But as you express a desire to be employed while in Europe if your services can . . . be made useful. The knowledge you acquired during your professorship in the Military Academy on the subject of engineering has sufficiently qualified you for procuring . . . information that may be highly important and valuable to this country. . . . It is desired that while in Europe . . . you will avail yourself of such opportunities as may be presented for acquiring by personal observation as well as through inquiries any information concerning roads, canals, bridges, the improvement of rivers and harbors, construction, labor-saving machinery, etc., which would be new to this country and of sufficient importance to render an acquisition desirable. . . . [14]

Travelling and honing his skills in France, Mahan extended his period of study to four years. During that time, although enjoying Parisian society and the friendship of Lafayette, Mahan reported to the chief engineer on canal construction, on bridges, on the process for curing wood used in naval construction, on foundries, and on concrete (*béton*) construction then practically unknown in America. Investigating the Saint-Etienne, France's railroad line, he discovered that French engineers had solved the problem of centrifugal force on curves by elevating the outer rail.[15] He made drawings of the new system of artillery carriages, and managed to investigate both the Ecole des Mines and the Ecole des Ponts et Chaussés. At this point in his investigations and reports, Mahan clearly reflected his own interests in the growing national goal of developing American resources by means of civil engineering. Later he would construct a solid curriculum in civil engineering at the U. S. Military Academy.

Nonetheless, he also began a painstaking study of the French system of educating officers—first in the theory of military art and science (as at the Ecole Polytechnique and St. Cyr), and then by attendance at schools of application (as at Metz for engineers and artillerymen, and Saumur for the cavalry). Aware that the French defeat in 1815 had forced a reassessment of military tactics, theory, and education in that country, Mahan proposed in his reports to Macomb that adopting a similar system of career military schools in January 1829 in America would be more than useful.[16] Amazingly, Mahan managed to get himself enrolled in the School of Application for Engineers and Artillery at Metz, where he remained for 16 months. Since many of the courses taught at the French schools were never permitted to appear in print, but were reproduced for the students' use by lithography, Mahan took voluminous notes, and before leaving Europe, procured a lithographic press for the Military Academy. For many years his own lectures would be turned out by lithography.

In 1832, Mahan was formally appointed professor of civil and military engineering and of the art of war, clearing the way for him to implement all that he had learned and assimilated in his studies so far. With respect to Mahan's teaching of the art of permanent fortification, the next four decades of his career were vital. During that time he attempted to impart to innumerable cadets the theories of fortification as they had developed over the centuries, and, when possible, to study the impact of technology upon them. The engineers he trained were those who would apply the theories they had learned at West Point to fortifications around the nation, and in some cases actually devise them. He was aware that he was teaching beginners in the study of fortification, describing his course in 1855 "as that little summary which we have time to teach here."[17] (Ironically, a twentieth-century student finds himself in exactly the same position as a cadet beginning in Mahan's course, confronting new terminology, a plethora of theory, and a great deal of geometry—a situation that renders Mahan's texts still valid.)

His first text on the subject was straightforward. After distinguishing between permanent and field fortifications, and defining the purpose of fortifications in general, Mahan introduced the technical vocabulary used in the design of a fortification—that is, the parts of a work such as the enceinte, the glacis, the scarp, the ditch, and the covered way—and elaborated on the historical systems of masters such as Vauban, Coromontaigne, Coehoorn, Carnot, and Montalembert.[18] A detailed description of a modernized, bastioned fortification—the design of which was known as the Noizet system after the professor who taught it at Metz—followed. By employing this specific example, Mahan hoped to produce a comprehensive and practical analysis of the problems encountered in building fortifications, forcing the students "to apply both the elementary principles of fortification and the geometrical methods that the engineer has to use as his principal tool" when designing a work.[19] As a result, a considerable amount of drawing and sketching was incorporated into his course (see Figure 5.3 on page 154).[20]

Mahan's teaching of the history and principles of permanent fortification to successive cadets and engineers was intended to convey the technical information required, and to describe the great practitioners of the art to date. He did, however, warn about too slavish an adherence to systems, "a too bigotted deference to authority and adherence to old ways," and argued that "to adhere rigorously to any elementary system is not only wrong, but, when this is done through national prejudice, it is puerile and absurd."[21] He hoped that American military engineers would choose the best and most adaptable of the European systems for their interests and therefore, chose not to teach the design of a specific American seacoast fortification as if it were a definitive style.

In time, his texts began to incorporate the changes in weaponry created by the growing range of siege artillery. Even before the Civil War, Mahan was aware of the likely impact of the new heavy caliber rifled artillery on masonry fortifications:

> The fragility of masonry, and the ease with which it can be ruined by distant batteries of heavy calibre, particularly when pierced with embrasures and loopholes, like the casemated caponnières and defensive barracks of the German system, must naturally incline engineers to limit its employment as much as possible, reserving its use for positions where it will not be subject to this exposure, or where

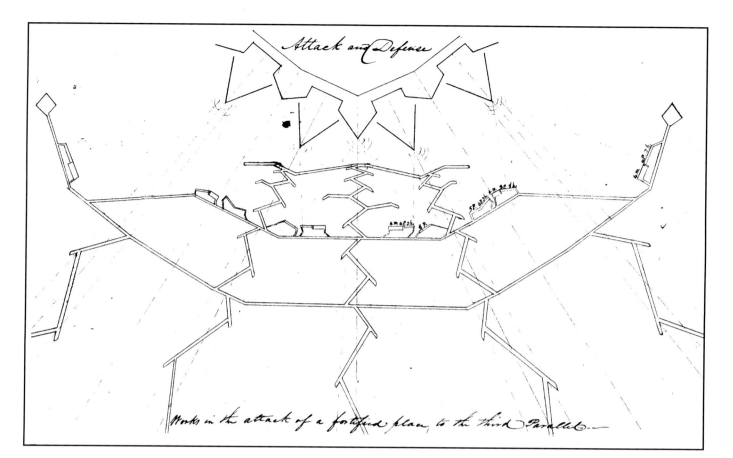

Figure 5.3   Extracts of the sort of drawing and work on fortification required by Mahan from his students. From the papers of George Lewis Welcker (1811–58). USMA 1836. *USMA Library, West Point, N.Y.*

it can be covered with an earthen mask that nothing may be appre-
hended from the besieger's heavy guns.[22]

In Mahan's opinion, works based on Montalembert's design would be completely at risk. The modernized bastioned trace, however, produced flanking
fire behind earthen parapets that absorbed the fire of heavy artillery, and
Mahan felt that the value of this design element of a fortification continued
to hold true, pointing to the events of the Crimean War as proof:

> There is nothing new in this capacity of earthen parapets. . . to with-
> stand for a long period, with such repairs as the besieged can find
> opportunity at night to give them, the effects of heavy artillery. So
> far from it, that it has been a well-settled maxim of engineering,
> from the time of Vauban, to cover all masonry by earthen masks,
> leaving the earthen parapets alone exposed to the enemy's guns.[23]

Modern siege artillery could, of course, damage the embrasures of the fortification, exposed by necessity since the defensive guns had to shoot from
them. Mahan suggested that iron casings around the embrasures might solve
the problem, but was concerned whether the iron could be made thick enough,
or whether the cost would be too exorbitant. Mahan had begun to ponder
seriously the impact of modern weaponry on fortifications, as revealed by a
letter he wrote to Joseph G. Swift in 1855. He reviewed the problems of how
to protect a fortification's artillery, given the new range of siege guns.
Conversely, he discussed the offensive capabilities bestowed on the fortress's
garrison by the rifled musket. By utilizing the Minié ball, the defender could
pick off sappers 600 to 1,000 yards away, thus continuing to maintain a balance between the defensive and the offensive forces. Mahan concluded that
the basic principles of permanent fortification still remained the same: works
must be strong enough to resist open assault and scaling; they must be protected by flanking fire; they must have bombproof shelters to protect the
guns and the garrison; and they must have secure and efficient routes of
communication both inside and outside the fort.[24]

Over the years Mahan did not escape criticism of the way he taught his
courses on permanent and field fortification.[25] However, his approach to the
question of the role of fortification in the development of national defense
policy, as generally revealed by the relevant chapters of his texts, seemed
quite sensible for his time. Fortifications, historically speaking, allowed the
state options on how to best utilize its forces in the most economical way,
both in a passive and offensive sense. For a nation like the United States with
a history of hostility toward large standing-armies, fortifications, both inland
as well as on the seacoast, were a particular necessity and the only option.
A combination of permanent works, mobile land forces, temporary fortifications, and floating batteries, chosen with a specific objective in mind, would
provide a deterrent force against invasion that could best serve the American
situation. In some seacoast situations, Montalembert towers, despite Mahan's
fear for their masonry design, could be acceptable; elsewhere, the tried and
true Vauban design using earth would serve better. During the Civil War,
Mahan was able to note with detail the effects of the new weaponry, especially with respect to his own teaching. He studied the mining and siege operations at Vicksburg and Petersburg, and wrote about the reduction of Fort
Wagner near Charleston with respect to the theories of siegecraft.[26]

Did the war drastically change Mahan's theories about permanent fortification? Events convinced him more than ever that the German (i.e., Montalembert) system that relied on casemated towers would shatter under the long range, accuracy, and penetrating power of the new artillery. Indeed, events during the Civil War were to confirm his opinions. Although Mahan argued that iron linings in the embrasures in floating batteries might help counter the new guns, he was aware that more long-term solutions such as new permanent fortifications to protect cities or arsenals would be considered too costly. Therefore, more reliance on field fortifications would be the answer, especially given the range and accuracy of small arms.[27] One study of Mahan has concluded that this last realization on the part of the professor about the increased importance of entrenched field fortifications "looked forward to operations of the type which became normal in W.W. I."[28]

Dennis Hart Mahan's death on September 16, 1871, ended an era at West Point. It marked, in a sense, the approach of a new era of technological change that would put an end to the entire subject that he had labored for so long to explain and to teach to his students and audiences. Nevertheless, his contributions to the military art of his time were significant and widespread. With respect to the history of fortifications, Mahan played an instrumental role in devising the most coherent, scientific, influential, and famous curriculum in America to teach the art and science of permanent fortification to a generation of American engineers and soldiers.

The Third System, 1815–1860

Most of the defenses constructed during the Second System were essentially complete by the outbreak of war in 1812. By 1815, practically every seaport of any importance in the United States had at least one or two fortifications that combined the features of the First and Second systems of defense.[29] Built, as has been noted, under the urgency of international crises and threats of war, many of these works were the results of short-lived, hasty designs intended to meet an emergency. In dramatic contrast, the fortifications of the next era—the so-called Third System—were built, beginning in 1817, for close to a half-century, and proceeded coherently and methodically from a program that elevated them to a position of the foremost importance in national defense. Indeed, the burning of Washington, D. C., by the British in 1812 had been traumatic. It reinforced the concept of deterrence that underlay all previous decisions to concentrate on seacoast defenses.

From the beginning, the more methodical nature of the Third System was apparent. Congress began by authorizing a special board of officers to create a third, "permanent," and comprehensive system of fortifications under a long-term program that continued until the Civil War.[30] This board was given the mandate to decide on the priority of fortification sites, to determine the designs, to dispatch the engineers to various works, and to supervise the construction. It represented a significant development in the history of fortifications in America: for the first time, a competent authority had been established to oversee virtually all forms of military fortifications from beginning to end. Such a specific group, despite changes in its composition or titles, remained in existence until the beginning of W.W. II.

The board designated to oversee future fortifications convened in late 1816 amidst controversy, because a French military engineer, Simon Bernard, with the rank of brigadier general, had been appointed to head it. Given the long-standing current of hostility toward foreign engineers, Bernard's appointment was tantamount to waving a red flag before some of the engineer-officers. Despite the fact that Bernard was well qualified, having served as a brigadier general under Napoleon and having been recommended by Lafayette, criticism of his appointment was immediate and angry. Major Christopher Van Deventer, aide-de-camp to Joseph G. Swift, wrote a letter to Thayer and McRee, then in France. In it he described the opposition to Bernard, and discussed Swift's threatened resignation over the issue:

> Herewith you will receive a copy of a letter from the Department of War deciding the postponement of any new and important Fortification until the arrival from France of a distinguished Engineer who shall revise and alter the plans already approved by the Government. . . . The letter from the War Department contains views and principles insulting to the General Swift and ruinous to the Corps he commands. . . . I need say but little to expose the evils to the service and the wrongs to Engineer Officers which will flow from the system of withdrawing confidence from American talent and exposing it exclusively in the presumption of adventurers. Nor need I detain you to portray injuries, such a course will inflict on the Mil'y reputation of our Academy and particularly on those who have sprung from that institution.[31]

Although in Europe at the time, Thayer wrote Swift counselling against hasty action and praising Bernard:

> Major Van Deventer intimated that you intended to resign. Such an event would, I fear, be an irretrievable blow to the prospects of the Corps. . . . If resignation becomes necessary it will be as the last resort and should be done by the whole corps in a body. As to General Bernard I believe him a most worthy gentleman, at least his appearance corresponds with his character which is that of a most amiable man and an officer of distinguished talents. I am disposed to believe that his conduct will be extremely concileating & that he will avoid any interference with the Corps. . . .[32]

Nonetheless, the Bernard board—composed of one naval officer and two engineers of the army, Lieutenant Colonel Joseph G. Totten and William McRee—undertook the task assigned to it, and issued its first complete report in February 1821.[33] Unlike the other members of the Bernard board, all of whom left it in the years that followed, Totten remained directly involved with the planning, design, and construction of seacoast fortifications for the 26 years he served as the chief engineer. The Third System was often referred to as the Totten System because of Totten's influence and continuity of service. In the report, 18 defensive works were listed as "of the most urgent necessity," but an additional 32 were projected for future construction under categories of lesser priority. Ultimately, the board drafted a monumental plan of harbor defense of the United States in which nearly 200 separate works were envisioned, guarding practically every harbor on the Atlantic and

Pacific seacoasts by 1850.[34] As was always the case with fortification projects, the board's hoped-for reach far exceeded its grasp (see Figure 5.4). This vast program was never really undertaken, primarily because of the expense involved and official indifference. Appropriations continued to be a problem, and before long, works from the First and Second systems inexorably replaced the projected works of the board's report. Many of the old harbor defenses, repaired and modified, were incorporated into the Third System, along with some detached batteries that were added as extra insurance.[35] These batteries were generally circular, semicircular, or crescent-shaped affairs, boasting as many as 20 or more guns in a row. Some were even more elaborate, with a single tier of casemate emplacements, such as the 40-gun casemated water battery at Fort Monroe.

Compared with the works of the First and Second systems, the principal new forts of the Third System were spectacular harbor defense fortifications, some of which were to play significant roles during the Civil War: for example, Fort Sumter (South Carolina), seen in Figure 5.5; Fort Pulaski (Georgia), seen in Figure 5.6; Fort Monroe (Virginia); Fort Pickens (Florida); and Fort Morgan and Fort Jackson (Louisiana) the latter of which is seen in Figure 5.7. Bernard, who had studied at the Ecole Polytechnique, working in collaboration with Joseph G. Totten and Guillaume Tell Poussin, who had been assigned to the Corps of Engineers as a topographic engineer, contributed to the construction of these forts during this period.[36] The objective of their design was to enable a fort to hold out against a regular siege for at least 10 to 50 days until help could arrive. These forts shared certain elements: durable construction from brick and stone, necessary to support the weight of numerous casemate emplacements; a high concentration of armaments, especially in the larger forts; and a design that specifically emphasized an enormous overall firepower. On the other hand, the forts of the Third System also reflected a great number of variations in individ-

Figure 5.4 Locations of some principal fortifications of the Third System, 1812–1860.

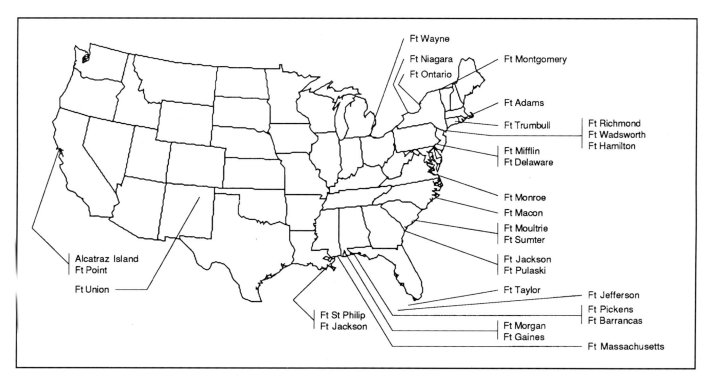

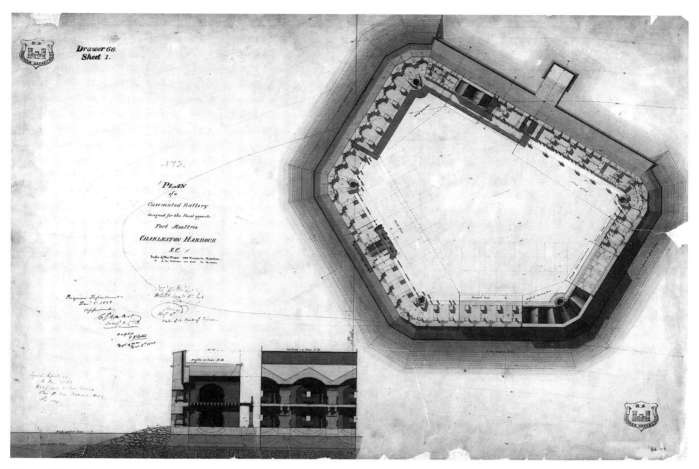

Figure 5.5   Forts of the Third System: Fort Sumter, South Carolina (1829), Simon Bernard and Joseph G. Totten, engineers. Plan and sections (1828). *National Archives, Washington, D.C.*

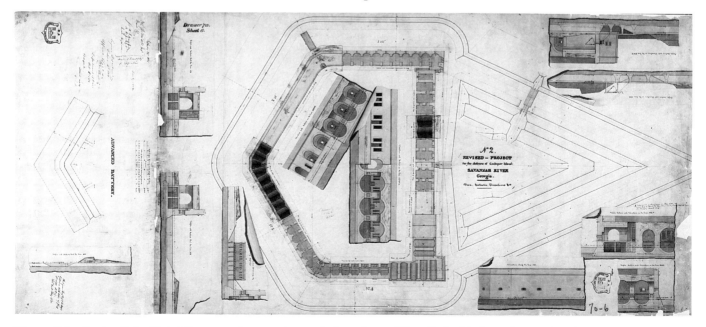

Figure 5.6   Forts of the Third System: plan, section and elevations of Fort Pulaski, Georgia (1829), Simon Bernard and Joseph G. Totten, engineers. *National Archives, Washington, D.C.*

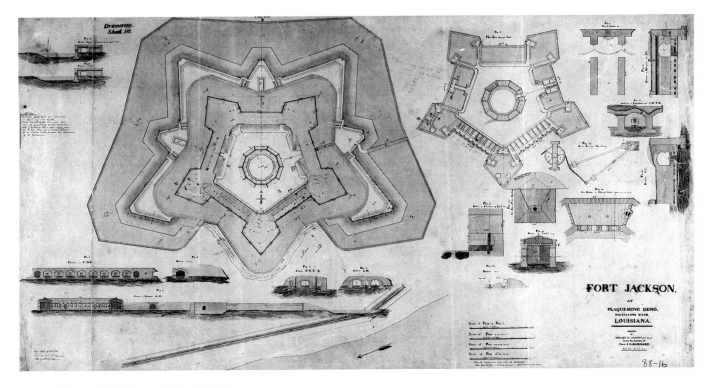

Figure 5.7 Forts of the Third System: Fort Jackson, Louisiana (1822), Simon Bernard, engineer. Plan, section and details drawn by Henry L. Smith. *National Archives, Washington D.C.*

ual design due to the different factors that came into play during construction. These included the topography of the site, the sort of area it was designed to protect, the year in which it was built, and the state of weapons technology when it was erected. Fort Monroe, for example, designed by Bernard, was an irregular hexagon with larger bastions at each salient and an additional bastion on the long southern front (see Figure 5.8). Fort Adams, near Newport, principally designed by Joseph G. Totten, displayed an irregular and prominently bastioned trace, with a single casemate tier, except along the face fronting the main channel where Totten placed an additional level of casemates. (See Figure 5.9.)

As the fortifications of the Third System continued, it became apparent that construction of very large forts was being abandoned for a number of reasons. The expansion of the railroads made it possible to move troops much more rapidly to support a besieged fort. As a result, huge fortifications designed to sustain long sieges were less important. Simultaneously, bastions tended to be reduced in size when the major portion of a fort's artillery was massed on the front with tiers of casemates. Fort Schuyler, begun in 1833 at the eastern entrance to New York harbor, was a good example, featuring three small bastions compared to the much larger ones at Fort Monroe and Fort Adams. Eventually, the general plan most common to the Third System forts, especially after the 1820s, was one based on a regular hexagon. It was often truncated on the landward side, as at Fort Pulaski near Savannah and at Fort Sumter in Charleston harbor. Sumter was designed as a brick fort with a five-sided polygonal trace (in effect, a truncated hexagon) with no bastions and multi-tiers of guns, very much in the style of Montalembert's theories. Fort Pulaski's trace was similar, with a large ravelin and rampart placed to protect the gorge that faced the land-

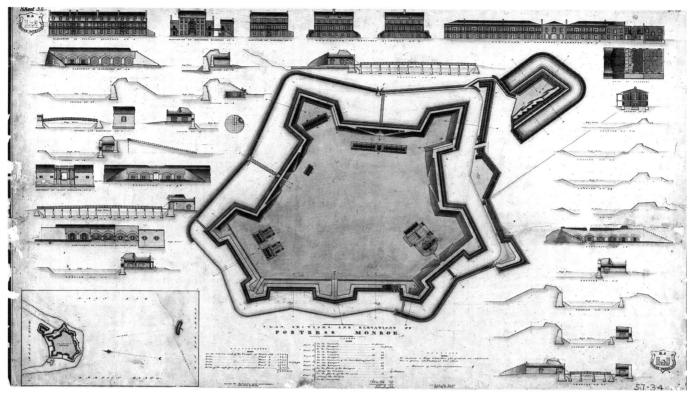

Figure 5.8   Forts of the Third System: Fort Monroe (1819–ca. 1847), Simon Bernard, engineer. Plan and section of fort and elevations of buildings drawn by George Driscoll. *National Archives, Washington D.C.*

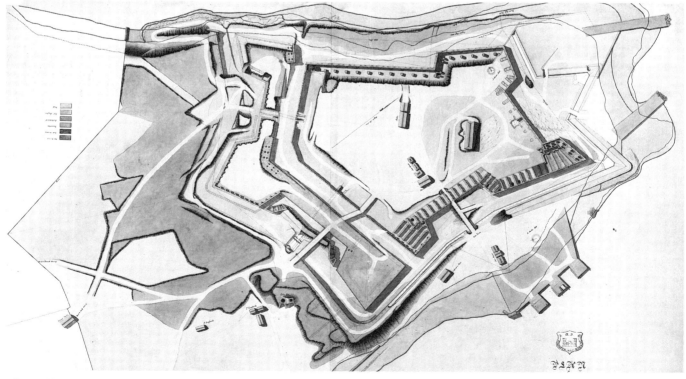

Figure 5.9   Forts of the Third System: Fort Adams, Rhode Island (1824–ca.1845), Simon Bernard and Joseph G. Totten, engineers. Plan of the state of the works on September 30, 1831. *National Archives, Washington, D.C.*

ward side of Cockspur Island, where the fort was located. Separating the ravelin from the main body, and completely surrounding both, was a wide ditch; the water for it was obtained by canal from the river and controlled by sluice gates. However, Fort Pulaski displayed only a single tier of casemates, since it was discovered that the soil on which it stood would not be able to hold the additional weight of more guns.[37]

Despite the depredations that future changes in technology were to bring to the forts of the Third System, and despite the fact that the original all-encompassing scheme of fortification proposed by the various engineer boards was never achieved, the forts of the Third System were significant for several reasons. First, they produced a distinctly American form of military architecture, which followed, on the whole, the precepts that Mahan had attempted to teach his students: understand the theoretical basis of all the best systems of fortifications and then adapt what was useful to the American landscape. Second, these forts were designed to be durable and expensive, and despite the ravages of the Civil War, many remain standing today. Their obsolescence could not have been foreseen, and so their design cannot be criticized from that standpoint. And, finally, although never tested by foreign invasion, they satisfied the nation for at least four decades that their very existence would deter a potential enemy, thus achieving the goal of that most basic policy of national defense in the nineteenth century. As the board of engineers summarized it: "However long it may be before sensible effects are produced, the result will be certain; and should no danger threaten the republic in our own days, future generations may owe the preservation of their country to the precaution of the forefathers. France was at least fifty years in completing her maritime and interior defences; but France on more than one occasion since the reign of Louis XIV has been saved by the fortifications erected by his power, and by the genius of Vauban."[38]

The Impact of the Civil War

The revolution in the technology of armament during the period between 1816 and the Civil War, must be mentioned briefly, primarily because of the effect it was to have on fortifications.[39] At the end of the War of 1812, the heavy cannon deployed in the seacoast fortifications were composed of 500 or so 24- and 32-pounders (see Figure 5.10), plus the few dozen 42- and 50-pounders at Castle Williams, a far cry from what would be required by the designs of the Third System.[40] During Tousard's tenure as inspector of artillery, efforts had been made to cast new cannon at such foundries as were able to produce them, but progress was slow.[41] In 1819, new 24-pounders, the largest cannon called for by the Bernard board in its initial plans, began to be manufactured in quantity. By 1829, the casting of 32-pounders began and, three years later, that of 42-pounders followed. For the moment the guns seemed to be keeping pace with the demands of fortification design.

It was during the years between 1840 and the beginning of the Civil War, as Mahan had noted, that such amazing progress in the technology of new weaponry occurred, both in the United States and abroad. George Bomford

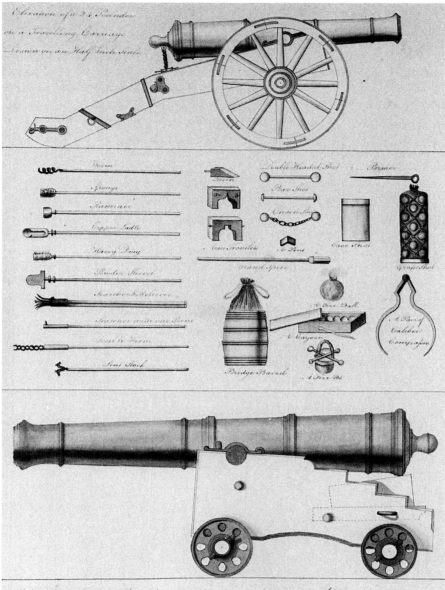

Figure 5.10 Drawings of the 24-pounders generally used in seacoast fortifications during the First and Second systems (Charnock).

and Thomas Rodman of the United States Army, and John Dahlgren of the Navy, made immense strides in the development of cast-iron, smoothbore ordnance. Shortly after 1840, Bomford introduced a versatile new gun of greater size, flexibility, and range than the standard 42- and 32-pounders. Known as "columbiads," these guns were produced in 10- and 8-inch calibers to fire either shot or shell at any angle between 0° and almost 40°. The result of this elevation increase was to triple the maximum range of shore guns, since the 10-inch model could exceed 3 miles, in contrast to the 42-pounder's maximum range of just over a mile. In addition, since they were able to fire both solid and explosive projectiles, they could be used in low-level casemates, in upper level barbette tiers, or in batteries on elevated sites.[42]

Thomas J. Rodman, an Army ordnance officer, made an equally significant contribution in the fields of armament design, metallurgy, and explosives. In the 1850s, he experimented on a new type of gun that, in the final analysis, so lessened the stress on the metal during firing that casting of one-piece iron guns in calibers as large as 15 and even 20 inches became possible. These guns, known as Rodmans, and produced just before the Civil War, were representative of cast-iron, smoothbore ordnance carried to its limit. The 15-inch caliber piece emerged as the most powerful military cannon in the world at that time, and was adopted in 1861 as the new standard seacoast weapon along with the 8- and 10-inch models. More than a thousand Rodman guns were used by the Union forces, not only at the harbors, but in inland forts as well; and after the Civil War, hundreds remained in use well into the 1880s as the primary coast defense armament.[43]

The development that totally revolutionized fortifications and ultimately became the nemesis of the whole art was the appearance of rifled guns. Despite the fact that it had been axiomatic since the fifteenth century that masonry must not be exposed to the battering of siege guns, seacoast fortifications had been regarded as exceptions because it was felt that naval cannon firing from moving vessels could not batter a seacoast fort with enough consistency or force to render it ineffective. Rifled guns, however, changed the situation totally.[44] They could deliver a much larger impact than smoothbores against a given target, and with greater range and accuracy. Robert P. Parrott, an Army ordnance officer, proved that rifled cannon, even the primitive muzzle-loading types of 1861–1865, were capable of accomplishing swiftly what it took smoothbores long, bloody bombardments to achieve—namely, the reduction of vertical walls to rubble. As a result, it was rediscovered that defenses constructed of earth or sand were superior to those of masonry in absorbing the impact of artillery; masonry shattered and ricocheted injurious stone splinters, and eventually became impossible to repair. Sandbags and makeshift earthwork emplacements, often backed by timbers, were used during the war years to defend against the new artillery.

The lessons learned at Fort Sumter and Fort Pulaski (see Figure 5.11) were the most dramatic. Federal artillery that had begun firing on Fort Pulaski on April 10, 1862, breached its thick walls on the second day. The

Figure 5.11 Interior of Fort Pulaski, Georgia, showing method of protecting casemates against artillery with heavy square timbers. *USMA Library, West Point, N.Y.*

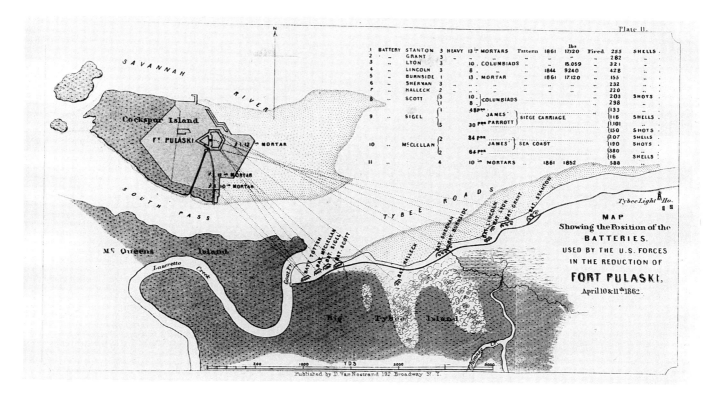

Figure 5.12 **Map showing the position of batteries used by the U.S. forces in the reduction of Fort Pulaski, April 10 and 11, 1862.** *USMA Library, West Point, N.Y.*

breach was effected by light James and Parrott rifles, assisted by 8 to 10-inch columbiads.[45] The destruction that had formerly taken many days to accomplish after siege batteries were set up took less than two days from a distance nearly twice the effective range of light smoothbores (see Figure 5.12).[46] It was an ironic development. Rifled cannon, which had been met with great skepticism by the military establishment, had in one stroke virtually made obsolete all the forts of the Third System. In fact, fortifications based on theory that had taken centuries to develop no longer appeared adequate. The effect of the rifled cannon on the architecture of forts in North America was to be as revolutionary as the invention of smoothbore cannon in the fifteenth century in Europe. Nevertheless, it would be some time after the Civil War before this fact was completely comprehended.

Despite the devastating impact of the rifled cannon, the siege of Fort Sumter provided some new concepts of defense in 1863, and, thus, slightly clouded the overall picture. Union batteries of rifled cannon were set up on Morris Island, well out of range of Fort Sumter's guns. In August, the Union rifles ostensibly reduced the fort to an island of brick debris in less than a week (see Figure 5.13). However, working at night, the Confederates essentially created an earthwork by covering the remaining casemates with mounds of heavy timbers, sandbags, and earth until the rifled cannon fire could no longer penetrate the soft masses of debris and earth. Sumter's evacuation in 1865 came as a consequence of Sherman's march through South Carolina, not because of Union artillery.

The impact of the Civil War—that is, the first use of new and powerful artillery—took time to be assimilated. The first conclusions drawn about fortifications were simple and obvious. A foreign engineer, Viktor E. K. R. von Scheliha, who served with the Confederate Army at Mobile, enumerated a

Figure 5.13   Appearance of Fort Sumter on Sunday afternoon, August 23, 1863. *USMA Library, West Point, N.Y.*

few conclusions about seacoast defense in a treatise he wrote on his wartime experiences: "First, exposed masonry is incapable of withstanding the fire of modern artillery; second, earth, especially sand-works, properly constructed, [is] better protection against modern artillery than the permanent fortifications built on the old plan; and third, no forts now built can keep out a large fleet unless the channel is obstructed."[47] In the years that followed, efforts were made to develop stronger fortifications through modification of old theories, and with innovations from the material at hand. Heavy rifles mounted on disappearing carriages, a system of submarine mines, and batteries of rapid-fire guns of small caliber to protect mined areas—all guarded by massive works of reinforced concrete—were physically incorporated into forts of the permanent system. However, the raw truth was that despite all these efforts, military architecture for defense was for the first time in history unable to keep pace with weapon design and technology. The old balance between the offensive and the defensive had, at last, been irretrievably broken.

Notes

[1.] Ambrose, *Duty, Honor, Country*, pp. 43–44. For further accounts of the events after 1812 that led to the court-martial of Partridge and the appointment of Thayer as superintendent, see also the appropriate chapters in Marcus Cunliffe, *Soldiers & Civilians: The Martial Spirit in America, 1775–1865* (Boston: Little, Brown & Co., 1968); Thomas J. Fleming, *West Point: The Men and Times of the United States Military Academy* (New York: William Morrow & Co., 1969); and Ernest R. DuPuy, *Men Of West Point: The First 150 Years of the United States Military Academy* (New York: William Sloane Associates, 1951).

[2.] Edgar Denton, III, "The Formative Years of the United States Military Academy, 1775–1833" (unpublished Ph.D. dissertation, Syracuse University, 1964), p. 10.

[3.] R. Ernest DuPuy, "West Point and Polytechnique," *Revue Historique de l'Armée*, Special Issue, 1957: *Fraternité d'armes franco-américaine*, p. 153.

[4.] Daniel Hovey Calhoun, *The American Civil Engineer* (Cambridge, Mass.: Technology Press, 1960), p. 45. After his dismissal from West Point, Alden Partridge went on in

1820 to found at Norwich, Vermont, the American Literary, Scientific, and Military Academy, devising his own engineering curriculum in the process. In 1824, Rensselaer Polytechnic Institute was also founded to teach civil engineering, but for many years West Point engineers continued to dominate the field. By 1831 the description of the civil branch of the course on engineering and the science of war at the U. S. Military Academy read as follows:

> Civil Engineering, viz.: the properties, preparation and use of materials; elementary parts of buildings; composition and distribution of buildings; art of construction; decorative architecture; manner of laying out and constructing roads; discussion of the different kinds of stone, iron, and wooden bridges, with the methods of construction; consideration of the obstacles impeding the navigation of rivers, and their remedies; details of the various constructions of a canal; survey, location, and construction of a canal; calculation of the economy of canal transportation; different kinds of railroads; survey, location, and construction of a line of railway; economy of transportation on railroads; construction of artificial and improvement of natural harbors. Calhoun, p. 41.

[5.] Thayer to Swift, October 10, 1815, *Thayer Papers*, 1808–1872, II, U. S. Military Academy Library, U.S.M.A, West Point.

[6.] McRee to Swift, December 18, 1816, *Thayer Papers*.

[7.] Ambrose, *Duty, Honor, Country*, pp. 55–61.

[8.] For an account of Thayer's administrative and intellectual innovations, see James L. Morrison, Jr., *"The Best School in the World": West Point, the Pre-Civil War Years, 1833–1866* (Ohio: Kent State University Press, 1986), pp. 3–4.

[9.] R. Ernest DuPuy, *Sylvanus Thayer, Father of Technology in the United States* (West Point: Association of Graduates, USMA, 1958), p. 2.

[10.] DuPuy, *Sylvanus Thayer*, pp. 4–6.

[11.] Denton, "The Formative Years of the United States Military Academy," p. 185.

[12.] For an account of these events, see Cunliffe, *Soldiers and Civilians*, pp. 261–262.

[13.] Thomas E. Griess, "Dennis Hart Mahan: West Point Professor and Advocate of Military Professionalism, 1830–1871," (unpublished Ph.D. dissertation, Duke University, 1968), p. 274. Years later, at an enquiry about Mahan's course of instruction and methods of teaching, various officers provided testimonials to Mahan's influence upon them. George McClellan stated that Mahan's course was better than any of those in the European schools he had visited, while another officer claimed that Mahan's texts were invariably used at all fortifications with which he had come into contact.

[14.] DuPuy, "West Point and Polytechnique," pp. 156–157.

[15.] Griess, "Dennis Hart Mahan," p. 123.

[16.] Griess, p. 126.

[17.] Mahan to Swift, February 17, 1855, in Dennis H. Mahan Papers, MSS Collections, U. S. Military Academy Library, USMA, West Point.

[18.] This general description of Mahan's course is taken from the following texts: D. H. Mahan, *Summary of the Course of Permanent Fortification*, (Lithographed at the U. S. Military Academy Press, 1850); the lithographed "Notes Supplementary to the Course on Permanent Fortification," in *Notes on Engineering*, 1840–1842; *An Elementary Course of Permanent Fortification*, 1863, a text prepared between 1857 and 1850; *An Elementary Course of Military Engineering*, Part II, 1867, which was essentially the same except for some comments on the American Civil War. (All of these texts were revised and edited over the years by various West Point professors of engineering, and different versions were issued by commercial publishing firms for general consumption.) Also, "Fortification-Land Defences-Profiles," *Army and Navy Journal*, I, (November 14, 1863); and "Systems of Fortification," *ibid*., I, (January 2, 1864).

[19.] Mahan, *Permanent Fortification*, 1863, p. 102.

[20.] One example of the complexity Mahan's course often required is the assignment entitled "Memoir on the Plan of the Front of Fortification in Horizontal Ground with Dry Ditches," prepared by Cadet Jacob Bailey (USMA 1832). The assignment ran to 12 pages and 28 sketches. Griess, "Dennis Hart Mahan," p. 262.

[21.] "Systems of Fortification," *Army and Navy Journal*, I, (January 2, 1864), p. 293.

[22.] Mahan, *Permanent Fortification*, 1863, p. 202.

[23.] "The Past, Present, and Future of Fortification," *Army and Navy Journal*, I, (December 26, 1863), p. 276.

[24.] Mahan to Swift, February 17, 1855, in Dennis H. Mahan Papers, USMA Library, West Point.

25. For an account of the events that occurred in 1857 when one of Mahan's assistants from 1855–1857, James St. Clair Morton, precipitated a series of incidents that involved then-President of the Board of Visitors William H. Chase, and Secretary of War Floyd, as well as Mahan, see Griess, "Dennis Hart Mahan," pp. 268–281. To summarize briefly: as abiding critics of Mahan's course of study and approach to permanent fortification, and fancying themselves experts in the field, Morton and Chase managed to have printed in an underhanded manner a report critical of Mahan's methods in the official board report for that year. The controversy that followed ended in a court of enquiry in 1858 (with Robert E. Lee as president), which met to consider the sufficiency and competence of Mahan's curriculum and methods.

26. Mahan, "Siege Operations against Fort Wagner," *Army and Navy Journal*, I, (October 24, 1863), p. 130.

27. Mahan, *Permanent Fortifications*, pp. 175–176; "The Past, Present, and Future of Fortification," *Army and Navy Journal*, I, (December 26, 1863), p. 276.

28. Griess, "Dennis Hart Mahan," p. 286.

29. Lewis, *Seacoast Fortifications*, pp. 139–141, has an appendix that most usefully lists every locality fortified under one or more of the Three Systems of fortification.

30. *ASP, MA*, II, p. 305.

31. Christopher Van Deventer to Thayer and McRee, June 4, 1816, *Thayer Papers*, I.

32. Thayer to Swift, August 12, 1816, *Thayer Papers*, I.

33. *ASP, MA*, II, pp. 308–310; p. 311.

34. Joseph G. Totten, *Report of the Chief Engineer on the Subject of National Defences* (Washington: A. B. Hamilton, 1851), pp. 86–89.

35. About two dozen of the old forts were directly repaired and included in the Third System. *ASP, MA*, II, pp. 310–312; III, pp. 257–260; Totten, *Report*, pp. 92–95.

36. Poussin arrived in the United States in 1814, and in 1816 worked under Benjamin Henry Latrobe as an inspector of art, sculpture, and decoration in Washington. Early in 1817 he was appointed to the Corps of Engineers with a rank of captain, and was associated with Simon Bernard for about 15 years.

37. Lewis, *Seacoast Fortifications*, p. 53.

38. *ASP, MA*, II, p. 308.

39. J. Leander Bishop, *A History of American Manufactures from 1608 to 1860* (3 vols. orig. published in 1868, reprinted, New York: Augustus M. Kelley, 1966), III, p. 98.

40. *ASP, MA*, 1, p. 821; II, p. 338 and p. 511.

41. Wade, "Artillerists and Engineers," pp. 232–233.

42. William E. Birkhimer, *Historical Sketch of the Organization Administration, Materiel and Tactics of the Artillery, United States Army* (Washington: Chapman,1884), p. 283.

43. Lewis, *Seacoast Fortifications*, p. 65.

44. "Rifling" was the spiral grooving of a weapon's bore to give a stabilizing spin to its projectiles; it had long been used to the advantage of small arms, but its application to cannon was not brought to a workable level until just before the Civil War.

45. Quincy A. Gillmore, *Official Report to the United States Engineer Department, on the Siege and Reduction of Fort Pulaski, Georgia, February, March and April, 1862* (New York: D. Van Nostrand, 1862). U. S. Engineer Department, Papers on Practical Engineering, No. 8, pp. 35–36.

46. Even Gillmore, who directed the siege, was amazed at the power of the rifles: "Had we possessed our present knowledge of their power, previous to the bombardment of Fort Pulaski, the eight weeks of laborious preparation for its reduction, could have been curtailed to one week, as heavy mortars and columbiads would have been omitted from the armament of the batteries as unsuitable for breaching at long range." *Official Report*, p. 51.

47. Viktor E. K. R. von Scheliha, *A Treatise on Coast Defence: Based on the Experience Gained by Officers of the Corps of Engineers of the Army of the Confederate States. . . .* (London: E. & F. N. Spon, 1868), p.15.

Conclusion 6

In the twentieth century, we have become so accustomed—some might say inured—to rapid change and obsolescence that the swift turnover of new technologies and discoveries creates barely a ripple in the public's awareness. It is an age of acceleration, one in which we have adapted to the world's being transformed even as we dwell in it. Nonetheless, despite this familiarity with the impact of change in modern times, one still confronts with considerable surprise the penultimate fact about permanent fortifications: an entire body of knowledge, namely the art and science of fortification, well over 400 years in the making, has been almost totally relegated to historical oblivion.

Centuries of studies, represented by formal treatises, manuals, dictionaries, atlases, and drawings—both theoretical and practical—have disappeared from common knowledge. An entire living discipline, once considered a fundamental part of a gentleman's education and of the military engineering curriculum, has been relegated to esoterica in libraries, referred to only by historians and military buffs. To be sure, many of the great fortresses that the art and science of fortification gave birth to remain as visible guardians over the cities, frontiers, rivers, and harbors they were constructed to protect. But they are now generally museum pieces, historical anachronisms of the twentieth century that have been restored so that visitors might acquire some grasp of the time, skill, and energy that went into designing them. How did this situation come about? What forces brought to an end the art and science of fortification as practiced since the fifteenth century?

Ironically, the fortification historian Christopher Duffy has maintained, "What is remarkable in the history of permanent fortification was not that it was changed so much by rifled artillery in the twenty years after 1860, but that it *changed so little* over the eight preceding generations. The masters of the early seventeenth century would have found nothing essentially unfamiliar with the enceinte of ninety-four bastioned forts that was cast about Paris in the 1840s or in the arguments that General Noizet put forward in his *Principes de Fortification* of 1859."[1] The explanation for both the long tenure of fortification and for its quick demise lay in its vulnerability to the impact of one specific historical factor: the balance between the defensive and the offensive with respect to fortress design and weapons technology. The history of fortification seesawed between innovations in weaponry and the military engineer's responses to those changes. As long as a workable balance between the tools available to a defender and to a besieger was maintained, the purpose behind designing and building a fortress remained valid. Perhaps the best image symbolizing this historical situation is that of a scale, one side representing the offense and the other, the defense. The objective of the practitioners of fortification was to keep the scale balanced toward the defensive, by rendering the fortress impregnable if possible; that of the opponents was to tip the balance toward the offensive, so as to achieve the fortress's destruction.

The golden age of fortification began, as has been pointed out, with the creation of a sudden imbalance between the available offensive weaponry and the castles and defensive strongholds that existed up to the fifteenth century. The new and highly mobile siege guns that appeared in Europe in the 1490s swiftly reduced castle walls to debris, and stimulated a new form of defense that aimed to both make use of, and yet counter, the new artillery—namely, the bastioned trace. It featured the innovation of a low, horizontal profile that offered a poor target for cannon shot, and at the same time provided broad platforms for mounting cannon so that the fortress could fire back at prospective besiegers with no element of its walls unprotected. The bastion design represented an excellent passive defense against the new artillery. And, in short order, the imbalance created by the new artillery was further redressed as engineers added various new elements of fortification that were intended to create a defense in depth. These included all those aspects of a fort, developed over the centuries, that were intended to keep an attacker from easily reaching the fortress walls: the covered way, the ramparts, the ditch, the ravelins, the hornworks, the glacis, and so forth.

The response of the military engineer and architect in modifying fortification design to meet the threat of artillery had been so successful by the mid-seventeenth century that the scale had, in fact, tipped slightly to the defensive side. Besiegers had now been placed at a clear disadvantage. The sappers and troops who undertook to dig the forward trenches of this period were routinely flung into bloody breach attacks in the face of the fortress's guns, and were cut down in large numbers. Siege guns had not particularly improved in design since their first appearance, and few scientific works dealt with the efficient emplacement of artillery to guide commanders planning an attack on a fortress. That is why the work of Vauban was so seminal in the seventeenth century. Not only did he ring France with a series of fortresses he had designed in a monumental defensive plan, but even more importantly, he also gathered together in a coherent system all the prevailing theories for besieging a fortification. Ultimately, his efforts more than counterbalanced the advantage fortresses held before his arrival on the scene. Vauban's pattern of zigzag approach and parallel support trenches, his strides in artillery emplacement for maximum efficiency in firepower, and his regularizing of the training of military engineers were exceptionally influential reforms. They gave rise to a firm belief among his contemporaries that a Vauban-style siege could not fail. So significant and successful were his innovations and designs that Vauban's successors, particularly in France, turned them into virtual holy writ, and throughout the next century refused to countenance any other theories if they were critical of his ideas.

Yet, despite individual innovations in design by engineers and military architects such as Cooehorn, Vauban, Carnot, Montalembert, Coromontaigne, and others between the seventeenth and early nineteenth centuries, the scales remained essentially balanced between the offensive and the defensive. Even though sieges were regarded ostensibly as having been reduced to a mechanical system, fortresses were still considered useful for a number of reasons. At a time when the mobility of armies was poor, roads often primitive, and siege trains interminably slow, a competent governor of an adequately prepared fortress garrison could delay an entire campaign by holding up an invading army. Admittedly, new factors that threatened to change this situation were beginning to be discernible. Some commanders, including, most prominently, Napoleon Bonaparte, demonstrated that it was possible to sidestep fortresses, gambling on the speed and movement of the new mass armies to successfully engage the enemy. In some cases entrenched camps were established, although at this stage they were really annexes to existing fortresses, and under their protection, rather than independent fortifications intended to keep the enemy away from the fortress itself. Nevertheless, it was still generally agreed that fortresses had a role to play. Vauban's ring of frontier fortresses was seen as having deterred the allied armies from crushing the French Revolution in its darkest days during the 1790s, a lesson that the Bernard board appropriated for America 30 years or so later.

As far as North America was concerned, the art and science of fortification was transferred in its entirety to the New World, with an emphasis on maintaining the same balance between the offensive and the defensive. Forts, designed on European models, were built under the stimulus of war and international crises to provide a deterrent against territorial inroads by other powers and against invasion. The concepts of fortification were transferred by various expedients to the educated classes of America, and valued for their help in the war for independence. Ultimately, the art and science of fortification was institutionalized at the U. S. Military Academy at West Point, and in the work done by the Corps of Engineers. This was, in fact, an extraordinary transfer of technology from Europe to America. It represented an impressive achievement, accomplished as it was despite the complexities created by a revolution, the building of a new republic, and the struggle to establish the institutions that would be capable of making use of fortification theory. That permanent fortifications, particularly on the seacoast, became and remained the very foundation of American defense policy for many years was of no small significance. Without them, the United States, with its abhorrence of standing armies and initially weak economy, would have been hard pressed to come up with an alternative or with a universally acceptable form of national defense.

It remained for the latter half of the nineteenth century to produce the scientific and social changes that were to spell the end of military fortification. Efficient networks of roads and railroads were developed, as were mobile armies, organized in semi-independent corps that could be moved quickly and separately. No longer could an army so easily be held up by a strategically placed fort. The development of new weapons was paced by the growing ability of nations to mass produce guns and ammunition in factories. Aware that the scales were tipping precariously toward the offensive, military engineers attempted to respond with a variety of modifications to fortification design, if not to theory. In Europe, semidetached works outside the

fortress became common—some so far removed from the principal fortification that they really became independent strong points of defense. As
rifled cannon became more lethal and increased the range of artillery in
general, and as the explosive shell multiplied its destructive effect, fortifications seemed incapable of protecting even the urban areas they had been
designed, in many cases, to guard. Since traditional fortress mechanisms
were no longer able to keep an enemy far enough away to prevent the economy or civilian population of a city from being threatened, defenders were
forced to devise new techniques whereby the enemy could be engaged at a
greater distance. Cities were surrounded with small but heavily armed
forts, strategically spaced so that approaches to urban areas could be sealed
off with tightly interlocking lanes of fire. (In America, coastal fortifications
were seen as providing a similar first line of defense for the populated areas
adjoining them.) General Henri Brialmont, sometimes called the "Belgian
Vauban of the nineteenth century," fortified the cities of Liège, Namur, and
Antwerp in this manner, providing much material for West Point textbooks.
He ringed these cities with heavily armed forts, built mostly underground
of concrete, at two-mile intervals and at an average distance of four miles
from the city.

Military engineers made other efforts to counter the onslaught of offensive power created by new technologies, whose progress appeared unremit-
ting. Some produced designs that called for great masses of iron to line gun
turrets, casemates, and masonry works. Others shifted the emphasis from
the fortification itself to the weapons contained inside it. Heavy guns of up
to 12-inch caliber, large numbers of mortars, and light-caliber rapid-fire
guns that were intended to cover fields of electrically controlled submarine
mines were experimented with in Europe and America. Individual clusters
of separate batteries were installed in strategic positions. Concrete or gran-
ite facings for the gun platforms and ammunition storage rooms were constructed to protect this armament from hostile artillery. It was hoped that
all these modifications would bolster the position of permanent defensive
works. Nonetheless, the long-lived concept of fixed and permanent fortifications continued to erode throughout W.W. I and W.W. II as the balance
shifted inexorably toward the offensive. New developments in weapons and
technology immeasurably speeded up the pace. Scientific discoveries were
appearing so rapidly that military engineers and tacticians were being hard
pressed to keep up with all that they implied. In the end, the airplane most
seriously undermined the theory behind permanent fortifications, until the
appearance of guided missiles dealt a final blow to the defensive theories
that had sustained it. After centuries of dramatic fluctuation, the contest
between the offense and the defense—at least with respect to fixed fortifications—seems to have ended at last. What the future will hold with
respect to this age-old struggle is another matter.

When examining the great remnants of these fortresses, one can only
wonder at the human ingenuity and energy that went into their design and
construction. The vast collection of material galvanized by the historical
contest between the offense and the defense is also staggering in its variety and complexity. It is unfortunate that so much of the richness of the
art of fortification and siegecraft has been rendered so arcane in our day.
Military architecture has been aptly described as the "architecture of defense
. . . characterized by beauty of form resulting from clarity of purpose."[2]

Perhaps this short history, with reference to the collection at West Point, will help revive interest in the art and science of fortification, at the very least for the part it played in the colorful history of the U. S. Military Academy and the nation.

Notes

[1] Duffy, *Fire and Stone*, p. 16.

[2] Robinson, *American Forts*, p. 184.

Glossary

Abatis. An obstacle made by placing cut trees or pointed poles lengthwise at a 45° angle to the ground in front of a defensive position, with sharpened ends pointed toward the enemy.

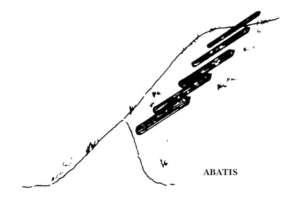

ABATIS

Approach. A trench, at least 10 feet in depth and width, dug toward a fortress. Approaches were intended to shield the besieger from the fortress's fire, and served as communication trenches for the movement of wagons and guns to the more advanced positions.

Banquette. A step or ledge at the base of the parapet of the rampart, of the covered way, or of a trench, from which fortress infantry could fire upon attackers.

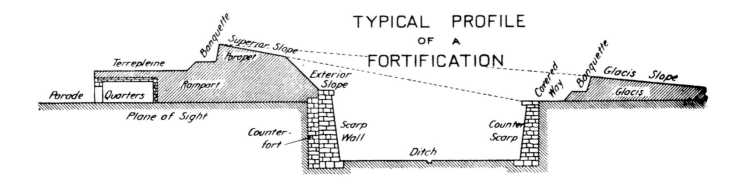

TYPICAL PROFILE OF A FORTIFICATION

Battlement An indented parapet with a series of openings, originally for shooting through, consisting of a regular alternation of merlons and crenels.

A, Merlon; B, Crenel; C, Loophole; D, Machicolation

Battlement. An indented parapet with a series of openings, originally for shooting through, consisting of a regular alternation of merlons and crenels.

Bastion. A four-sided projection from the main rampart in an enceinte of a fortress, consisting of two faces and two flanks.

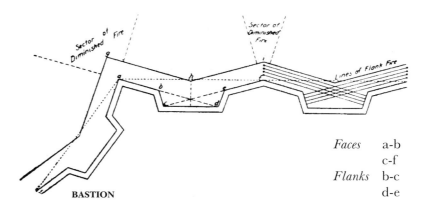

BASTION

Faces a-b
c-f
Flanks b-c
d-e

Berm. The narrow ledge between the ditch and the base of the parapet, designed to prevent earth and debris from falling into the ditch when the parapet was struck by enemy fire.

Bombard. The early artillery piece that fired stones or other projectiles.

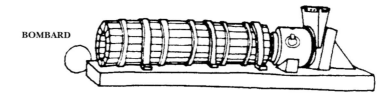

BOMBARD

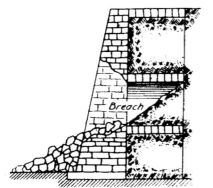

Breach. A hole or gap blown in the rampart or wall of a fortification by cannon fire or mining, wide enough for a body of troops to enter the works of a fortress.

Caponnière.

1. A covered passage from the main wall with rifle ports for muskets, intended to provide communication with the outworks.
2. A strong casemated work of 6- or 7-foot parapets sloping perpendicularly down to the ditch in order to provide additional flanking fire for the ditch.

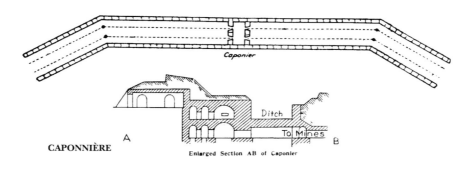

CAPONNIÈRE

Enlarged Section AB of Caponier

Casemate. A bombproof chamber, generally built into the thickness of the ramparts, used as barracks or gun positions. It housed cannons that fired through embrasures in the scarp. Vaulted in permanent fortifications, casemates also appeared in tiers in seacoast defenses of the nineteenth century

Cavalier. A raised work built on the terreplein of a bastion or of a curtain where an artillery battery would be placed.

Chemin de ronde. A narrow passage on top of the scarp wall at the base of the exterior slope of a rampart. Protected by a small parapet, soldiers used this to make their rounds, to observe the glacis at close range, and to defend against attempts at escalade.

Chevaux-de-frise. Defensive obstructions mostly used in field fortifications to check cavalry charges, but also used to close breaches. These were large pieces of timber, 10–12 feet long, into which were driven many long wooden pins tipped with iron points.

CHEVAUX-DE-FRISE

Circumvallation. A line of entrenchments cut by besiegers in the surrounding country to prevent a relieving force's surprising of the besiegers' camp.

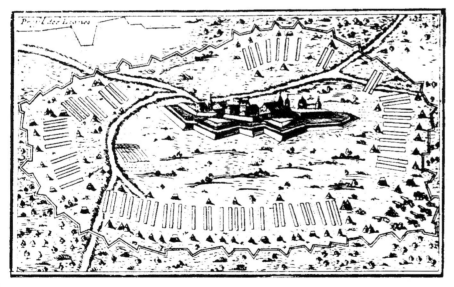

CIRCUMVALLATION

Citadel. A small but strong work of four or five sides, usually within a fortress or town, intended to dominate and protect the town if the main works fell.

Contravallation. A line of entrenchments made at the beginning of a siege facing the fortification that was under attack in order to prevent a sortie or assault from the fortification.

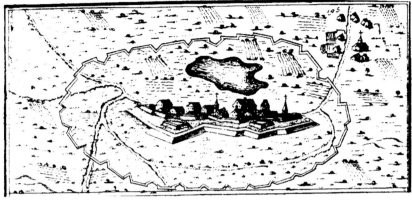

CONTRAVALLATION

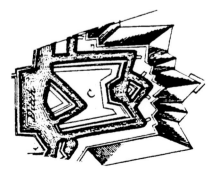

SCARP WALL WITH COUNTERFORT

Counterfort. Interior buttresses built behind scarp walls in order to strengthen them.

Counterscarp. The outer wall or slope of the ditch, the side away from the body of the place. The counterscarp was usually faced with stone or brick to make the besiegers' descent into the ditch more difficult, and might also support the covered way.

Counterscarp gallery. A work situated behind the counterscarp from which the ditch could be enfiladed with reverse fire.

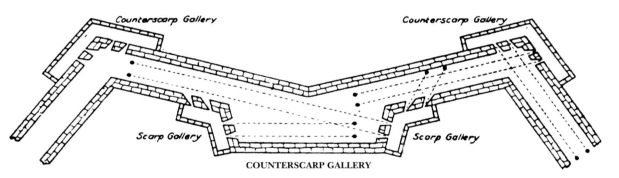

COUNTERSCARP GALLERY

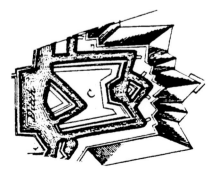

CROWNWORK

Covered way. A broad "road" extending around the counterscarp of the ditch and protected by the parapet from enemy fire, intended to form a "communication" around the place. At its foot was the banquette, used to cover the glacis with musket fire to prevent the enemy from approaching the counterscarp of the ditch. It also functioned as a place of assembly for sorties. Also called the *via coperta*.

Crenellation. Embrasures or gaps in a parapet through which archers or musketeers could fire.

Crownwork. An outwork not unlike a crown, with two fronts and two branches. The fronts were composed of two half-bastions and one whole one, and generally placed in front of the curtain or bastion. They were intended to enclose buildings that could not be brought within the body of the place, to cover the town gates, or to occupy ground that might be advantageous to the enemy.

Curtain. The main wall of a defensive work, lying between two adjacent bastions, towers, or gates.

Cuvette *(cunette)*. A narrow ditch sunk in the bottom of a dry ditch for the purpose of drainage.

Demilune. A work constructed to cover the curtain and shoulders of the bastion. It was composed of two faces forming a salient angle toward the country, had two demigorges formed by the counterscarp, and was surrounded by a ditch. The demilune was sometimes termed a ravelin.

Ditch. A wide, deep trench around a defensive work. The dirt from its excavation was used to form the rampart and parapet, and when it was filled with water, it was known as a wet ditch.

Embrasure. An opening cut through a parapet or wall through which cannon or other guns could be fired. The sides of an embrasure were flared outward to protect the defenders from attacking fire, and to provide a broader sweep or range of fire.

Enceinte. The walls, ramparts, and parapets that formed the main enclosure of a fortification (or castle).

Enfilade. Artillery or musket fire that swept a line of troops or the length of a work from one end to the other. The naval equivalent would be "to rake."

Face (of a bastion). The exposed outer wall between the flanked angle and the shoulder angle; also one of the two sides of the bastion that converged to a salient angle pointing outwards toward the country, and was situated on the line of defense.

Fascine. A long cylindrical bundle of sticks or brush firmly bound together at short, regular intervals, and used in building earthworks and batteries, and in strengthening ramparts. Fascines were also used to fill ditches during a siege or assault on a fortified position.

CONSTRUCTION OF FASCINES

Fausse-braye. A low, outer rampart, usually built of earth, that stood in front of the curtain wall. It provided shelter for troops firing against the besiegers before they entered the ditch. Under bombardment, debris from the wall behind tended to wound its defenders, and by the end of the seventeenth century, its use was largely abandoned by engineers.

Fieldwork. Temporary fortifications constructed in the field.

Flank (of a bastion). The section of the bastion between the face and the curtain, from which the ditch in front of the adjacent curtain and the flank and face of the opposite bastion were defended.

Flèche. See **Redan.**

Fraise (storm poles). Palisades of pointed timbers between the main wall and the ditch or other earthwork, directed horizontally or slightly inclining toward the attackers. The purpose was to hinder an enemy assault, but to avoid providing, at the same time, the sort of protection that an abatis might afford.

Gabion. A cylindrical wicker basket filled with earth and used during sieges to form parapets and so forth in fieldworks.

GABION

Glacis. A gentle (less than 45°) bank, sloping away from the parapet of the covered way. Its purpose was to expose an attacker to fire from the defenders. Since considerable time and labor went into removal of trees and scrub growth, and grading the soil, glacis were normally found only around permanent fortifications.

Gorge. The neck or the open rear part of a bastion or other outwork.

Hornwork. An important outwork made up of a bastioned front—two demibastions and a curtain—and two long sides called branches.

Investment. The process of isolating a fortress at the beginning of a siege by cutting off roads and taking control of all routes around it, so that it could not receive relief.

INVESTMENT

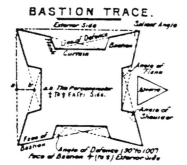

LINE OF DEFENSE

Line of defense. Theoretical line extending from the flanked angle of a bastion along a face to the point of the adjacent bastion. This line of fire determined the position of the face of the bastion relative to the flank that would defend it.

Machicolation. Projecting galleries in the face of a wall from which missiles, molten lead, etc., could be dropped upon attackers at the base of the wall.

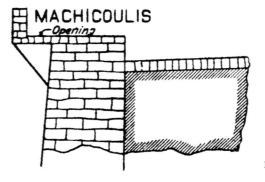

MACHICOLATION

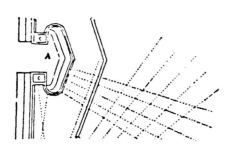

ORILLON

Orillon. A curved projection ("ear") placed at the shoulder of a bastion, designed to cover a retired flank from fire.

Outwork. A work inside the glacis but outside the body of the place.

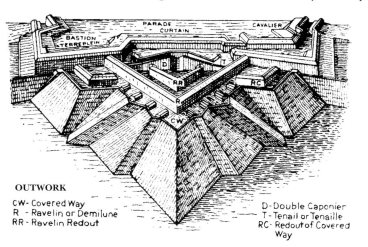

OUTWORK

CW- Covered Way
R - Ravelin or Demilune
RR - Ravelin Redout

D- Double Caponier
T - Tenail or Tenaille
RC- Redout of Covered Way

Parallel trench. A wide and deep trench dug by besiegers parallel to the fortress under attack. From it, zigzag approaches were dug to the next, more forward, parallel as the siege progressed.

Parapet. A wall of earth or masonry on top of the rampart providing protection behind which troops could fire.

Polygonal trace. A fortification design devised by Montalembert consisting of faces forming salient angles (the outward points of a bastion) or re-entering angles (angles pointing toward the interior of a fortification) of small depth, flanked by a powerful caponnière.

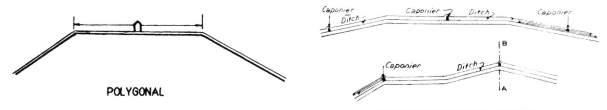

POLYGONAL

TRACES OF POLYGONAL FRONTS

Rampart. A thick wall formed from earth excavated from the ditch to protect the enclosed area from artillery fire and to elevate defenders to a commanding position overlooking the approaches to a fortification. Usually a rampart was capped with a stone or earth parapet. Its presence signified a permanent defense.

Ravelin. A low, V-shaped outwork consisting of two faces that formed a salient angle, the ravelin was placed outside the ditch of a fortification to cover the portion of a wall (i.e. the curtain) between two bastions.

RAVELIN

Redan. A simple V-shaped fieldwork with two faces that formed a salient angle. Usually used in the fortifying of walls where it was not necessary to build bastions, the redan pointed toward the enemy and was open to the rear (basically the same as a flèche).

Re-entering (re-entrant) angle. An angle pointing toward the interior of a fortification.

Redoubt.

1. A small work in a bastion or a ravelin.
2. A small independent outwork, usually an earthwork of square or polygonal shape, with little or no means of flanking defense. Redoubts were used to fortify a hilltop or pass, or any other main avenue of enemy approach.

Re-entering place of arms. A larger space in the covered way, found at the re-entering or salient angles of the covered way, designed for troops to assemble and engage in a sortie.

Relieving arches. Tiers of arches built in the rear of the scarp wall and between the counterforts, intended to make it more difficult for attackers to make breaches in the wall.

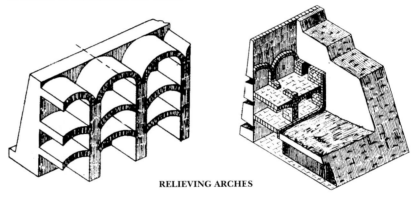

RELIEVING ARCHES

Revetment. A facing of earth, sandbags, or stone built to protect an embankment (for example, the sides of the ditch or parapet) against bomb splinters and so forth.

Ricochet fire. The art of firing cannon so that the missiles dropped over the parapet of a fortification and bounced along its length. The ricochet was intended to wreak havoc among the enemy fortifications and troops as it skipped along the ground.

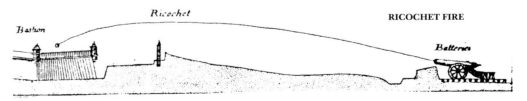

RICOCHET FIRE

Salient. Two lines of works meeting and pointing toward the country, away from the center of fortification.

Salient angle. An angle pointing out toward the field.

Sally port. An opening or underground passage that led from the inner to the outer works. Cut into the glacis, it was a gateway through which a large number of troops could pass when making a sortie.

Sap. A narrow trench cut by besiegers to protect their approaches toward a fortification during a siege.

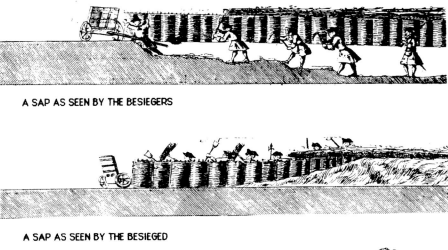

A SAP AS SEEN BY THE BESIEGERS

A SAP AS SEEN BY THE BESIEGED

Scarp. Also "escarp," that is, the part of the facing of a fortification that fronted the exterior, from the bottom of the ditch to the parapet of that wall.

Semi-detached scarp. A scarp wall with loopholes constructed in its upper part so that soldiers could fire into the ditch or across the ditch toward the covered way and the glacis.

SEMI-DETACHED SCARP

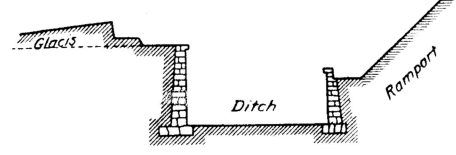

Shoulder angle. The interior angle formed by the meeting of a flank and a face of a bastion. An orillon sometimes supported the shoulder.

Storm poles. See **Fraises.**

Star fort. An enclosed work with a trace made up of a series of salient and re-entering angles.

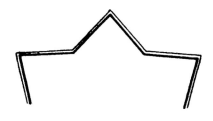

STAR FORT

Tenaille. A small low-lying work, placed in a main ditch between adjoining bastions to provide cover from the curtain wall.

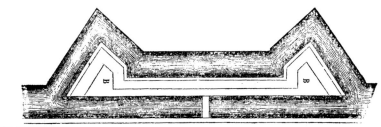

TWO TENAILLES

Tenaille trace. A succession of redans (V-shaped works, open to the rear) joined at right angles to form a front of defense that resembled the teeth of a saw.

TENAILLE

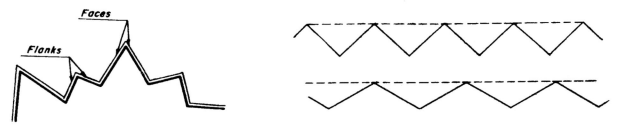

TRACES OF TENAILLE LINES

Terreplein. The top or horizontal surface of the earthen rampart, situated behind the parapet and used as a support for the cannon.

Tour bastionnée. A masonry tower, several stories high, with gun platforms higher than the curtain ramparts.

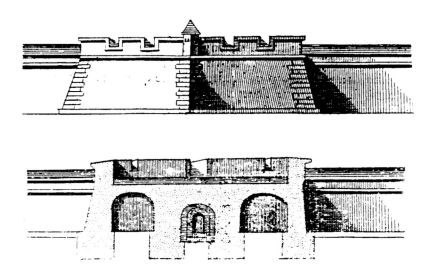

TOUR BASTIONNÈE

Trace. The plan on which fortifications were arranged on the ground.

Traverse. A barrier (earthen bank or wall) constructed across a covered way, a terreplein, etc., to protect troops and guns from enemy flanking fire (enfilade).

Trous de loup. Field fortifications comprised of a series of pits designed to hold pointed stakes projecting from the bottom.

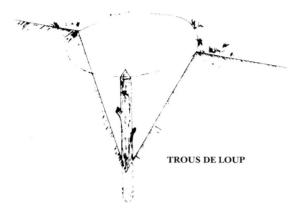

TROUS DE LOUP

Via coperta. See **Covered way.**

A Select Bibliography

One of the most visible effects of nearly four centuries of interest in the art and science of fortification was the flood of literature produced on the subject. Written by both professional military engineers and by enthusiastic amateurs, this literature was aimed at a general audience and took a number of forms: memoirs, treatises, manuals, illustrated manuscripts, histories, dictionaries, encyclopedias, and so forth.

The books selected for this bibliography represent only a portion of the material on fortifications housed by the U. S. Military Academy Library at West Point, but they are among the most seminal and distinguished in the field. Because of the amount of material involved, it has been necessary to omit, for example, most of the works available on ancient fortifications, on modern field fortifications, and on artillery, as well as voluminous maps and manuscripts relating to permanent fortifications in general.

Alghisi, Galasso. *Delle fortificatione* (Venice, 1570).

Allent, Pierre A. *Histoire du Corps impérial du génie* (Paris, 1805).

Almon, John. *A New Military Dictionary* (London, 1760).

Analyse de l'ouvrage intitulé réflexions critiques sur l' art moderne de fortifier (Strasbourg, 1805).

Architecture militaire, ou l'art de fortifier (n.p., 1741).

Augoyat, A. M., ed. *Traité des sièges et de l'attaque des places par le Maréchal de Vauban*, 2 vols. (Paris, 1892).

——. *Aperçu historique sur les fortifications, les ingénieurs et sur le corps du génie en France*, 3 vols. (Paris, 1860–1864).

Bardet de Villeneuve. *Traité de l'attaque et la défense des places* (The Hague, 1742).

Barker, John. *Treasury of Fortification* (London, 1707).

Barnard, John. *The Dangers and Defences of New York* (New York, 1859).

Belair, Alexandre de. *Éléments de fortification* (Paris, 1792).

——. *Éléments de fortification*, 2d. ed. (Paris, 1793).

Belidor, Bernard de. *Le Bombardier français* (Amsterdam,1734).

——. *Oeuvres diverses . . . concernant l'artillerie et le génie* (Amsterdam, 1764).

——. *La Science des ingénieurs* (Paris, 1739).

Bernard, Jean F. *Nouvelle manière de fortifier les places* (Paris, 1689).

Blomfield, Reginald T. *Sebastien le Prestre de Vauban, 1633–1707* (London, 1938).

Blondel, A. *Nouvelle manière de fortifier les places* (Paris, 1683).

Boillot, Joseph. *Artifices de feu, et divers instruments de guerre* (Strasbourg, 1602).

Borgo, Carlo. *Analisi ed esame ragionato dell'arte della fortificazione e difesa delle piazze* (Venice, 1777).

Bousmard, Henri. *Essai général de fortification, et d'attaque et défense des places* (Berlin, 1797).

Brialmont, Alexis. *Études sur la défense des états et sur la fortification*, 3 vols. (Paris, 1863).

——————. *La Fortification à fosses secs*, 2 vols. (Brussels, 1872).

——————. *La Fortification du temps présent* (Brussels, 1885).

——————. *Manuel de fortification de campagne* (Brussels, 1879).

——————. *Traité de fortification polygonale*, 3 vols. (Paris, 1869).

Brioys, Jean. *Nouvelle manière de fortification* (Metz, 1666).

Bubilan. *La Science de la guerre* (Turin, 1744).

Burgoyne, John. *Introduction to the Art of Fortification* (London, 1745).

Busca, Gabriele. *Della espugnatione et difesa delle fortezze* (Turin, 1598).

——————. *Instruttione de bombardiere* (Turin, 1598).

——————. *L'Architettura militare* (Milan, 1619).

Cambray, Chevalier de. *Manière de fortifier* (Amsterdam, 1687). English translations of this volume appeared in two pirated editions entitled: *The New Method of Fortification* (London, 1722).

Capra, Alessandro. *La Nuova architettura militare* (Bologna, 1683).

Carnot, Lazare. *De la défence des places fortes* (Paris, 1812).

——————. *Mémoire sur la fortification primitive* (Paris, 1823).

——————. *A Treatise on the Defence of Fortified Places* (London, 1814).

Cataneo, Pietro. *Dell'arte militare, libri cinque* (Brescia, 1608).

Charnock, John. *Military Architecture*, 2 vols. (n.p., 1800?) MS copy in 2 folio volumes with hand-colored plates.

Chase, William H. *Brief Memoir Explanatory of a New Trace of a Front of Fortification in Place of the Present Bastioned Front* (New Orleans, 1846).

Clarke, George S. *Fortification* (London, 1890).

Coehoorn, Menno. *New Method of Fortification* (London, 1705).

Cormontaigne, Louis de. *Architecture militaire, ou l'art de fortifier* (The Hague, 1741).

——————. *Mémorial pour la fortification permanente passagère* (Paris, 1809).

D'Arçon, C. le Michaud. *Considérations militaires et politiques sur les fortifications* (Paris, 1795).

——————. *Réponse aux mémoires de M. de Montalembert* (Paris, 1790).

De'Marchi, Francesco. *Della architettura militare* (Brescia, 1599).

Deidier, l'Abbé. *Le Parfait ingénieur français* (Paris, 1736).

Deschales, Claude. *L'Art de fortifier, de défendre, et d'attaquer les places* (Paris, 1676).

Desprez de S. Savin, P.S. *Nouvelle école militaire* (Paris, 1735).

Diderot, J. et J. Le Rond d'Alembert. *Encyclopédie: Art militaire* (n.p., n.d.).

Dögen, Matthias. *Architectura militaris moderna* (Amsterdam, 1647).

Douglas, Howard. *Observations on the Motives, Errors and Tendency of M. Carnot's Principles of Defence* (London, 1819).

——————. *Observations on Modern Systems of Fortification* (London, 1859).

Dubreuil, Jean. *L'Art universel des fortifications* (Paris, 1674).

Duffy, Christopher. *Fire and Stone: The Science of Fortress Warfare 1660–1860*

(Newton Abbot, 1975).

————. *Siege Warfare: The Fortress in the Early Modern World 1494–1660* (London, 1979).

————. *The Fortress in the Age of Vauban and Frederick the Great 1660–1789* (London, 1985).

Dürer, Albrecht. *Alberti Dureri pictoris et architecti praestantissimi de vrbivs, arcibvs, castellisque condendis* (Paris, 1535).

————. *Etliche Underricht, zu Befestigung der Stett, Schloss und Flecken* (Nuremberg, 1527).

The Elements of Fortification (Philadelphia, 1801).

The Elements of Fortification, trans. Jonathan Williams (Philadelphia, 1810).

Erlam, J.S. *Outlines of Military Fortification* (London, 1855).

Errard, Jean. *La fortification demonstree et reduicte en art* (Paris, 1620).

Fallois, Joseph. *L'Ecole de la fortification* (Dresden, 1768).

Fer, Nicolas de. *Introduction à la fortification* (Paris, 1723).

Fernandez De Medrano, Sebastian. *El architecto perfecto en el arte militar* (Antwerp, 1708).

Fieberger, G. *Permanent Fortification* (West Point, N. Y., 1916).

Floriani, Pietro. *Difesa et offesa delle piazze* (Venice, 1654).

Fortification and Military Discipline (London, 1688).

Fortification de Paris (Paris, 1833).

Fourcroy de Ramecourt, Charles. *Mémoires sur la fortification perpendiculaire* (Paris, 1786).

Fournier, George. *Traité des fortifications* (Paris, 1648).

France. Institut géographique national. *Catalogue de la galerie des plans en relief des places fortes* (Paris and Nancy, 1900).

Freitag, Adam. *Architectura Militaris Nova et Aucta. (Neue Vermehrte Fortification)* (Amsterdam, 1665).

————. *L'Architecture militaire ou la fortification nouvelle* (Leyden, 1635).

Gay de Vernon, Simon. *Traité élémentaire d'art militaire et de fortification* (Paris, 1805).

Gillmore, Q.A. *Official Report to the United States Engineer Department of the Siege and Reduction of Fort Pulaski, Georgia: February, March and April 1862* (New York, 1862).

Gillot, C.L. *Traité de fortification souterraine* (Paris, 1805).

Glenie, James. *A Few Concise Observations on Military Construction* (London, 1800).

————. *A Short Essay of the Modes of Defense Best Adapted to the Situation and Circumstances of this Island* (London, 1785).

Goldman, Nicholas. *La Nouvelle fortification* (Leyden, 1645).

Goulon, Louis. *Bericht von Belagerung und Vertheidigung einer Vestung* (Nuremberg, 1737).

————. *Mémoires pour l'attaque, et la défense d'une place* (The Hague, 1730).

————. *Memoirs of Monsieur Goulon* (London, 1745).

Groote, Alex von. *Neovallia Dialogo* (Munich, 1617).

Guarini, Guarino. *Trattato di fortificatione che hora si usa in Fiandra, Francia, e Italia* (Turin, 1676).

Hale, John R. *Renaissance Fortification: Art or Engineering?* (London, 1977).

Halévy, Daniel. *Vauban* (Paris, 1923).

Hennert, Johann. *Dissertation sur la fortification permanente, la fortification de campagne, et la portée des bombes* (Utrecht, 1795).

Herbort, Jean de. *Nouvelles méthodes pour fortifier les places* (Frankfurt, 1735).

Hogg, Ian V. *Fortress: A History of Military Defence* (New York, 1977).

Holden, Edward S. *Notes on the Bastion System of Fortification* (New York, 1872).

Holliday, Francis. *An Easy Introduction to Fortification and Practical Gunnery* (London, 1774).

Huchtenburg, Jean et du Mont, J. *Batailles gagnées par le Serenissime Prince Eugene de Savoye* (The Hague, 1725).

Hughes, Quentin. *A Chronology of Events in Fortification from 1800 to 1914 and an Illustrated English Glossary of Terms used in Military Architecture* (Liverpool, 1980).

——————. *Military Architecture* (New York, 1975).

Ive, Paul. *The Practise of Fortification* (London, 1589).

Lallemand, Henri. *Complete Treatise upon Artillery* (New York, 1819–1820).

Landmann, Isaac. *The Principles of Fortification*, 6th ed. (London, 1831).

Landsberg, Johann H. *Les fortifications de tout le monde* (Dresden, 1737).

——————. *Nouveau projet d'une citadelle confrontée contre celle de Lille* (The Hague, 1714).

Lanteri, Giacomo. *Delle offese et diffese delle città, et fortezze* (Venice, 1601).

Leblond, Guillaume. *Eléments de fortification*, 3rd ed. (Paris, 1742).

——————. *Eléments de la guerre des sièges*, comprised of *I, L'Artillerie raisonnée; II, L'Attaque des places; III, La Défense des places* (Paris, 1743).

——————. *The Military Engineer* (London, 1759).

——————. *Traité de l'artillerie* (Paris, 1743).

——————. *Traité de la défense des places* (Paris, 1743).

Lewis, Emanuel R. *Seacoast Fortifications of the United States* (Washington, D. C., 1970).

Luffman, John. *Plans of the Principal Fortresses in the Netherlands and on the French Frontier* (London, 1816).

Maggi, Girolamo and Iacomo Castriotto. *Della forticatione delle città . . . Libri III* (Venice, 1564).

Mahan, Dennis Hart. *A Complete Treatise on Field Fortification* (New York, 1836).

——————. *Descriptive Geometry, as Applied to the Drawing of Fortification and Stereotomy* (New York, 1868).

——————. *An Elementary Course of Permanent Fortification* (New York, 1874).

——————. *Notes Supplementary to the Course of Permanent Fortification* (West Point, N. Y., 1841).

——————. *A Summary of the Course of Permanent Fortification, and of the Attack and Defense of Permanent Works for the Use of the Cadets of the U.S. Military Academy* (West Point, N. Y., n.d.).

——————. *A Treatise on Field Fortification* (New York, 1852).

Maigret. *Traité de la sûreté et conservation des états, par le moyen des forteresses* (Paris, 1770).

Mallet (A. Manesson). *Les Travaux de Mars*, 3 vols. (Paris, 1685).

Mandar, Charles F. *De l'Architecture de forteresses ou l'art de fortifier les places* (Paris, 1804).

——————. *Essai sur la fortification* (Paris, 1801).

Marolois, Samuel. *The Art of Fortification or Architecture Militaire as well*

Offensive as Defensive (London, 1642).

——————. *Fortification* (Amsterdam, 1628).

——————. *Oeuvres mathématiques traitant de la géometrie et fortification* (Leyden, 1628).

Mitchell, William A. *Elements of Fortification* (West Point, N. Y., 1923).

——————. *Fortification* (Washington, D. C., 1927).

Montalembert, Marc Réné. *La Fortification perpendiculaire*, 11 vols. (Paris, 1776–1793).

Moore, Jonas. *Modern Fortification* (London, 1689).

Morlet, Hippolyte. *Réflexions critiques sur l'art moderne de fortifier* (Paris, 1804).

Morrison, George. *An Essay on Fortification* (Woolwich, 1746).

Morton, James St. Clair. *Memoir on American Fortification*. (Washington, D. C., 1859).

Muller, John. *The Attack and Defense of Fortified Places*, 4th ed. (London, 1791).

——————. *The Field Engineer of M. le Chevalier de Clairac* (London, 1773).

——————. *System of Mathematics, Fortification and Artillery* (London, 1757).

——————. *A Treatise Containing the Practical Part of Fortification* (London, 1755).

——————. *A Treatise Containing the Elementary Part of Fortification, Regular, and Irregular*, 2nd ed. (London, 1756).

Naudin. *L'ingénieur français* (Paris, 1695).

Noizet, G. *Elémens de fortifications*, 2 vols. (Paris, 1811).

——————. *Mémoire en réponse à l'ouvrage du Général . . . Prevost de Vernois ayant pour titre, De la fortification depuis Vauban* (Paris, 1862).

——————. *Principes de fortification* (Paris, 1859).

——————. *Résumés des leçons de la l. et 3. partie du cours de fortification permanente par . . . Noizet*. Ecole d'application de l'artillerie et du génie (Metz, 1842).

——————. *Traité complet de fortification*, 2 vols., 3rd ed. (Paris, 1817–1818).

Officiers du Corps royal du génie. *Mémoires sur la fortification perpendiculaire* (Paris, 1786).

Ozanam, Jacques. *La fortification régulière et irrégulière* (Paris, 1720).

Pagan, Blaise. *Les fortifications* (Paris, 1645).

Parent, Michel and Jacques Verroust. *Vauban* (Paris, 1971).

Pasley, Charles W. *A Course of Elementary Fortification*, Vol. 1, 2nd ed. (London, 1822).

——————. *Course of Instruction* (London, 1814–1817).

Pleydell, J.C. *An Essay on Field Fortification* (London, 1768).

Prevost de Vernois. *De la fortification depuis Vauban*, 3 vols. (Paris, 1861).

Quincy, Marquis de. *L'Art de la guerre* (The Hague, 1716).

Rimpler, Georg. *Rimplers . . . Sämtliche Schrifften von der Fortification* (Dresden, 1724).

Robinson, Willard B. *American Forts: Architectural Form and Function* (Urbana, Illinois, 1976).

Rocque, Mary Ann, ed. *A Set of Plans and Forts in America* (n.p., 1777).

Rossetti, Donato. *Fortificazione a Rovescio* (Turin, 1678).

Royal Military Academy, Woolwich. *Text Book of Fortification and Military Engineering*, 2 vols. (London, 1878).

Rozard. *Nouvelle fortification françoise* (Nuremberg, 1731).

Saint Julien, Chevalier de. *Architecture militaire* (The Hague, 1750).

Sardi, Pietro. *Corno dogale della architettura militare* (Venice, 1639).

Sautai, M.T. *L'Oeuvre de Vauban à Lille* (Paris, 1911).

Savart, M. *Cours élémentaire de fortification.* 3rd ed. (Paris, 1828).

Saxe, Maurice de. *Remarques sur un nouveau système de fortification* (The Hague, 1757).

Séa. *Mémoire sur la fortification permanente* (St. Petersburg, 1811).

Sellon, Emile M. *Mémorial de l'ingénieur militaire* (Paris, 1849).

Smith, George. *A Universal Military Dictionary* (London, 1779).

Speckle, Daniel. *Architectura von Vestungen* (Strasbourg, 1608).

Stevin, Simon. *Castrametatio* (Rotterdam, 1617).

——————. *Nieuwe Maniere vom Sterctebau door Spilschluysen* (Rotterdam, 1617).

——————. *Wasser-Bau* (Leyden, 1618).

Stone, Nicholas. *Enchiridion of Fortification* (London,1645).

Sturm, Leonhard C. *Architectura militaris* (Nuremberg, 1736).

——————. *Der wahre Vauban* (Nuremberg, 1737).

——————. *Le véritable Vauban* (The Hague, 1708).

Teliakoffsky, A. *Manuel de fortification permanente,* 2 vols. (St. Petersburg, 1849).

Tensini, Francesco. *La Fortificatione* (Venice, 1624).

Theti, Carlo. *Discorsi delle fortificationi* (Venice, 1575).

——————. *Discorsi delle fortificationi, espugnationi, e difese della città* (Venice, 1617).

Tielke, Johann G. *The Field Engineer* (London, 1789).

Tousard, Louis de. *American Artillerist's Companion,* 2 vols. (Philadelphia, 1809).

Turenne, Prince de. *An Introduction to the Art of Fortification* (London, 1745). (This copy owned by General J. Burgoyne, with MSS notes and tables).

Turpin de Crissé. *Essai sur l'art de la guerre,* 2 vols. (Paris, 1754).

U.S. Congress, House Committee on Military Affairs. *Permanent Fortifications and Sea-Coast Defences* (Washington, D. C., 1862).

U.S. Congress, House Committee on Ways and Means. *Report of General Joseph G. Swift of the Sums Required for the Several Fortifications in the United States, and the Buildings at West Point* (Washington, D. C., 1815).

U.S. Engineer School. *Pamphlet on the Evolution of the Art of Fortification* (Washington, D. C., 1919).

U.S. Military Academy, Engineering Department. *Notes on Permanent Fortifications* (West Point, N. Y., 1946).

——————. *Permanent Fortifications as Elements in the Defense of States* (West Point, N. Y., 18–?).

——————. *Subject Pamphlet of Fortification* (West Point, N. Y., 1931).

Vauban, Sebastien Prestre de. *Le Directeur-Général des fortifications,* printed as appendix to L. Goulon's *Mémoires pour l'attaque et la défense d'une place* (The Hague, 1730).

——————. *Oisivetés,* 3 vols. (Paris, 1845). This work contains papers by Vauban on all sorts of subjects, including the topic of the attack and defense of fortresses.

In his later years, Vauban put together his notes on attack and defense in a *mémoire* titled *Traité de fortifications, Attaque et défense des places*, which was to be treated as a state document, not for publication. Eventually, this work was published in various forms and versions, to include:

—————. *Mémoire pour servir d'instruction dans la conduite des sièges et dans la défense des places* (Leyden, 1740). This work has been translated by George A. Rothrock as *A Manual of Siegecraft and Fortification* (Ann Arbor, 1968).

—————. *Mémoires inédits du Maréchal de Vauban,* M. Augoyat ed. (Paris, 1841).

—————. *Oeuvres militaires:* Vol 1. *Traité de l'attaque des places;* Vol 2. *Traité de la défense des places;* Vol 3. *Traité des mines* (Paris, 1796).

—————. *Traité de l'attaque et de la défense des places* (The Hague, 1742).

—————. *Traité de l'attaque et de la défense des places,* de Valage, ed. (Paris, 1829).

—————. *Traité de l'attaque et de la deffence des places.* MS copy, *Executé par le Seigneur de Lussac, Ingénieur du Roy* (n.p, n.d.).

—————. *Traité des sièges: sur l'attaque et la défense des places de guerre,* MS copy (n.p., n.d.).

Ville, Antoine de. *De la charge des gouverneurs des places* (Paris, 1639).

Viollet-Le-Duc, E.E. *Annals of a Fortress* (London, 1875).

—————. *Mémoire sur la défense de Paris* (Paris, 1871).

Ward, Robert. *Animadversions—The Second Booke* (London, 1639).

Williams, Jonathan. *Letter from Col. Jonathan Williams, on the Subject of Fortifying and Protecting the Harbour of New York* (New York, 1807).

—————. *Plan of Col. Jonathan Williams, for Fortifying the Narrows, Between Long and Staten Islands* (New York, 1807).

Yule, Henry. *Fortification* (Edinburgh and London, 1851).

Zastrow, Heinrich. *Histoire de la fortification permanente,* 2 vols. (Paris, 1856).

Index

Italicized page numbers indicate illustrations.

Abatis, 97
Abraham, Plains of, 92
Adams, John (United States), 94, 122, 128
Adams, John Quincy (United States), 128
Alexander, Brigadier General William. *See* Stirling, Lord.
Alexandria (Va.), 133
Allen, Ethan (United States), 94
American Artillerist's Companion (Tousard), 129
    frontispiece, *129*
American Fortification,
    First System, 115-124
    Second System, 132-139
    Third System, 156-162
American Revolution, 5, 6, 81, 92, 93, 94, 96, 98, 109,
    115, 117, 118, 121, 125
    Charleston, 97, 98
    Fortification and seigecraft, 92-98
    Saratoga, 96
    Valley Forge, 96, 97
    West Point, 96, 97
    Yorktown, 96, 97
Amherst, Major General (England), 90, 92
Amiens
    citadel of, 30
    fortress of, 29, 30
Angle bastion, 16, 40
Angular salient, 16
Annapolis, 133
Anse de Foulon, 92
Antwerp. *See* Rebellion, Dutch Protestant.
Architectura Militaris, 28
    frontispiece, *28*

Architectura Militaris Moderna. See Dögen, Matthias.
    frontispiece, *28*
Architectura von Vestungen (Speckle), 21
    frontispiece, *21*
Armistead, Lieutenant Walter K. (United States), 132
Arnold, Benedict (United States), 94
    (England), 108

Badajoz, siege at, 55
Banquette, 12, 15, 34
Barron, Captain William A. (United States), 128, 130,
    131, 132
Bastion, 16, 17, 20, 21, 31, 34, 36, 44
    attacked, 54
    detached. *See* Counterguard.
    traces, *17*, 62, 63, 73, 155
Bastion du Roi, 87
Batteries, 50, 53, *67*, 86, 91, 107, 166
    casemate, 16
    Chain, 101, 103
    Lanthorn, 101
    South, 101
    water, 101
Battlements, 12
Bavaria, Marlborough's devastation of, 55
Bedlow's Island, 133, 138
Belidor, Forest de (France), 45, 62, 71
Bérard, Claudius (United States), 151
Bergen Op Zoom, 59, *69*
Bernard, Simon (United States), 150, 157, 158, 162
Bloomfield, General (United States), 140
(Le) Bombardier français (Belidor), 71

Bomford, George (United States), 162-163
Bonn, siege of, 59
Borgia, Cesare (Italy), 11
Boston Grenadier Corps, the, 94
Bougainville, Louis-Antoine de (France), 91
Boulogne, fortress of, 29
Bouquet, Colonel Henry (England), 90
Bourbon restoration, the, 75
Braddock, Lieutenant Colonel (England), 92
    Major General (England), 90
Brandenburg, Elector of, 59
Breda. *See* Rebellion, Dutch Protestant.
Brialmont, General Henri, 172
Brussels, French attack of, 53
Burbeck, Henry (United States), 130
Burnet, Governor William (United States), 88

Calais, fortress of, 29
Calhoun, Secretary (of war) John C., 150
Cambray, Louis Antoine de (United States), 96, 98
Caponnière, 35, 134
Carnot, Lazare (France), 71, 74, 153, 171
    career, 75
    theories of fortification, 75, 92
Casemates, 72, 134
Castillo de San Marcos, *83*
Castle Island, 118
Castle of Milan, *15*
Castle Williams, 121, 136-*137*, 138, 142, 162
Castles, examples of, *13*
Castriotto, Fusto (Italy), 19
Cataneo, Pietro (Italy), 19-20
Catholics, 29
Cavaliers, 54
Cellini, Benvenuto (Italy), 11
Charles VII, King (France), 3, 9
Charleston
    American Revolution, 97, 98
    British surrender of, 58
    plan of, *97*
Charon, 107
Chartres, sieges of, 30
Chartier, Michel. *See* Lotbinière, Sieur de.
Chemin de ronde, 37
Chevaux-de-frise, 100
Chew House, British attack of, 94-95
Civil War, impact of, 162-166
Clerville, Chevalier de (France), 39
Clinton, George (United States), 100
Clinton, Sir Henry (England), 100, 105
Clinton, Colonel James (United States), 99, 100

Cockspur Island, 162
Coehoorn, Baron Menno van (Netherlands), 46, 48, 49, 59, 61, 153, 173
    fortification by, *60*
Coevorden, fortress of, *26,* 59
Cologne, 2
Commonwealth of Massachusetts, 121
Condé, Prince de (France), 39
Congress (United States), 115, 116, 117, 118, 119, 120, 121, 122, 125, 132, 133, 135, 137, 140, 148, 156
    Committee on Peace Arrangements, 116, 119, 120
    Corps of Artillerists and Engineers, 125, 126, 127, 128
    Corps of Invalids, 116
    General Survey Act, 148
Considérations militaires et politiques sur les fortifications (d'Arcon), 75
Constantinople, siege of, 3
Constitution Island, 99, 100, 102
Copernicus, 2
Cormontaigne, Louis de (France), 62, 75, 153, 171
Cornwallis, Lord (England), 97, 105, 106-107, 109
Corps of Engineers, 117, 130, 131, 132, 133, 135, 136, 138, 139, 140, 148, 149, 150, 151, 158, 171
Counterforts, 15
Counterguard, 44
Counterscarp, 15, 20
Covered way. *See* Via coperta.
Crenellations, 12
Crownworks, 36, *43*
Crown Hill, 102
Crozet, Claude (United States), 149, 151
Curtain walls, 12, 16, 34
Cuvette, 35

da Urbino, Francesco Paciotto (Italy), 18
da Vinci, Leonardo (Italy), 11
Dahlgren, John (United States), 163
d'Arcon, Michaud (France), 74, 75
de Béthune, Maximilian. *See* Sully, Duke of.
de Chastillon, Claude (France), 30
de'Marchi, Francesco (Italy), 19-21
de'Medici, Cosimo (Italy), 11
de Saint-Luc, d'Espinai (France), 30
de Turenne, Maréchal (France), 31
de Ville, Chevalier (France), 32
Deane, Silas (United States), 96
Dearborn, Secretary (of war) Henry (United States), 129, 130, 131, 132, 133, 135
Della Architettura Militare, 20
Demibastion, 86

Demilune, 25, 40, *56*
Detached forts, 73
di Sanmicheli, Michele (Italy), 18
Dögen, Matthias (Germany), 28
Dransy, Lieutenant Peter A. (United States), 130
Dry ditch. *See* Cuvette.
Duffy, Christopher, 169
Dunkirk, Battle of, 31
Duportail, Louis Lebègue (United States), 96, 97, 98, 100, 102-103, 104, 105, 116, 118, 125
Duquesne, Marquis de (France), 84

Earthen rampart, 24
Ecole des Mines, 152
Ecole des Ponts, 152
Ecole du Corps Royale du Génie, the (at Mézières), 62, 74, 76, 96, 101, 104, 105, 116
Ecole Polytechnique, 149, 151, 152, 158
Eléments d'algèbre (Lacroix), 150
Ellis Island, 133
Enceinte, 17, 18, 21, 25, 28, 32
Enfiladed, 17
England
    colonial fortification, 87-89
    fortification and siegecraft (American Revolution), 92-98
    impact of French and Indian War, 89-92
    printing, growth of, 2, 4
Entrenched camp, 74
Errard, Jean de Bar-le-Duc (France), 30-31
    bastions designed by, *31*
    fortification by, *30*
Escalade, 14
Essai de geometrie analytique (Biot), 150
Essex, 142
Eustis, Secretary (of war) William (United States), 137-138, 139

Fascines, 48, 52
Fausse-braye, 24-25
Fieldwork, 13
Firepower, 33, 34, 134
Flanking fire, 16
Flanks, 16, 36
Foncin, Jean (United States), 123, 133
Fontenelle (France), 40-41
Forbes, Brigadier John (England), 90
Fort Adams, 131, 133, 160
Fort Allen, 120
Fort Beauséjour (England and France), 89

Fort Bowyer, 141, 142
Fort Carillon. *See* Fort Ticonderoga.
Fort Charles, 84
Fort Columbus. *See* Fort Jay.
Fort Crown Point. *See* Fort Saint-Frédéric, 85
Fort Cumberland, 88
Fort Duquesne, 85, 86
    plan of, *85*
Fort Frontenac, 90
Fort Greene, 121
Fort Independence, 133
Fort Jackson, 158
Fort Jay, 121, 126
Fort Johnston, 132
Fort Kingston. *See* Fort Frontenac.
Fort Matanzas, 84
Fort Maurepas, 84
Fort McClary, 136
Fort McHenry, 122, 123, *124*, 133, 141, 142
Fort Mechanic, 121
Fort Meigs, 102
Fort Mifflin, 121, 122, *123*
    plan of, 123
Fort Monroe, 158, 160
Fort Montgomery-Fort Clinton, 100
    map of, *126*
    plan of, *103*
Fort Morgan, 158
Fort Moultrie, 121
Fort Necessity, 87-88
Fort Niagara, 86, 129
    plan of, *86*
Fort Ontario, 89
    plan of, *89*
Fort Oswego, 88, 90
Fort Pickens, 158
Fort Pinckney, 121
Fort Pitt, 89, 90
Fort Presqu'Ile, 84
Fort Prince George, 85
Fort Pulaski, 158, 160, 162, *164*
Fort Putnam, 102, 103, 104, 126
Fort Rivière au Boeuf, 84
Fort Saint-Frédéric, 85
Fort Saint Philip, 141, 142
Fort San Carlos de Austria, 84
Fort Schuyler, 60, 160
Fort Stanwix, 88. *See also* Fort Schuyler.
Fort Sumner, 120
Fort Sumter, 158, 160, 164, 165, *166*
Fort Ticonderoga, 86

plan of, *86*
Fort Toulouse, 84
Fort Warren, 121
Fort Washington, 141. *See* Goat Island.
Fort Webb, 102
Fort Whetstone, 121, 123
Fort William and Mary, 121
Fort William Henry, 88, 90
    plans of, *88*
Fort Wolcott, 133
Fort Wyllys, 102, 103
(La) Fortification demonstrée et reducite en art (Errard), 30
Fortification, development of
    Dutch design, 22-27
    French design, 29-32
    German design, 27-28
    Italian design, 18-21
Fortification, Dutch, *25*
Fortification, theory and practice, (United States)
    military role, 149-156
Fortification, types, *18, 19, 74*
(La) Fortification perpendiculaire (Montalembert), 72, *73,* 134
    frontispiece, *72*
Fortifications (de Ville), 32
    frontispiece, *32*
Fortifications
    bastioned, *34*
    locations of colonial, *82*
    locations of First System, *120*
    locations of Second System, *137*
    locations of Third System, *158*
    student work on, *154*
(Les) Fortifications du Comte de Pagan, 31
Forts,
    all-masonry, 134
    pentagonal, *20*
    star, 119, *124,* 136
Fourcroy, Charles-René de (de Ramecourt), 62, 74, 75
Fraises, 24, 97
France, 39, 43, 45, 46, 49, 61, 62, 71, 73, 74, 75, 76, 93, 149, 150, 152
    colonial fortification, 84-87
    fortification design, 29-32, 79
    invades Naples, 9
    impact of French and Indian Wars, 89-92
    improved weaponry, 8-9
    printing, growth of, 2, 4
François, Blaise. *See* Pagan, Comte de.
Franklin, Benjamin (United States), 95, 96
Frederick the Great (Prussia), 74

French Republic, the, 75
French Revolution, the, 61, 62, 73, 76

Gabions, 48, 51, 52
Gallatin, Commissioner Albert (United States), 150
Gallatin, Gaspard de (France), 105
Gates, General Horatio (United States), 93
Georgia, 138, 140
Glacis, 19, 20, 34, 36, 119
Goat Island, 118, 121
Gordon, Henry, 89
Gouvion, Jean-Baptiste (United States), 96, 105
Governor's Island, 121, 133, 136
Grant, General (Ulyssess S.) (United States), 92
Gratiot, Charles (United States), 133
Green Mountain Boys, the, 94
Greene, Major General Nathaniel (United States), 93, 97
Grenoble, fortress of, 29
Gridley, Richard (United States), 94, 95
Groningen, 59
Guicciardini, Francesco (Italy), 9-10

Hamilton, Alexander (United States), 107, 116, 117, 128
Henri IV, King (France), 29, 30
Herlin, L.A. (Germany), 28
Hornwork, 25
Howe, General Sir William (England), 94, 97
Hudson Highlands, 98, 99, 100, 101
Hudson River, 98, 100, 101, 103, 104, 126, 136
Huguenots, 29
Hundred Year's War, Normandy, French invasion of, 2

Isle d'Orléans, 92
Italy
    bastion, development of, 11-18
    invaded by France, 9
    printing, growth of, 2, 4
    Renaissance, 10, 11, 32
    School of Engineers, 19-21, 40, 79
Izard, Captain George (United States), 131

Jackson Administration, the, 151
Jacobin government, 75
Jefferson, President Thomas (United States), 129, 130, 132, 134, 135-136

Keep, 12
Knox, General Henry (United States), 93, 94, 105, 116
    Secretary (of war), 119-120, 121, 125

Knox Battery. *See* South Battery.
Kosciuszko, Thaddeus (United States), 96, 101, 102, 103

Laumoy, Chevalier du (United States), 96, 97, 98
Laurens, Colonel (United States), 108
Lee, General Charles (United States), 93, 95
L'Enfant, Pierre-Charles (United States), 96, 97, 98, 122, 133
Leopard, H.M.S., 135
Léry, Chaussegros de (France), 91-92
Lévis Heights, the, 92
Levy, Simon M. (United States), 131
Leyritz, Alexander de (United States), 123
Liège, 61
Lille, siege of, 46, 47, 49, 53, 54
Line of circumvallation, *14,* 22
Line of contravallation, *14,* 22
Line of defense, 17
Lotbinière, Sieur de (Canada), 86
Louis XIV, King (France), 28, 29, 31, 32, 39, 47, 48, 58, 59, 61
Louis XV, King (France), 62
Louis-Philippe, King (France), 75
Louisbourg, 86-87, 91, 121
    plan of, *87*
Louvois, Marquis de (France), 39
Luxembourg, Duke of (France), 48

Machiavelli, Niccolo (Italy), 5, 8
Machicolated, 12
Machin, Thomas (United States), 100, 102
Macomb, Second Lieutenant Alexander (United States), 130, 132, 152
Madison, James (United States), 116
    president, 139, 140, 147
Maggi, Girolamo (Italy), 19
Mahan, Dennis Hart (United States), *151*-156, 162
Mainz, 2
Manhattan Island, 133, 136
(La) Manière de fortification de M. Vauban, 41
Mannheim, 59
Mansfield, Captain James (United States), 130, 131, 132
Marlborough, Duke of (England), 46, 48
Martalaer's Rock. *See* Constitution Island.
Maryland, 40
Maubeuge, 37
Maurice (of Nassau), 22, 26, 59
Mazarin, Cardinal, 39
McHenry, Secretary (of war) James (United States), 122, 127, 128
McRee, William (United States), 140, 148, 149, 150, 157

Menin, (French occupation of), 31
Michelangelo (Italy), 11
Milan
    Castle of, (Viollet-le-Duc), 15
    Duke of, 11
    Duomo, 11
Monroe, Secretary (of war) James (United States), 147-148
Montalembert, Marc-René, Marquis de (France)
    coastal towers of, *72*
    theories of fortification, 72-75, 92, 134-135, 136, 142, 153, 155, 156, 160, 171
Monte San Giovanni, 10
Montgomery, General Richard (United States), 93
Montmélian, fortress of, 29, 30
Morris Island, 165
Mount Defiance, 95
Mud Island, 118, 122

Namur
    capture of, 58
    defense of 59, 61
    Fort William, 59
    siege of, 45, 46, 48, 49, 53, 55
Napoleon, 75, 105, 135, 149, 171
    empire, the Napoleonic, 75
    wars, 74, 75, 76
Narragansett Bay, 138
Netherlands
    fortification design, 22-27
    printing, growth of, 2, 4
Neuf-Brisach, 45
New London, 108, 121
New Method of Fortification, (English translation), 59
Newport, 138
Nieuwe Vestingbouw (Coehoorn), 59
Nimjegen, 59
Niven, Captain (United States), 96
Noizet, General (France), 169
Nouvelle fortification (Coehoorn), 59
Nuremberg, 2

O'Hara, General (England), 108
Oosterhout. *See* Rebellion, Dutch Protestant.
Orillon, 21
Ostend. *See* Rebellion, Dutch Protestant.
Ostend, siege of, 24
Ottoman Turks, 3
Oudenarde
    fortification of, 22
    occupation of (by France), 31

See also Rebellion, Dutch Protestant.
Outworks, *19, 25,* 26, 32, 35, *43,* 44, 119

Pagan, Comte de (France), 31-32
Parallel trench, 45, *46,* 50, 58
Parapet, 15, 34, 155
Parrott, Robert P. (United States), 164
Partridge, Lieutenant Alden (United States), 136, 140, 147, 150
Paul III, Pope, 20
Pickering, Secretary (of war), Thomas, 125, 126, 127
Pierrier, 53
Plum Point, 100
Pollopel Island, 100
Polygonal system, 74
Popolopen Creek-Anthony's Nose, 100
Portcullis, 83
Pouchot, Francois (Canada), 86
Poussin, Guillaume Tell (United States), 158
Pré carré, 43
President, S.S., 142
Principes de Fortification (Noizet), 169
Printing, mechanical duplication, 2
Profiles, sketches of, *33, 40*
Putnam, Colonel Rufus (United States), 95, 100
Putnam, Major General Israel (United States), 95, 100, 101
Pyrenées, Peace of the (Treaty), 31

Quebec, 91
plan of, *91*

Radière, Louis de Shaix la (United States), 96, 100, 101
Rampart, 15, *17,* 75
Ravelin, 19, 25, 40
Rebellion, Dutch Protestant, 22
Redoubt, 35, 40
Re-entering place of arms, 20
Relieving arches, 15, 16
Revetted, 35
Rhine, 45, 75
Ricochet fire, 50, *66*
Rimpler, Georg (Germany), 27
Rimpler trace, the, 27
Rivardi, John Jacob (J.J.) Ulrich (United States), 123, 125, 127, 130
Rochambeau, Comte de (France), 105
Rochefontaine, Lieutenant Colonel Stephen, 120, 121, 125, 126, 127, 133
Rodman, Thomas J. (United States), 163-164

Romans, Bernard (United States), 95, 99, 100
Royal Navy, 92, 118

Saint Peter's, 11
Saint-Simon (France), 40
Sandbags, 164, 165
Sappers (volunteer trenchmakers), 50, 51-52, 53, 54, 61, 170
Saps, *66*
tools and techniques of construction, *50*
Sardi, Pietro (Italy), 19
Savoy, Prince of, 46, 48, 54
Saxe, Marshal Maurice de (France), 71
Scammell, Colonel Alexander (United States), 108
Scarp, 15
semidetached, 36
Scheliha, Viktor E.K.R. von (United States), 165
School of Application for Engineers and Artillery, 150, 152
Sforza, Ludovico (Italy), 11
Sherburne's Redoubt, 102
Siege operations, 45-58, *66, 68*
attack approaches, *51*
attack of a place, *14*
fourteenth century, *12*
fifteenth century, *13*
sixteenth century, *23*
tools and materials of, *49*
views of, *56-57*
South Battery, 101
South Carolina, 138, 140
Speckle, Daniel, 21, 27
Steenbergen. *See* Rebellion, Dutch Protestant.
Stevin, Simon (Netherlands), 22
Stirling, Lord (United States), 100
Storm poles. *See* Fraises, 27
Strasbourg, 2
Sturm, Leonhard Christoph (Germany), 27
Sully, Duke of (France), 29
Swift, Joseph G. (United States), 128, *131,* 132, 136, 140, 147, 149, 150, 155, 157

Tappan, Christopher (United States), 99
Tarleton, Colonel (England), 105
Tartaglia, Niccolo (Italy), 19
Tenaille, 28, 35, *37,* 40
Terra Nova. *See* Namur.
Terrepleins, 27
Thayer, Sylvanus (United States), 140, 147, 148, *149,* 150, 151, 157
Totten, Joseph (United States), *131,* 140, 150, 160

Totten System, the, 157
Toulon
     capture of, 75
     fortress of, 29, 45
Tournai. *See* Rebellion, Dutch Protestant.
Tours bastionées, 37, 40, 44, 45, *65*
Tousard, Colonel Louis de (United States), 122, 123,
     125, 127, 129-130, 133, 162
Traces, types of, *28*
Traité de l'attaque des places (Vauban), 41, 45
Traité de la defense des places (Vauban), 41, 47
Traité de la Defense des places fortes (Carnot), 75
*Traité de la science de la guerre et de la fortification
     des places* (Vernon), 150
Traité de mécanique (Francoeur), 150
Traité des machines (Hachette), 150
Traité des mines (Vauban), 41
Traité du Calcul différentiel et intégral (Lacroix), 150
Trous de loup, 97

United States Military Philosophical Society, the,
     133, 135

Valley Forge, 101
Van Deventer, Christopher (United States), 157
Vauban, Sebastien le Prestre de (France) 28, 32, 38, *41,*
     59, 61, 123, 134, 153, 155, 170, 171
     defensive engineer, 41-45
     fortifications, contributions to, 39-40, *44,* 119
     fortresses by, a map of, *42*
     legacy and successors, 61, 62, 71-76
     siege warfare, offensive tactics, 45-58
Vaudément, Prince de (France), 48
Vaudreuil, Marquis de (France), 90, 92
Vendée
     insurrection of, 75
Verville, Jean-Francois du Verger (Canada), 86-87
Via coperta, 20, 34

Wadsworth, Major Decius (United States), 130, 131, 132
War of 1812, 133, 162
     impact of, 139-141
Warin, Joseph, 127
Washington, George
     after American Revolution, 115, 116, 117
     and West Point, 98, 100, 101, 104
     French and Indian Wars, 90
     General, American Revolution, 93, 94 95, 96, 97
     Lieutenant Colonel, 88
     Major, 84
     Yorktown, 105, 107, 108
Wayne, General Anthony (United States), 93
Weaponry
     cannon, 4, *9,* 14, 19, 33, 34, 36, 43, 44, 53, 71, 85,
          89, 92, 107, 119, *163,* 170
     cast-iron shot, 8
     gunpowder, 3, 4, 8, 11, 14, 44, 47, 90
     longbow, 8
     magazines, 49, 53, 119
     musket, 4, 36, 43, 45, 52, 53, 82
     pike, 4
     rifled guns, 164, 165
     rifled ordnance, 8
     siege guns, 47, 50, 90, 155, 170
     siege trains, 46, 49
     technical improvements in, 9
West Point
     Fort Arnold (Benedict), 101, 102, 126
     Fort Independence, 100
     Fort Montgomery-Fort Clinton, 100
     fortifications at, 98-104
     U.S. Military Academy at, 6, 117, 125, 129, 130, 131,
          132, 136, 140, 147, 148, 149, 150, 151, 152, 172, 173
     Verplanck's Point, 100
Westerloo. *See* Rebellion, Dutch Protestant.
Wet ditch, 24, 26, 27, 35, 59
William III, King (England), 46, 48, 59
William the Silent, 59
Williams, Jonathan (United States), 122, 129-130, 131,
     133, 134, 135-136, 138, 139, 140
Wilson, Lieutenant James (United States), 130, 131-132
Wilson, Lieutenant William (United States), 127, 132
Wolfe, Major General James (England), 91, 92

York River, 104-105, 106
Yorktown. *See* American Revolution.
     British surrender of, 58
     siege at, 104-109
Ypres (French occupation of), 31